Credit Repair Kit FOR DUMMIES®

by Steve Bucci

Foreword by Terry Savage

WILEY

Wiley Publishing, Inc.

Credit Repair Kit For Dummies®

Published by
Wiley Publishing, Inc.
111 River St.
Hoboken, NJ 07030-5774
www.wiley.com

Copyright © 2006 by Wiley Publishing, Inc., Indianapolis, Indiana

Published simultaneously in Canada

For general information on our other products and services, please contact our Customer Care Department within the U.S. at 800-762-2974, outside the U.S. at 317-572-3993, or fax 317-572-4002.

For technical support, please visit www.wiley.com/techsupport.

Wiley also publishes its books in a variety of electronic formats. Some content that appears in print may not be available in electronic books.

Library of Congress Control Number: 2005933522

ISBN-13: 978-0-7645-9908-8

ISBN-10: 0-7645-9908-9

Manufactured in the United States of America

10 9 8 7 6 5 4

1B/RY/RR/QV/IN

WILEY

About the Author

Steve Bucci is president of the Houston, Texas–based Money Management International Financial Education Foundation, a nonprofit organization that operates to educate the general public on sound personal-financial skills and money-management principles by developing, delivering, and supporting programs that teach those skills and principles. He is also Visiting Executive in Residence at the University of Rhode Island's Center for Personal Financial Education.

Steve also writes a popular weekly column as the Debt Advisor for the financial mega-site Bankrate.com. His column is featured frequently on America Online, Yahoo! Personal Finance, and other Web sites. The Scripps-Howard newspaper syndicate distributes his column nationally.

Steve was formerly president of Consumer Credit Counseling Service of Southern New England, the founder of the Consumer Credit Counseling Service of Rhode Island, and the founder of the University of Rhode Island Center for Personal Financial Education. The Center is a joint venture with the University of Rhode Island and Money Management International, Inc.

He began his career in counseling at the Yale Psychiatric Institute before switching to the more profitable business of management consulting and then developing both publicly-offered and privately-offered investment products in the insurance/financial-services industries. Steve returned to helping individuals in 1991, this time using his financial experience when he launched Rhode Island's first private, nonprofit, financial counseling agency.

Steve was a director of the CDNE Education Foundation, the National Foundation for Credit Counseling, and the Better Business Bureau of Rhode Island. He graduated from East Providence Senior High School and the University of Rhode Island at Kingston, where he received his B.A. and M.A. degrees. He and his wife, Barbara, live with their two cats, Big Al and Stinky, in the seaside community of Narragansett, Rhode Island.

Dedication

This book is dedicated to my gorgeous wife, Barbara, who for some unknown reason, thinks I can do anything; my two sons, Steve and Geoff, who know better but won't tell her; my new daughter-in-law Grace Ki Hye, whose smile outshines the sun; my mom, Grace, whose legendary cooking may someday become a *Mother's Guide to Italian Cooking;* and my father, Jim Bucci, who knew I had a book in there somewhere but passed away at 85 last year and didn't live to see this book or the Red Sox win the World Series.

Author's Acknowledgments

Writing a book is like grabbing a tiger by the tail: Once you've grabbed on, you don't dare let go! I was fortunate to have the support and assistance of a large number of colleagues who encouraged me and, in at least one case, took a risk in the belief that I could tame this beast. My thanks to them all, and my particular thanks to Ivan Hand of Money Management International, who shares my passion for financial literacy; Jessica Faust, my agent, who saw things I did not; Kristin DiSpirito, who researched and edited the CD content; Betsy Sheldon, who polished my text on its way to editing; Mike Staten, Ph.D., at the Georgetown Credit Research Center who provided his technical-editing expertise; Ron Ramos, who advised me with insightful comments; my delightful and understanding editors at John Wiley & Sons, especially Elizabeth Kuball and Tracy Boggier; and Barbara Newman, Ph.D., at the University of Rhode Island, who offered me shelter, encouragement, and the benefit of her wisdom.

Publisher's Acknowledgments

We're proud of this book; please send us your comments through our Dummies online registration form located at www.dummies.com/register/.

Some of the people who helped bring this book to market include the following:

Acquisitions, Editorial, and Media Development

Project Editor: Elizabeth Kuball

Acquisitions Editor: Tracy Boggier

Technical Editor: Michael Staten, Ph.D.

Media Project Supervisor: Laura Moss

Media Development Specialists: Kate Jenkins, Angie Denny

Editorial Manager: Michelle Hacker

Editorial Supervisor and Reprint Editor: Carmen Krikorian

Media Development Manager: Laura VanWinkle

Editorial Assistant: Hanna Scott, Nadine Bell

Consultant: Betsy Sheldon

Cover Photos: © Geoff Brightling/ Photographer's Choice/Getty Images

Cartoons: Rich Tennant (www.the5thwave.com)

Composition Services

Project Coordinator: Kathryn Shanks

Layout and Graphics: Carl Byers, Andrea Dahl, Mary Gillot, Stephanie D. Jumper, Barbara Moore, Brent Savage,

Proofreaders: Leeann Harney, Carl William Pierce, TECHBOOKS Production Services

Indexer: TECHBOOKS Production Services

Publishing and Editorial for Consumer Dummies

Diane Graves Steele, Vice President and Publisher, Consumer Dummies

Joyce Pepple, Acquisitions Director, Consumer Dummies

Kristin A. Cocks, Product Development Director, Consumer Dummies

Michael Spring, Vice President and Publisher, Travel

Kelly Regan, Editorial Director, Travel

Publishing for Technology Dummies

Andy Cummings, Vice President and Publisher, Dummies Technology/General User

Composition Services

Gerry Fahey, Vice President of Production Services

Debbie Stailey, Director of Composition Services

Contents at a Glance

Table of Contents

Part IV: Building and Maintaining Good Credit 179

Chapter 10: Getting Back in Good Credit Standing 181

Chapter 11: Budgeting for Your Future 197

Foreword

Someone's watching every move you make with your money! You probably think your personal finances are just that: personal. But every purchase you make on your credit card, every mortgage payment you send, every doctor's bill you pay, and every insurance application you submit is being monitored, reported, and scored. That's the nature of our credit-centered financial system.

Of course, you could just use cash for all your purchases. But how would you buy a home, rent a car, or make hotel reservations? Having good credit and using it wisely is essential these days.

It's so easy to get off to a bad start. Few schools teach kids about money. Their first lessons come from sitting in a car seat and watching Mom put a card into a machine in the bank's drive-thru. Money doesn't grow on trees anymore; it comes out of ATMs! By the time teens are ready for college, they're handed credit-card applications along with their books and the school sweatshirt.

In my years as a nationally syndicated personal-finance columnist for the *Chicago Sun-Times,* I've heard so many sad stories about lives ruined by debt. Bankruptcy has become an epidemic — and new, more-stringent laws haven't stemmed the tide. After all, if our federal government runs budget deficits, and our largest companies file for bankruptcy, how is the average consumer supposed to resist the dangers of debt?

Getting overloaded with debt is so easy. It's like quicksand: easy to walk into and very tough to pull yourself out. And if you aren't careful, you could fall into an even worse trap: unscrupulous "fix-it" companies that actually make your situation even worse.

That's why I'm delighted you've picked up this book. Written by a pro in language you can understand, it will give you honest answers to all your credit questions. Whether you're just starting out in life, or feeling overwhelmed by financial problems, this is the resource that will guide you to the correct answers.

Steve Bucci is currently the President of the Money Management International Financial Education Foundation (www.mmifoundation.org), which provides funds and materials for essential money-management education. In addition, he is helping to build one of the nation's largest credit-counseling services, Money Management International. Best of all, it's affiliated with both the National Foundation for Consumer Credit and the Association of Independent

Consumer Credit Counseling Agencies — the umbrella associations for credit counseling nationwide. All of their counselors are accredited — and trained to help you find the best way out of debt.

But isn't it better to avoid credit problems in the first place? That's why this book should be required reading for everyone — from high school students and their parents to senior citizens. After all, as Benjamin Franklin said in *Poor Richard's Almanac:* "Creditors have better memories than debtors."

If you don't use credit wisely, your creditors and the collectors they assign to your case will make your life miserable. But if you understand and manage your credit well, you've started down the road to financial success.

Terry Savage
Nationally syndicated *Chicago Sun-Times* columnist
Author of *The Savage Truth on Money* and *The Savage Number: How Much Money Do You Need to Retire?* (both published by Wiley)

Introduction

*Y*ou deserve some credit — and I mean that in two ways:

- ✔ **You deserve credit for picking up this book.** Whether you have found yourself struggling to pay creditors, you have a loved one in credit trouble, or you're simply trying to *avoid* credit problems, kudos to you for your proactive approach.

- ✔ **You deserve credit — that unique institution embraced by Americans that protects one of our most inalienable of rights: the pursuit of happiness.** Credit, defined by Webster as "permission for a customer to have goods or services that will be paid for at a later date," allows you to realize major life goals, such as owning a home, having a car, or getting an education — goals you might never achieve in a lifetime if it weren't for credit.

So, yes, in my view, you — as a hard-working, responsible citizen — deserve credit. What you *don't* deserve are the disastrous consequences of bad credit. And that is what this book is all about — showing you how to repair your damaged credit or, better yet, avoid damaging your credit in the first place.

Credit Repair Kit For Dummies comes at a critical time. The confluence of many forces has created a challenging landscape for the American consumer: The advent of new technology makes online bill-paying and financial transactions easier than ever — at the same time it makes it easier than ever for unscrupulous types to hack into your personal data, imperiling your credit information and increasing the possibility of identity theft. New laws protect consumers and increase your rights to your credit information; other laws make bankruptcy a nearly impossible option for many credit-strapped individuals. And despite increased restrictions on direct-mail solicitations and telemarketers, you're bombarded with more offers for credit than ever before.

It's no wonder that you and so many others are looking for up-to-date, useful, and proven answers from a trusted and known resource. And you need not look any further than this book.

About This Book

The modern world of consumerism is a minefield of credit perils — from identity theft to too-good-to-be-true lending terms to debt-settlement plans. Most consumers need an experienced guide to help them navigate that minefield without incurring collateral damage to their credit.

In this book, I serve as that guide. After nearly two decades of administering to hundreds and thousands of shell-shocked credit refugees, I've helped individuals work through all aspects of financial challenges, from creating a household budget for the first time to negotiating the complexities of bankruptcy. In *Credit Repair Kit For Dummies,* I share my experience to get you over those hurdles, too.

The advice in this book is for *anyone* seeking easy-to-understand, no-nonsense, straightforward advice about repairing your credit. But I don't limit my focus to turning around a less-than-stellar credit report. I pack the pages with plenty of powerful action plans for *avoiding* bad credit.

So, why this book?

- Because you may be drowning in collection calls and notices — and this book reveals your rights to fend off the callers.

- Because you may need the advice of an experienced advisor to guide you through your debt situation — and this book tells you how to find a good credit-counseling agency.

- Because you may have inaccurate data in your credit record — and this book offers tips on cleaning up your credit report.

- Because you may be the victim of identity theft — and this book provides valuable information to protect your personal data.

- Because you may be on the brink of credit trouble — and this book gives you budgeting and spending advice that can pull you back from the edge.

- Because you may be in serious credit despair — and this book offers you solid and level-headed advice about your options.

- Because the time is right for you to make a difference in your credit and your financial peace of mind — and this book helps you do just that.

There are two final reasons why you should buy this book:

✔ In 2005, major changes were made to the rules for bankruptcy, your rights in case of identity theft, and your rights to dispute and clean up your credit report. This book spells it all out in clear, easy-to-understand language.

✔ The *For Dummies* series is a trusted, proven, understandable resource that you and more than 100 million readers have relied upon successfully for years.

Conventions Used In This Book

To make this book as simple to follow and as convenient as possible, I've used the following conventions throughout:

✔ All Web addresses and e-mail addresses appear in `monofont`.

✔ New terms appear in *italics* and are closely followed by an easy-to-understand definition.

What You're Not to Read

You can safely skip the sidebars, which are text enclosed in a shaded gray box. These provide supporting or entertaining information that isn't critical to your understanding of the topic.

You can also skip anything marked by a Technical Stuff icon — more on that later in this Introduction.

Foolish Assumptions

In writing this book, I assume that you don't have a formal education in credit or personal finance. If you do, however, I believe that you can still find useful insights in these pages that make this book well worth the read.

I also assume that you're reading this book because you or someone you care about is at a point in life where credit is important. This doesn't mean that your credit must be out of control to benefit from this book. It may simply mean that you're wise enough to know that additional, up-to-date knowledge ensures that your credit stays healthy.

An understanding of your credit and how the credit system works may be especially important during certain life situations. I assume that this book is of value for:

- ✔ Anyone whose personal information is a concern or has been compromised or stolen

- ✔ Anyone establishing credit for the first time, from young adults to new immigrants

- ✔ Anyone who is already in or will soon be in a marriage or partnership

- ✔ Anyone who has recently been or will soon be divorced

- ✔ Anyone with a student loan

- ✔ Anyone in the process of a job hunt

- ✔ Anyone dealing with medical issues and bills

- ✔ Anyone who has lost a spouse or life partner

- ✔ Anyone who wants to know more about maintaining good credit

- ✔ Anyone who is concerned about the credit status of a loved one

How This Book Is Organized

This book is divided into 5 major parts with 19 chapters and an appendix. I wrote *Credit Repair Kit For Dummies* so that you could choose to read only the topics of interest to you — or the entire book.

At your fingertips is everything you need to get your credit back on the right track with simple, easy-to-understand tips and action steps. This book is packed with information to help you at whatever state or stage your credit is in. You can skip over any of the parts and go directly to the topics of most interest to you, or you can start at the beginning and determine exactly where your credit stands, figure out what to do now, and maybe even get some insights and tips to prepare for what credit has in store for you in the months and years ahead.

Part 1: Understanding Credit: The Good, the Bad, and the Ugly

In this part, I tell you all about credit — your own personal credit and the importance of knowing how your credit behavior is reported to the credit bureaus. I put the two critical credit tools — credit reports and credit scores — under the microscope, and walk you through all the working parts so you have a clearer understanding of how they're used to evaluate your creditworthiness. Lastly, I help you determine if professional advice would benefit you or a loved one.

Part II: Finding Out Where You Stand

To know where you need to go, you need to know where you are. Getting hold of your credit report, the reasons for doing so, and what your credit score means are the focus of this part. I fill you in on what information is contained in your credit report, how it's reported, and who can view that information. Additionally, I show you how to interpret your credit score and — most importantly — how to improve it. I also introduce the other consumer credit-reporting agencies that report information used for insurance, medicine, gambling, employment, checking accounts, and even renting.

Part III: Doing Damage Control

If you have damaged credit, you've come to the right part. The chapters in this part are dedicated to helping you stop further destruction and turn around your credit as quickly as possible to produce a positive credit report and credit score. I outline your rights under the new FACT Act, and I explain how to use them to ensure your credit report reflects accurate, updated information. I show you how to deal with those aggressive bill collectors, and I detail your rights under the Fair Debt Collection Practices Act. Lastly, I offer information to help determine if bankruptcy is the right decision for you.

Part IV: Building and Maintaining Good Credit

This part is for anyone — whether you've recovered your credit or you've always maintained a positive credit history. Here I provide a guidebook for planning a future that will meet your financial goals. I also give you proven techniques to build your credit, control your finances, and avoid the pitfalls of identity theft. I show you how to spend with confidence, stay within your means, and save for the things you want. I also present strategies to help get you through the many financial challenges that life throws at you, including marriage, divorce, unemployment, and more.

Part V: The Part of Tens

If you like concise information, and you want to improve your credit, you'll enjoy and benefit from this part. I offer quick-reference items to help you identify ways to improve your credit, avoid identity theft, and deal with financial emergencies. I also give you steps to take if you're a victim of identity theft, warning signs your credit may be in trouble, and tips for getting quality professional credit and debt help.

Appendixes

In Appendix A, I've compiled a list of commonly used terms I believe are useful in your understanding of credit. Although I define these terms in the text where they first appear, you may use this glossary for frequent reference if you come across the term elsewhere in this book — or even in other resources.

In Appendix B, I fill you in on the CD-ROM that comes with this book, letting you know what you can find there and how to access the information.

Icons Used in This Book

Icons are those little pictures you see sprinkled in the margins through this book. Here's what they mean:

Anything marked with this icon flags credit-industry jargon you may hear bandied about by credit counselors, debt collectors, and your Uncle Milo. Read the definitions I provide, and you'll be able to bandy right back.

The CD that comes with this book is jam-packed with all kinds of useful information that I reference throughout the chapters ahead. Whenever I mention a useful tool available on the CD, I use this icon.

This icon denotes critical information that you really need to take away with you. Considering the state of my own overcrowded memory, I wouldn't ask you to remember anything unless it was really important.

This image of a credit professional — okay, fine, of a Dummies Man — shows up whenever I go into more detail on a concept or rule. If you don't care about the details of how something works or where it came from, feel free to skip these gems. My wife, when she reads this book, will not read one of them because she is just too busy and tells me that she really has more important things to do.

This bull's-eye lets you know that you're reading on-target advice, often little-known insights or recommendations that I've picked up over the years.

This icon serves as a warning — telling you to avoid something that's potentially harmful. These paragraphs are worth reading if only to be able to point out to your family or friends what they're doing wrong.

Where to Go from Here

You get to choose what happens next. You may want to start with Chapter 1, which gives you an overview of credit repair and what topics are covered in more detail throughout the book. If you're considering getting some outside assistance with a credit-related issue but you don't know where to look, I highly recommend Chapter 3. If you're living through one of the significant events that life has a habit of turning up — such as unemployment, divorce, or marriage — check out the sound advice and strategies in Chapter 12. If you have specific concerns, you can find your topic in the table of contents or, if you're really specific about what you want to know, in the index.

With the information in *Credit Repair Kit For Dummies,* I'm confident you can turn around your credit situation and clean up your credit report. And if your credit is good, I'm certain that, with this book by your side, you can stay on that positive path. Either way, I wish you all the best in achieving your life dreams through the responsible use of credit. You deserve it.

Finally, feel free to contact me with any questions or concerns you may have regarding any of the topics covered in this book. I'm genuinely concerned about you and your credit life. I'll be glad to make specific recommendations or forward your issues or concerns to appropriate resources if I can't help. You can e-mail me at `CreditRepairForDummies@moneymanagement.org` or you may write to me at:

Steve Bucci, President
Money Management International Financial Education Foundation,
9009 West Loop South, Suite 700
Houston, TX 77096-1719
Attention: *Credit Repair Kit For Dummies*

Part I

Understanding Credit: The Good, the Bad, and the Ugly

The 5th Wave   By Rich Tennant

WHENEVER CARL USED HIS CREDIT CARD, THE RESULTS WERE ALWAYS DISASTROUS.

In this part . . .

1 define credit, how to determine how yours is doing, and why it's so important for you to know. I describe the basic workings of credit, including details about your personal credit report and the major and minor national bureaus that report your credit history to lenders and others, such as employers and insurance companies. In this part, you discover how you can improve your credit report for maximum benefit to you. I also spell out the details of credit scores — what's good and what's not — and what you can do to get the very best credit score. Finally, I give you the scoop on credit counselors, clarifying what they can — and *can't* — do for your financial and credit well-being.

Chapter 1

The ABCs of Credit

Good credit. Bad credit. Damaged credit. Repaired credit. No matter how *you* define it right now, credit is a big part of your life. Got a credit card? No doubt, more than one. Do you carry a mortgage on a home? If so, most likely it's your biggest credit commitment. Making payments on a car? More proof, my friend, that you and credit are on intimate terms.

And that's not a bad thing by any stretch of the imagination. *Credit* — the opportunity to obtain something now by committing to pay for it in the future — is a fabulous tool that, when used to your advantage, allows you to enjoy and achieve much in the material world. Approached with knowledge and understanding of how it works, credit is a valuable and, in many cases, unavoidable tool in your financial life. Imagine trying to figure out a complicated bench saw without instructions. Ouch! Imagine if first-time home-buyers had to save $264,000 (the national average for the cost of a new home in 2004, according to the Federal Housing Finance Board) before taking ownership and stepping over the threshold. If that were the case, it's likely they'd be using a walker to enter their new abode — at an assisted-living facility!

Indeed, credit can be a valuable friend. It can also be a vindictive foe. Credit is widely misunderstood and, perhaps even more to the point, widely misused. Instead of using it as a helpful tool, many consumers have unknowingly *abused* credit and, in turn, have found themselves abused by their credit behavior. Opening up numerous lines of credit, maxing out lines of credit, making payments late (or skipping them altogether), and defaulting on loans can lead to devastating results — results that can cut off future options for borrowing, increase the cost of borrowing, and hurt in seemingly unrelated ways (losing a job opportunity or a marriage, for example).

In this chapter and in this book, I aim to help you whether you've compromised your credit, you've had it compromised by the actions of others, or you're just concerned that what you don't know may hurt you. But I go beyond the steps you need to follow for repairing your own credit. I fill you in on the basics of credit, defining the concept and providing you with the fundamental principles and terms. I show you how to identify whether you're on the road to credit trouble. Then, after I've guided you out of the mire of credit reports and scores, late payments, collection calls, and scam-artist practices, I move on to lessons in rebuilding and maintaining good credit — as helpful to readers with credit troubles as to those with spotless records. And I hit on one of the number-one credit concerns in the country today: identity theft.

You *can* repair your credit. Not by tricks or subterfuge, but through knowledge, good spending, reasonable budgeting, and safe borrowing practices. The end result? The impeccable credit standing you need to accomplish what you want to do. It is my pleasure to be your guide through this jungle of tangled terms, perplexing players, and sometimes dangerous predators.

Defining Credit: Spending Tomorrow's Money Today

Credit has its origins in the Latin word *credo*, which means, "I believe." The real underlying issues of credit are: Do you do what you promise? Are you believable and trustworthy? Have you worked hard to have a good reputation? Little is more precious to a person than being believed — and that's what credit is all about.

You (and Webster's) can also define credit as:

- Recognition given for some action or quality; a source of pride or honor; trustworthiness; credibility

- To believe or trust; to bring honor or esteem; to reflect well upon

- Permission for a customer to have goods or services that will be paid for at a later date

- The reputation of a person or firm for paying bills or other financial obligations

Pretty nice stuff. You'd like some of this, I bet.

The concept of credit is simple: You receive something *now* in return for your promise to pay for it *later*. Credit does not increase your income. It allows you to conveniently spend money that you've already saved — or to spend the money today that you know you'll earn tomorrow.

Because businesses make money when you use credit, they encourage you to use it as often as possible. In order for creditors to make as much money as possible, they would like you to spend as much as you can — as fast as you can. Helping you to spend your future earnings today is their basic plan. This plan may make them very happy — but it may not do the same for you.

Many types of credit are available to consumers today. This, I'm sure, is no surprise to you — I suspect you receive as many offers for various types of credit cards and lines of credit as I do. But despite the endless variations and terms there appear to be, most credit can be classified into one of two major types:

✔ **Secured credit:** As the name implies, *security* is involved — that is, the lender has some protection if you default on the loan. Your secured loan is backed by property, not just your word. Generally, the interest rates for secured credit are lower and the *term* (the length of time before you have to pay it all off) may be longer, because the risk of loss is lessened by the lender's ability to take back whatever you bought. In this category fall house mortgages and car loans.

✔ **Unsecured credit:** This type of credit is usually more expensive, shorter-term, and considered a higher risk by the lender. Because it is backed by your promise to repay it — but not by property — lenders are more vulnerable if you default. Credit cards fall into this category.

Chances are, you've always looked at credit from your own perspective — the viewpoint of the *borrower*. From where you're standing, you may be the hero, saving the day for a business that's begging you to buy. You acquiesce to take some stock off their hands at their fire sale, going-out-of-business closeout, grand-opening special, or end-of-month clearance — and they make money, right? From the lender's perspective, however, you represent a risk. Yes, your business is sought after, but the lender takes a chance by giving you something now for a promise to pay later. If you fail to keep your promise, the lender loses.

The degree of doubt between the lender making money and losing money dictates the terms of the credit. But how does a lender gauge the likelihood of your paying on time and as promised? The lender needs to know three things about you to gauge the risk you represent:

✔ **Your character:** Do you do what you promise? Are you reliable and honest?

✔ **Your capacity:** How much debt can you handle given your income and other obligations?

✔ **Your collateral:** What cash or property could be used to repay the debt if your income dries up?

But where can this information be had — especially if the lender doesn't know your sterling attributes firsthand? The answer: your credit report and, increasingly, your credit score. That's why, as you stand in the checkout line to open up that line of credit that allows you to buy the new dining room suite on a 90-day-same-as-cash special, you have to fill out and sign some paperwork and wait a few minutes for your credit to check out.

Sometimes, however, a few unscrupulous creditors try to take advantage of you and charge you more than the market price for the credit you want. Why? Because they like to make money. So, how do *you* know if you're being overcharged? The same way the lenders decide whether to offer you credit and what to charge you for it: by looking at your credit report and credit score.

Meeting the Cast of Characters in the Credit Story

So before I get any further into the saga of credit and all its complicated plot twists, allow me to introduce the characters. In most lending transactions, three players have lead roles: the buyer (that's you), the lender, and the credit reporter.

The buyer: In the beginning, there was stuff

The cycle of credit begins with the buyer — a person who wants something (that's you!). A house, a car, a plasma TV . . . it doesn't matter what the thing is — the definitive factor is that paying for it up front isn't convenient or possible. Maybe you just don't have the cash with you and you want the item now, perhaps because it's on sale now. Or maybe you haven't even earned the money to pay for the purchase, but you know you will and you don't want to pass up the chance.

"Hmm," you calculate as you gaze longingly at the coveted find. "I really want to get this now. If I wait until I have the money, it might be sold or the price might have gone up, so it only makes sense to buy it now." Or, if you're generous (or making excuses), you might say, "My sweetie would love this thing — and *me,* if I bought this. Who cares that I don't have the money right now? I will someday. I just know it."

ENTER CREDITORS, STAGE RIGHT.

The creditors: Heroes to the rescue

The creditor spots your desire a mile away, and it stirs the compassionate capitalist within him. "Hey," says the businessperson. "No need for you to do without. We have financing. We just need to take down a little information, do a quick credit check, and you can walk out the door with this thing you're lusting after."

If businesses can't sell you something or lend you money, they can't make a profit. So believe it or not, they really do want to loan you money. But there's that risk factor: They need to find out how risky a proposition you may be. In order to get the rundown on your credit risk, they called the credit bureau.

ENTER CREDIT BUREAU, STAGE LEFT.

The credit bureaus: In a supporting role

The merchant was most likely contacting one of three major credit-reporting bureaus — Equifax, Experian, or TransUnion — to get the credit lowdown on you. The credit bureaus make the current lending system work by providing fast, reliable, and inexpensive information about you to lenders and others.

The information in your credit report is reported by lenders doing business with one or more bureaus and put into what is the equivalent of your electronic credit history file folder. This file of data is called your *credit report,* and I devote a good portion of this book to credit reports. (See Chapter 2 for the full-blown story.)

Over the years, as more information has built up in credit reports and faster decision-making has been found to result in more sales, lenders have increasingly looked for shortcuts in the underwriting process that still offer protection from bad lending decisions. This need was met by the *credit score,* a shorthand version of all the information in your credit report. The credit score predicts the likelihood of your defaulting on a loan. The lower the score, the more likely you are to default. The higher the score, the better the odds for an on-time payback. By far, the most-used score today is the FICO score, which I cover in detail in Chapter 2. FICO scores range from 300 to 850.

ON THE CD

Power to the people: Knowing your rights

When it comes to credit, you have rights — a lot of them. Two big laws address your rights pertaining to your credit standing:

✔ **Fair Credit Reporting Act (FCRA):** The Fair Credit Reporting Act ensures fairness in lending.

✔ **Fair and Accurate Credit Transactions Act (FACTA, or the FACT Act):** The FACT Act is an update of the FCRA. It addresses credit-report accuracy and entitles you to access your data and dispute it. It also addresses the problem of identity theft and gives you leverage to deal with this crime if it happens to you.

I discuss these laws throughout this book, but if want the nitty-gritty details, you can find copies of these acts on the CD that came with this book.

In Chapter 4, I tell you about an additional 20 bureaus that have information about you. They're known as the *national specialty consumer reporting bureaus,* and they contain information on everything from how much you gamble to what medical condition you may have.

Understanding the Consequences of Bad Credit

Over the last 15 years, I've seen the underside of credit up close. During that time, I started a local credit-counseling agency that grew into a regional consumer resource and helped thousands of individuals and couples from all walks of life with credit issues. More recently, during the last few years, I've gotten questions from consumers just like you from all over the country — questions about their credit-related problems and opportunities — through my weekly "Debt Advisor" column that appears in newspapers and on the financial megasite Bankrate.com. I've witnessed time and again the devastating effects of credit gone bad.

Aside from the obvious increase in borrowing costs and maybe a hassle getting a credit card, what are the very real costs of bad credit? The extra interest you'll have to pay is only the tip of the iceberg. The real cost of bad credit is in reduced opportunities, family stress, and having to associate with lenders who, more often than not, see you as a mark to be taken for a ride and dumped before you do it to them. And, believe me, they're better at it than you are.

In this section, I fill you in on some of the unpleasant consequences of bad credit.

Fees

From your perspective as the borrower in trouble, this makes no sense at all. You're having a short-term problem making ends meet, so what do your creditors do to help you? They add some fat fees onto your balance. Thank you very much.

How do these fees help you? They don't. The fees helps the *creditor* in two ways:

- They focus your attention on *their* bill, instead of someone else's.
- The creditor gets compensated for the extra risk you just became.

As bad as the fees can be on your credit cards, they can be even worse on your secured loans. If you fall behind in your house payment three months, you can be hit with huge fees to the tune of thousands of dollars.

Secured lenders tend to be low-key. Don't let that calm voice or polite, non-threatening letter lull you into complacency. They're low-key because they don't *have* to shout — they'll very quietly take your home or other collateral, unlike the credit-card guys, who can be heard across the street. Pay attention to the quiet guy, and take action.

Late fees, over-limit fees, legal fees, repo fees, penalty fees, deficiency payments, and default rates: When the fees show up, its time to get serious. Call the creditor and ask to have the fees waived. Explain your plan to get current and let them know that you need their help, not their fees.

Chapter 11 of this book helps you put together a budget, so you know exactly how much you can afford. If you have a problem developing a budget, your creditors will accept a debt-management plan, which you work out with the help of a credit-counseling agency (see Chapter 3). Take action early enough in the game while you're still considered a desirable customer, and you're more likely to have success getting the fees removed.

Higher interest rates

Consider two home buyers: one with a credit score of 720, the other with a credit score of 619. Both are able to obtain a 30-year mortgage. But the happy new homeowner with the lower score won't be so happy to learn that, because of that lower score, he'll pay over $60,000 more in interest over the life of the loan. Why? Because the mortgage company offers an interest rate of 5.93 percent to the individual with the 720 score — and an interest rate of 8.53 percent to the borrower with the 619 score.

The concept works basically the same in any lending situation. What impact would these scores have on a new car loan? A 60-month interest rate almost *triples* for the 619 score versus the 720 score!

All of this information is based on what you did yesterday, last year, maybe even ten years ago. Do something unpleasant while you have a variable-rate line of credit outstanding, and it will take your breath away. Got a low interest rate on your credit card? Carrying a high balance because the rate is low? Go ahead, miss a payment or two and watch the rate climb to the mid- to upper 20s — percent, that is! After all, you made a mistake. So it's makeup time for the lender.

You think that getting your rate hiked for a minor infraction is unfair? That's not the end of it. Under the policy of *universal default* if you have an issue with one lender, all your lenders can hike your rates as well. Yes, even though you're still paying the others on time and as agreed! In fact, some companies even use a deteriorated credit score as reason to escalate your rates to the penalty level. Yep. Even though you're paying that loan on time, a change in your credit score (perhaps from too many account inquiries or closing some old accounts) gives the creditor that has a universal default policy full rein to hike up your interest rates. All the more reason to pay all bills on time and keep track of your credit report and credit score on a regular basis.

Sub-prime loans

Students with the highest SAT and ACT scores get their choice of the most prestigious colleges. Lending institutions aren't so different — consumers with the highest credit scores get their choice of the best borrowing opportunities and lowest interest rates.

Shopping around for the best lender becomes even more important when your score may not be as attractive as it could be. You may, for instance, find that you're offered what is known as a *sub-prime loan,* because your current risk profile makes you a high risk. With more flexibility stemming from loose credit, lenders may say yes to a loan, but at a higher — or sub-prime — cost. (In a time of tight credit, you might not qualify for a loan at all.)

My dictionary says that a sub-prime loan is "a loan that is offered at a rate above prime to individuals who do not qualify for prime rates." Wasn't that a big help? My own definition is this: A sub-prime loan is an expensive loan that you don't want if you have any choice in the matter.

You may be an innocent victim of sub-prime rates

The saddest stories of sub-prime abuse are of individuals who are "prime" but don't know it. Typically, they're in vulnerable groups: immigrants, minorities, people who don't have a familiarity with credit and their own status. The lender usually opens the conversation with some reference like "Considering your credit history . . . " or "This is a great rate for you."

When you hear words like this, consider it a warning. If you have your credit report and know your score, you can ask the hard questions back. Such as, "What is your criteria for the advertised rate?" Know *your* score and you'll know "the score," when you apply for a loan. If the offer is sub-prime and your credit report and score indicate that you deserve prime (according to either the lender's criteria or your own shopping around), I suggest you reassess your lender.

Some businesses make a lot of money putting people into more expensive loans than they qualify for. Called a *premium,* overcharging you can mean big bonuses for mortgage or car lenders. But this won't happen to you if you have the facts and know where you stand.

The Federal Home Loan Mortgage Corporation (known as Freddie Mac) estimates that as many as one-third of borrowers who end up in sub-prime loans could have received better loan terms, but due to lack of competition, ignorance of their own creditworthiness, failure to shop around, and so on, they did not. Some experts think that figure is as high as 50 percent.

Two guys walk into a hardware store and pick up the same screwdriver. (No, this isn't the beginning of a joke — unless you have a pretty sick sense of humor.) At the checkout counter, the first guy pays $10. The cashier rings up the second guy's screwdriver at $15. Seem fair? Not likely. But this is exactly what happens when you apply for credit with lenders who charge you more than your friend because of what's on your credit report. Whether it's a screwdriver or a new car, I don't need to tell you what you're *really* getting with a sub-prime loan.

Lost employment opportunities

Prospective lenders aren't the only ones who judge you based on your credit report and credit score. Potential employers check out your credit report, too. Why is that, you ask? After all, they're in position to pay *you,* not the other way around. But businesses reason that the way you handle your finances is a reflection of your behavior in other areas of your life. If you're late paying your bills, you may be late for work. If you default on your car loan, you may not follow through with an important assignment.

Even if your credit woes can be explained, bad credit is a distraction from the employer's perspective, and it detracts from worker productivity. Recent research shows that employees with credit problems are significantly less productive on the job than those without. So, the easy way out for the employer is to not bother to find out what's going on, but to hire someone with good credit instead.

Increasingly, credit checks are a standard part of the hiring — and even promotion — process at companies large and small throughout the United States.

Higher insurance premiums

The brain trust at the insurance companies (known as *actuaries*), love their numbers. They sniff out a trend, sometimes even before it happens, and slap a charge on it faster than my cat can catch a mouse — and, let me tell, you she's *fast!*

The fact that a strong correlation exists between bad credit and reported claims has not escaped the attention of these people. The upshot: Bad credit will cost you a bundle in insurance-premium increases and may result in your insurance being denied.

Some states have gotten very excited about safe drivers and homeowners getting premium increases with no claims being reported. They've outlawed or restricted the use of credit reports and scores in setting insurance prices. The states are still battling with this issue and it is difficult to say whether current laws will be overturned, upheld or more will be added. Currently a majority of states have something on the books about using credit report information in determining access to insurance, insurance rates or underwriting. Fair Isaac has developed an Insurance Score. The score is calculated by taking information from your credit report, but the formula is different from the one used to figure your credit score. Insurance scores range from 500 to 997 with 626 to 775 being average. To find out if scores are used in your state, contact your local state insurance department.

More financial stress *may* be distracting and *may* result in more accidents. Is it a sign that if you're fastidious about your credit you'll be the same about car and home maintenance? There are a number of studies underway, including one at the Fair Trade Commission, trying to determine if this practice is kosher. Time will tell. But in the meantime, bad credit can cost you when it comes to insurance premiums.

Divorce

Would your better half dump you because of bad credit? Maybe not, but one thing is sure: Half of all marriages end in divorce, and the biggest cause of fighting in a marriage is due to financial issues — as in bad credit.

Spouses want to be proud of their mates. And with credit playing a bigger role in so many aspects of modern American life, living with bad credit has to be a bit like living under a cloud. I advise couples who are serious about pursuing a life together to talk about their attitudes on money and credit use. Sweeping this topic under the rug is too easy. Having a credit card refused for payment (often in front of others), worrying about which card still has some room on it, or getting collection calls in the sanctuary of your home can be part of the credit nightmare you face as a couple. If you can't seem to find the words to talk about this sensitive topic or agree on a solution, get some professional advice before it becomes too late (see Chapter 3 for more information).

As a former counselor, I've seen too many people ruin otherwise promising marriages over money and credit. I can't help but offer some advice on bad credit and marriage:

✔ Get a credit report before you marry.

✔ Discuss money and agree on goals.

✔ Find out if your honey is a spender or a saver.

✔ Fix your credit before it fixes you (as in "My cat is going to get fixed").

I cover this topic in more detail in Chapter 12.

Identity Theft: The Crime That Turns Good Credit Bad

Touted loudly as one of the largest and fastest growing of crimes in the United States, identity theft is, indeed, a serious problem that can devastate your credit and your ability to get loans, employment, insurance, and some security clearances and licenses without your ever having done anything to deserve it. An identity theft can also put you on the defensive, burdening you with the responsibility of proof — that you are not the person collectors are after. Chapter 13 specifically addresses these issues — but for now, read on.

Protecting your identity from theft

To avoid the havoc wreaked by identity theft, your best bet is to avoid being a victim of identity theft altogether. Consider these tips:

- **Protect your financial information at home.** Don't leave credit-card numbers and statements, Social Security information, bank-account information, and other financial data unprotected. Most identity theft is low-tech (that is, paper-based). And most is carried out by people you know: friends, relatives (I've always worried about some of my aunts), acquaintances, coworkers, and people you invite into your home for a variety of reasons.

   Shred statements before putting them in the trash and lock your sensitive information away. Using your computer more (as long as you use it properly and password-protect information), is an even better way to avoid theft.

- **Watch the mail.** Sending and receiving financial statements and bills in your household mail can be risky. Most people think that no one is watching their unprotected mailboxes. And most are right, but that leaves the rest of you with sensitive account numbers and documents containing your Social Security number sitting all day in an unlocked mailbox outside your home or apartment. By comparison, e-mail is much safer.

Taking action if you're victimized

If you're a victim of identity theft, you may first discover that fact through a collection call on an account you never opened or unusual activity on a credit card or credit report. When you suspect your identity has been compromised, respond immediately. Here are some tips:

- **Write down everything.** This process may not be quick or simple, but it is critical.

- **Call any creditors affected and close your accounts.** Don't forget ATM and debit cards — you have higher limits of liability for these than you do credit cards, so they're particularly important.

- **Call a credit bureau and place a fraud alert.** The bureau you contact will inform the other two bureaus. A credit report will be sent to you after you make your call.

- **If you're in a state that allows you to freeze your credit report, do it.** (You can unfreeze it later.) If you live in a no-freeze state, you can add a victim's statement to your credit report. This tells anyone getting your report that there is a problem with your file.

- **Call the police and make out a report.** Some creditors and collectors require this to take action. Be sure to get a copy of the report.

Taking Charge of Your Credit

Now that you have a better understanding of the perils and pitfalls of credit, you *can* take charge of your credit! By following some very basic actions — some of which have an element of fun and inspiration — you can harness the power of credit to your advantage:

- ✔ Borrowing when it suits your needs without paying outrageous interest rates

- ✔ Taking advantage of lucrative lending offers such as "same-as-cash" and "no-money-down" offers typically available only to those with stellar credit histories

- ✔ Achieving your life dreams, whether owning that vine-covered cottage or sending your offspring to an Ivy League university

It all begins with the simple steps I cover in the following sections.

Setting your financial goals

Your financial goals serve as a beacon to you and keep you on course. You've heard the saying "If you don't know where you're going, any road will take you there." Well, if you don't have clear objectives when it comes to how you want to spend and save your money, you risk veering off on that rocky and perilous path to bad credit. Your goals — whether as grand as starting your own business or as modest as buying a new refrigerator — help you keep your eye on the horizon and guide you to your destination. Chapter 11 helps you put together a list of your goals, for the near and far-off future.

Creating a budget

Call it a spending plan, if you like, but however you refer to it, be sure to see it as a positive *enabler,* rather than a restriction or a barrier. The purpose of the budget is to get you to arrive at your goal. If, for example, your goal is to take a beach vacation next year, putting money aside each paycheck and limiting spending on restaurants and clothing are as important in getting you there as filling the gas tank and turning the car on the highway that leads to the shore.

Start with an understanding of how much income you have to work with, and then allocate it as necessary for living expenses. If you have debt, set aside part of your income to retire that debt just as quickly as you can.

Then, just as important as your expenses and debt commitment, be sure you contribute to your own savings plans: one toward an emergency fund (in case of job loss or illness, for example); the others, for your goals (your kids, your honey, your retirement). Make saving as automatic as possible (an IRA or 401[k] for retirement, for example); the money can come right out of your paycheck. Use payroll deduction as an easy way to do this — and try to put at least half of your future raises in savings. You can spend the other half.

In Chapter 11, I walk you through creating your own personal budget.

Obtaining and maintaining your credit reports and credit score

Like your annual medical exam, this data serves as your routine credit checkup — only you're wise to schedule this exam every four months. Get it more often if you have a need — a big purchase on the horizon or a job change, for example. Pay for it, if you have to. It won't kill you. For information about ordering your credit reports and credit score, read Chapter 4.

Read your credit reports — every word. Errors do happen and when you're dealing with billions of pieces of data a month, they can happen a lot. Do you count your change when you check out at the supermarket or a restaurant? Your credit report is no small change. Dispute the errors, outdated information, and negative stuff that belongs to someone else's report.

Check for signs of identity theft and take immediate action if you discover evidence that someone else is using your good name. Chapter 13 of this book addresses identity theft in detail.

Being a good credit citizen

You're already so many other good things: a good person, a mother or father, a boyfriend or girlfriend, a spouse, a sibling, a worker. Do you really need someone telling you to be a good borrower, too? The answer: Yes.

I bet you knew I was going to say that, didn't you? The reason is not about you, but about the environment you're in. Taking the credit that is offered, using the credit that is offered, even not using credit at all can get you into trouble. So how do you know what's "good"? You weren't born with the credit gene that enabled you to understand the correct road to follow like so many migrating birds.

Being a good credit citizen means being responsible as a borrower, responsible to yourself and those who share your life. This starts with goals, a future vision of your life and knowing which financial tools to use, in what measure, and when.

Here are my top ten good-citizen credit practices:

✔ Set goals.

✔ Have a spending plan or budget.

✔ Use long-term credit for long-term uses. Don't use a home-equity line to buy sneakers or eat out (see Chapter 10 for more on home-equity lines).

✔ Use short-term credit for short-term uses. Pay off your credit-card balances as quickly as you can.

✔ Save money for future goals and needs.

✔ Pay your bills on time.

✔ Pay at least the amount due. Always set a time by which you will pay off a debt; don't let the creditor set the time for you, because it may be forever.

✔ Watch out for the seven warning signs of bad credit:

- Using credit cards for daily expenses and not paying the balance every month

- Not knowing how much you owe

- Using cash advances to pay credit-card bills or for daily expenses

- Only paying the minimum due on credit cards, or paying less than the minimum

- Getting calls from your creditors

- Spending more than 20 percent of your take-home pay on credit payments, excluding your mortgage

- Arguing about money at home

✔ Never fight over credit or money.

✔ Get help as soon as you think you may need it — not as a last resort.

Reading the rest of this book

This book will help you gain the knowledge you need to be in charge. Read it. I wrote it for *you*. Honest.

Chapter 2

The Ins and Outs of Credit Reports

*M*any people put their credit reports in the same category as IQ results, SAT scores, school report cards, job reviews, and cholesterol readings — in other words, information that doesn't seem all that relevant to their day-to-day life. They figure that if they're looking to buy a home, they need to know what shape their credit is in. But for most times, knowing about their credit history just isn't that important. Right? Unfortunately, these people couldn't be more wrong.

In this chapter, I explain why you need to be on intimate terms with your credit report. Speaking of intimate, consider two hypothetical life situations to illustrate my point:

✔ Let's say you signed up for a dating service. Now, what if all the information available to your prospective dates is given to them by people you've dated in the past? What if the quality of the dates you get in the future are directly tied to what all the people you've dumped (or been dumped by) say about you? Starting to sweat a little?

✔ Let's say you're applying for a job. Your salary, job title, and the size of your office will be tied directly to what's on your résumé. But what if you didn't write your résumé — your past employers did, and what if they've mixed your personnel file with the file of that person who was fired for sexual harassment? Can you imagine walking into that job interview without any idea what your former boss may have reported or whether it was correct?

Meeting your life partner, landing a great job — these situations are ones in which you have a great deal of personal investment and interest in a successful outcome. Kind of like getting a good mortgage rate so you can afford that dream home.

I'm not saying you're guaranteed to *like* the outcome of the date or the job interview — but at least you know it's based on information you're privy to. Likewise with your credit report. You can't rewrite your own credit history, but you *can* be knowledgeable about what a credit report is and how much weight it carries as you try to negotiate your way through the financial universe. You *can* be savvy to situations that could cost you thousands of dollars more or deny you opportunities. And you *can* catch inaccuracies on your report (a common situation) and correct them.

Your credit report doesn't come into play just when you want to borrow money. A bad credit report may affect what you pay for insurance, whether you can rent the apartment of your choice, or whether you'll be hired for certain jobs. Heck, a particularly finance-conscious romantic prospect might even nix you for a bad credit history! It's a fact, Jack: Your credit score can cost you thousands of dollars and deny you opportunities you never even knew you missed. Clearly, what you don't know *can* hurt you.

There is no excuse for not knowing what's in your credit report. You should have a current copy of your credit report from each of the three credit bureaus (Equifax, Experian, and TransUnion). And don't even think about saying you can't afford it, because you can now request your credit report from each credit bureau once a year for *free*.

So, what's in your report? Is the information correct — or even yours? And if not, what can you do to fix it? Settle in for some facts that will open your eyes and save you money, time, and frustration.

What Is a Credit Report, Anyway?

In its most basic sense, your credit report is your financial life history of borrowing money. This information is gathered, managed, maintained, and shared by a credit-reporting bureau or agency. Trust me: You don't have to lift a finger to create it or disseminate it. There are actually as many as 20 credit-reporting bureaus; most are specialty reporting agencies (I introduce you to some of these at the end of this chapter). The following three are considered the biggies:

- **Equifax** (www.equifax.com; 800-685-1111)
- **Experian** (www.experian.com; 888-397-3742)
- **TransUnion** (www.transunion.com; 800-888-4213)

Every day, businesses rely on the information in your credit report to help them decide whether to lend you money and at what price (otherwise known as the *interest rate* and *loan terms*). But because the information in your credit report can be sliced and diced many ways, your report becomes an important tool that serves different purposes for different people:

✔ For a lender, your credit report is a tool to determine how likely you are to repay the loan, and it's an indicator of how much interest and what fees to charge you based on the risk profile you represent.

✔ For an insurance company, your credit report is a tool to predict how likely you are to have an accident or file a claim.

✔ For an employer, your credit report is a tool to predict whether you'll be a trustworthy employee.

✔ For a landlord, your credit report is a tool to determine whether you're likely to pay the rent on time.

✔ For you, your credit report is a tool to help you understand how you've handled your finances in the past and how you're likely to handle them in the future.

A picture is worth a thousand words: What your credit report says about you

As a snapshot of your financial life, your credit report may also indirectly predict your potential behaviors in other areas of your life. The fact that you have a history of making credit-card payments late may tell a prospective landlord that you're likely to be late with your rent, too. A history of defaulted loans may suggest to a potential boss that you aren't someone who follows through with commitments. If you've declared bankruptcy because your finances are out of control, perhaps you're out of control in other ways, too.

This snapshot, which brings into focus the details of your spending and borrowing, and even suggests your personal life patterns, also paints a *bigger* picture of two important factors — characteristics that are critical to employers, landlords, lenders, and others. I cover these two critical characteristics in the following sections.

Do you do what you promise?

Your credit history is an indicator of whether you're someone who follows through with commitments — a characteristic important to most people, whether they're looking for a reliable worker, a responsible nanny, a dependable renter, or a faithful mate. Needless to say, a person or company considering lending you a sizeable sum of money will want to know the same.

Based in large part on your history of following through with your financial promises, you'll be assigned a credit score. People with higher scores generally get the best terms, including lower interest rates and reduced minimum down payments. People with low credit scores can usually get credit in today's economy, but they pay higher interest rates and possibly additional fees or insurance.

Do you do it on time?

When it comes to your credit score, following through with your promises is only half of the game. The other half is doing it on time. It's a fact in the lending business that the more overdue the payment, the more likely it will not be paid at all — or paid in full. This is why, as you get further behind in your payments, lenders become more anxious about collecting the amount you owe. In fact, if you're sufficiently delinquent, the lender may want you to pay back the entire amount at once rather than as originally scheduled. (When it comes to money, your creditors' faith in you is only 30 to 90 days long.) So, the longer you take to do what you promised, the more it costs you and the more damage you do to your credit score.

Uncovering the details in your credit report

Many people believe that your credit report contains the intimate personal details of your life, ferreted out from interviews with your neighbors, your ex, and your business associates. Not true! You can rest assured that your credit report does not reveal whether you tend to drink too much at office parties, whether you sport a tattoo, or whether you had an eye lift or indulged in a wild fling on your last vacation to Mexico.

The information in your credit report is specific, purely factual, and limited in scope. What it lacks in scope, however, it makes up for in sheer volume of material and length of time it covers. When I talk to high school, college, or technical-school students, I tell them that if they cut a class, chances are no one will notice, but if they fail to pay a bill on time, a multibillion-dollar industry will notice, record it, and tell everyone who asks about them for the next seven years!

Here's the short take on what's in your credit report:

- ✓ **Personal identification information** such as your name, Social Security number, addresses (present and past), and your most recent employment history.
- ✓ **Public-record information** on tax liens, judgments, bankruptcies, child-support orders, and other official information.

✔ **Collection activity** for accounts that have been sent to collection agencies for handling.

✔ **Information about each credit account,** open or closed (also known as *trade lines*), such as whom you owe, the type of account (such as a mortgage or installment account), whether the account is *joint* (shared with another person) or just in your name, how much you owe, your monthly payment, how you've paid (on time or late), and your credit limits.

✔ **A list of the companies that have requested your credit file** either for promotional purposes (like sending you a hot offer) or in response to your request for more or new credit. *Note:* The companies that look at your report for promotional purposes don't appear on the report that prospective creditors see, but they do appear on the copy you can request for your own review.

✔ **An optional message from you** that can be up to 100 words in length and that explains any extenuating circumstances for any negative listings on your report.

✔ **An optional credit score.** Your credit score is, strictly speaking, not part of your credit report but an add-on that you have to ask for. Just as the information in your credit report may vary from one bureau to another, so your score may vary. (I cover the importance of your credit score later in this chapter.)

Credit reports used to be very difficult to read. Most of the data appeared in a nearly indecipherable numeric code, which was mystifying to the average reader. Today, although there's still room for improvement, credit reports are more readily understood by the average person. Each of the three major credit-reporting agencies reports similar credit information but each in its own unique format. *Remember:* The credit-reporting agencies are competing with each other for business, so they have to differentiate their products.

Among the list of items *not* included in your credit report are your lifestyle choices, religion, national origin, political affiliation, sexual preferences, friends, and relatives. Additionally, the three major credit-reporting agencies do not collect or transmit data on your medical history, checking or savings accounts, brokerage accounts, or similar financial records.

On the CD, you can view a sample credit report from TransUnion. You can see sample credit reports from Equifax and Experian online:

✔ **Equifax:** Go to `www.equifax.com` and, from the "Products" drop-down menu, click on "Equifax Credit Report"; then click on "See Equifax Credit Report sample."

✔ **Experian:** Go to `www.experian.com/consumer_online_products/credit_report.html` and click on "View Sample Report."

Understanding How Bad Stuff Gets in Your Credit Report

Whether you're new to the world of credit or you're an experienced borrower, you need to keep a few key concepts in mind as you look over your credit report. Like the person who can't see the forest because there are too many trees, when you get your hands on your credit report you may be blinded by the amount of information. In the following sections, I help you focus on what matters and let go of what doesn't.

Nobody's perfect: Don't expect a straight-A report card

You aren't perfect. (I hate to have to be the one to tell you this, but if you aren't married, someone had to!) The same goes for your credit report — and lack of perfection isn't a big deal as long as your credit report shows more smooth patches than bumps. No matter how early you mail off that bill payment, it can still arrive late or get lost, which means you can expect to find some negative information on your credit report from time to time. The good news is that you can still be eligible for plenty of loans at competitive rates and terms without having a flawless credit report or qualifying for credit sainthood.

But how many bad marks are okay? How long do they stay? And how will they be interpreted by lenders who view your report?

Let's say you're a well-heeled, easy-going gal and you loan your boyfriend $5,000 for a very worthy cause. He promises to pay you back monthly over two years. But after four months without a payment, it's likely that two things will happen: He'll no longer be your sweetie and you'll have mentally written off any chance of collecting the debt. Plus, if you're smart, you'll think twice before loaning money to a friend again. You might even mention the negative experience to your friends, especially if they were thinking of floating him a loan.

If you were to run into your ex-boyfriend sometime down the road, you'd probably mention the $5,000 — after all, you want your money back, and he still owes you! Whether you'd ask him to join you for dinner is another matter and might depend on his showing you some good-faith gesture!

In business, as in love, trust and faithful performance are keys to success. A creditor can tell your future and current creditors any repayment information that is correct and accurate through your credit report, in the same way that you would warn your friends about your ex-boyfriend. That information or warning may be modified at any time, as long as the new information is correct and accurate.

Just how much does a mistake cost you when it comes to your credit report? Well, it depends on your history. Along with the credit report, and all the information that it contains, lenders can also buy a *credit score* based on the information in the report. That score comes from a mathematical equation that evaluates much of the information on your credit report at that particular credit bureau. By comparing this information to the patterns in zillions of past credit reports, the score tells the lender your level of future credit risk.

The most widely used of these credit scores is the FICO score. In order for a FICO score to be calculated on your credit report, it must contain at least one account which has been open for six months or greater and the report must contain at least one account that has been updated in the past six months.

So, people with a lot of information in their credit files will find that a lot of good credit experiences will lessen the effect of a single negative item. Score one for the old folks with long credit histories! If you're a young person with only a few trade lines and months of credit history (sometimes called a *thin file*), a negative event will have a much larger effect in relation to the information available. Many young people think the world is stacked against them. In this case, it's true — but to be fair, it's also stacked against anyone with a limited credit history, regardless of age.

FICO takes into account more than 20 factors when building your score and the importance of each one is dependent on the other factors and the volume of data and length of your history. (I cover the factors that affect your credit score later in this chapter.)

Checking for errors: Creditors aren't perfect, either

Other people make mistakes, too. Even banks and credit-card payment processors! Considering that about 4.5 billion pieces of data are added to credit reports every month, it shouldn't be a big surprise that incorrect information may show up on your credit report. And I won't even get into the unrelated problem of errors caused as a result of identify theft. (I address this at length in Chapter 13.) There have been a number of conflicting studies on what percentage of reports contain errors and of those, how many were serious enough to affect either the terms under which credit was granted or if it was granted at all. So, you may have errors on your report or not. And they may be serious or not. But unless you are feeling really lucky, I strongly suggest you find out what's in your report.

Still, credit-reporting agencies have a vested interest in the accuracy of the information they report. **Remember:** They sell it, and their reputations are on the line if their information is consistently inaccurate. If credit-reporting agencies consistently provide error-riddled data, those who grant credit won't be as eager to pay money to get or use a bureau's credit reports.

Getting a copy of your credit report gives you a chance to check for these errors and — better yet — get them corrected! You can have inaccurate information removed by one of two methods: contacting the credit bureau or contacting the creditor.

Contacting the credit bureau

If you notice incorrect information on your credit report, contact the credit bureau that reported the inaccurate information. Each of the three major bureaus allows you to dispute information in your credit report on its Web site, or you can call the bureau's toll-free number (see "What Is a Credit Report, Anyway?" earlier in this chapter). If you make your dispute online, you'll need to have a copy of your credit report available; there is information on the report that will allow the bureau to confirm your identity without a signature. If you opt to call the toll-free number, you're unlikely to get a live person on the other end — this stuff is heavily automated — but you'll be told what information and documentation you need in order submit a written request. After you properly notify the credit bureau, you can count on action.

Credit-reporting agencies are required by the Fair Credit Reporting Act to investigate any disputed listings. The credit bureau must verify the item in question with the creditor *at no cost* to you, the consumer. The law requires that the creditor respond and verify the entry within 30 days, or the information must be removed from your credit report, and the credit-reporting agency has to notify you of the outcome. If information in the report has been changed or deleted, you also get a *free* copy of the revised report.

Contacting the creditor

Another way to remove inaccurate information from your credit report is outlined under the Fair and Accurate Credit Transactions Act (FACT Act or FACTA), passed in 2003 and rolled out in pieces through 2005. Under these new FACTA provisions, you can deal directly with the creditor who reported the negative information in the first place. Contact information is contained on your latest billing statement from that creditor.

I strongly suggest you do everything in writing, return-receipt requested. After you dispute the information, the reporting creditor must look into the matter and cannot continue to report the negative information while it's investigating your dispute.

For new delinquencies, FACTA now requires that you be notified if negative information is reported to a credit bureau. That said, you may have to look closely to even see this new notice. Anyone who extends credit to you must send you a one-time notice either before or not later than 30 days after negative information — including late payments, missed payments, partial payments, or any other form of default — is furnished to a credit bureau. This includes collection agencies, as long as they report to a credit bureau. The notice may look something like this:

✔ **Before negative information is reported:** "We may report information about your account to credit bureaus. Late payments, missed payments, or other defaults on your account may be reflected in your credit report."

✔ **After negative information is reported:** "We have told a credit bureau about a late payment, missed payment, or other default on your account. This information may be reflected in your credit report."

The notice is not a substitute for your own close monitoring of your credit reports, bank accounts, and credit-card statements.

Looking at the accurate information

Most of the information in your credit report will be accurate. There is a popular misconception out there that data stays on your credit report for seven years and then drops off. What really happens is that negative data will stay on your credit report for seven years, although a few items are different, such as a Chapter 7 bankruptcy, which will stay on for ten years. Even though the negative information is out there for a long time, as the months and years roll by, the information becomes less important to your credit profile. The fact that you were late in paying your credit-card bill one time three years ago will not concern most creditors. Positive information, however — the good stuff we all like to see — stays on your report for a much longer time. Some positive data may be on your report for 10, 20, or even 30 years, depending on whether you keep your account open and depending on each bureau's policy.

Negative information might, however, be used by unscrupulous lenders as a reason to put you into a higher-cost (and more profitable for them) loan, even though you qualify for a less-expensive one. This is just one example of a situation in which understanding your credit score can save you money. The scenario can go something like this: You're looking for a loan for a big-ticket item. Instead of going from bank to bank and wasting days of precious free time or risking being turned down after filling out long applications and explaining about the $5,000 your ex-boyfriend owes you, you go to a trusted financial advisor who knows how these things work. She pulls your credit report and shops for a loan for you. The answer that you're given is that this is "a great deal considering your credit score." Translated, this means you're being charged a higher-than-market rate because of your imperfect credit score. If you don't know what your score is and what rate that score will entitle you to in the marketplace, you may be taken advantage of. So read on and get the skinny on credit scores, which have a big effect on your interest rates and terms.

You Can Call Me HAL: Computer Models and How to Decipher Your Credit Score

With billions of pieces of data floating around, it's little wonder that the people who use this data to make decisions turned to computers to help make sense of it all. Starting back in the 1950s, some companies, including one called Fair Isaac Corporation, began to *model* credit data in hopes of predicting payment behavior. (A model uses a series of formulas based on some basic assumptions to simulate and understand future behavior or to make predictions. Weathermen use models to predict your weather for tomorrow. Usually, the credit guys are more accurate because they're predicting the likelihood of something happening in the next year or so.) Today, the three major credit bureaus use the scoring model provided by Fair Isaac — known as the *FICO score*. Your FICO score is a three-digit number that rules a good portion of your financial life, for better or worse.

Understanding what your credit score is made up of is an important step in ensuring that yours is the best it can be. Until recently, the proprietary formula for FICO scores was a well-guarded secret. Creditors were concerned that if you knew the formula, you might be tempted to manipulate the information to distort the outcome in your favor. Well, that may or may not be the case, but if creditors are looking for good behavior on your part, I think it only makes sense to tell you what constitutes good behavior. In 2001, Fair Isaac agreed with me, with a little help from some regulators, and disclosed the factors and weightings used to determine your credit score. In this section, I give you the skinny.

FICO scores range from 300 to 850. The higher the number, the better the credit rating. Based on the general population's FICO scores, the ranges and percentages of scores are as follows:

- ✔ Twenty percent have scores above 780.
- ✔ Twenty percent have scores in the range of 745 to 780.
- ✔ Twenty percent have scores in the range of 690 to 744.
- ✔ Twenty percent have scores in the range of 620 to 689.
- ✔ Twenty percent have scores below 620.

A person may have no credit score at all, because he doesn't have enough of a credit history. In order for a FICO score to be calculated, you need to have at least one account that has been open for at least six months and you need at least one account that has been updated in the past six months. Although having no credit history will make it difficult for you to get credit initially, you'll find it a lot easier to build credit for the first time than to repair a bad credit history (which is like being two runs down in a ballgame and trying to catch up).

Fleshing out FICO-score components

Your FICO score is made up of five components (see Figure 2-1):

✔ **Paying on time (35 percent):** Payment history is considered the most significant factor when determining whether an individual is a good credit risk. This category includes the number and severity of any late payments, the amount past due, and whether the accounts were repaid as agreed. The more problems, the lower the score.

✔ **Amount and type of debt (30 percent):** The amount owed is the next most important factor in your credit score. This includes the total amount you owe; the amount you owe by account type (such as revolving, installment, or mortgage); the number of accounts on which you're carrying a balance; and the proportion of the credit lines used. For example, in the case of installment credit, *proportion of balance* means the amount remaining on the loan in relation to the original amount of the loan. For revolving debt, such as a credit card, it would be the amount you currently owe in relation to your credit limit. You want a low balance amount owed in relation to your amount of credit available. Having credit cards with no balances ups your limits and your score.

✔ **The length of time you've been using credit (15 percent):** The number of years you've been using credit and the type of accounts you have also influence your score. Accounts that have been open for at least two years will help to increase your score.

✔ **The variety of accounts (10 percent):** The mix of credit accounts is a part of each of the other factors. Riskier types of credit will mean lower scores. For example, if most of your debt is in the form of revolving credit or finance-company loans, your score will be lower than if your debt is from student loans and mortgage loans. Also, the lender will give more weight to your performance on its type of loan. So, a credit-card issuer looks at your experience with other credit cards more closely and a mortgagee will look pay closer attention to how you pay mortgages or secured loans. An ideal mix of accounts will have many types of different credit used.

✔ **The number and types of accounts you've opened recently, generally in the last 6 months or so (10 percent):** The number of new credit applications you've filled out, any increases in credit lines requested by you (unsolicited one's don't count) and the types and number of new credit accounts you have will affect your credit score. The reasoning here is that if you're applying for several accounts at the same time, and you're approved for all of them, you may not be able to afford your new debt load.

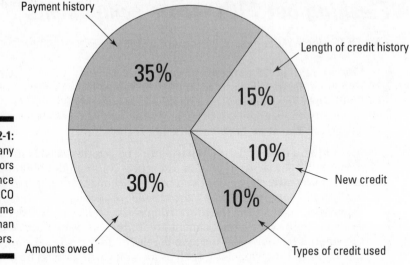

Payment history

Length of credit history

35%

15%

10%

Figure 2-1:
Many
factors
influence
your FICO
score, some
more than
others.

30%

10%

New credit

Amounts owed

Types of credit used

Are you a "normal" credit risk?

How normal are you? Ask your mother and your best friend, and you'll get two different answers. Ask Fair Isaac, and you'll get a statistically accurate snapshot. For them normal is not so much an average number as it is a range into which a large percentage of borrowers fall. If you fall outside the range, this does not mean that you are in any way abnormal, but just that your standard deviation (whatever that is) is outside of a range.

Well, I did ask and they tell me that you're "normal" if you

- ✔ **Have a total of 11 credit accounts that report to a credit bureau.** These include credit cards (such as department-store charge cards, gas cards, or bank cards) and installment loans (auto loans, mortgage loans, student loans, and so on). *Not* included are savings and checking accounts (typically not reported to a credit bureau). Of these 11 credit obligations, 7 are likely to be credit cards and 4 are likely to be installment loans.

- ✔ **Have never been reported as 30 or more days late on a payment.** Sixty percent of people fall into this category.

- ✔ **Have been 30 days late but never 60 or more days overdue on any credit obligation.** Twenty percent meet this criteria.

- ✔ **Carry a credit-card balance of less than $1,000.** About half of credit-card holders do this.

✔ **Have access to an average of $12,190 in credit lines on all credit cards combined.**

✔ **Have had a credit card or loan from the same source for 13 years.** This indicates you've been managing credit for some time.

Chances are that you don't fit all the preceding criteria. That's not a problem. *Remember:* Normal is more of a statistical term than a description of quality. You can still be stellar while not being "normal." Ask your spouse if you don't believe me.

Are you a "higher-than-normal" credit risk?

You are other than normal (I suggest you confirm this with your friends, not your mother) if you:

✔ **Have a credit history shorter than two years.** Only 5 percent of consumers do.

✔ **Have total card balances in excess of $10,000.** Another dubious distinction shared by about 10 percent of card holders. The issue here is that you're better off carrying a balance on an installment loan or line of credit rather than a credit card. If you're using your cards this way, the lender may wonder why. It's like driving a car in second gear all the time. Yes, you can do it, but it may indicate that you could use some additional drivers ed. The same applies here. Use your credit cards for short-term borrowing, and use other, more-appropriate types of credit for carrying balances long-term.

✔ **Have ever had a loan or account closed by the lender due to default.** If this happened to you, you're among only 10 percent of your fellow borrowers. (And those are not the people you want be among!)

✔ **Have had a loan or account that was 90 or more days overdue.** Only 15 percent of people reach this point.

Although the exact effect of any one action is hard to pinpoint, missing even one payment can knock 50 to 100 points off a good score. Something as commonplace as a bankruptcy (well over 1 million people file bankruptcy each year) can knock 200 points, or more, off a credit score.

For more-specific details on improving your credit score, many sources now offer "score simulator" products. These tools can help you determine how specific actions would affect your score. Two sources for these simulators are www.bankrate.com and www.myfico.com.

If you're neither "normal" nor "bad"

If you're not "normal" and not "higher than normal" from a conventional credit-profile standpoint, don't worry. FICO has a score for you, too: It's the FICO Expansion score, a credit-risk score based upon nontraditional consumer credit data (in other words, not based on data from the three major national credit bureaus). The purpose of this new score is to predict the credit risk of consumers who don't have a traditional FICO score. The use of FICO Expansion scores gives millions of new consumers an opportunity to access credit without extensive credit histories including:

- ✔ Young people just entering the credit market
- ✔ New arrivals and immigrants to the United States
- ✔ People who previously had mostly joint credit and are now widowed or divorced
- ✔ People who used cash rather than credit most or all of the time

More information on the FICO Expansion score is available in Chapter 5.

Looking at other credit scores: A FICO score by any other name is not a FICO score

There is considerable competition in the credit-reporting business. Even in the credit-scoring business where Fair Isaac is the 600-pound gorilla, others are trying to steal the bananas right out of Isaac's mouth. These other, non-FICO scores are proprietary models that credit bureaus offer to their customers.

What most people don't know, until they try to use these other credit scores with a lender (or go blind reading the fine print), is that these proprietary scores are only provided to consumers and not lenders. The lender scores, which are almost all FICO-derived, can vary greatly from the proprietary bureau scores. So be sure you're getting a FICO score.

Even if you're sure you're getting a FICO score, do yourself a big favor and find out from your lender of choice which bureau's report it uses. Just as the information about an individual can differ across the three companies, so can the FICO score. My suggestion is to get all three FICO scores while you're at it. That way, you have all the information you need. You can get these three scores as part of a package deal at www.myfico.com.

When you get to insurance companies, all bets are off. Yes, they use credit scores. And, yes, they may use a Fair Isaac model. But after that, the actuarial department can tinker to its mathematical heart's content. No one knows exactly what factors into the insurance-company decision (or into the mind of an actuary for that matter) to raise your rates or deny you insurance.

Credit scores are part but not all of the equation, and the factors are not made public. If you're concerned about insurance scores, you may want to order an ATTRACT Insurance Score from the ChoiceTrust Web site (`www.choicetrust.com`); the scores range from 200 to 997.

Examining Specialized Credit Bureaus

In the world of credit reports, there are the "big three" credit-reporting bureaus: Equifax, Experian, and TransUnion. But specialty credit-reporting bureaus, which are covered by the Fair Credit Reporting Act and the Fair and Accurate Credit Transaction Act, also exist. In fact, to allow for the large number and to allow for even more to come under the law, they aren't specifically named by the Federal Trade Commission as the big three are — the list would be too long and it would change frequently. Specialized credit bureaus report data about you in areas such as gambling, checking, medical, and insurance experience.

Exploring all these specialized bureaus would require a book of its own, but I do want to give you a sampling of what's out there. In the following sections, I fill you in on two types that are worth knowing about.

Getting to know the national check registries

One of my favorite stories as a kid was the original 1932 *Tarzan, The Ape Man,* in which the big guy goes to the elephant graveyard. The legend was that when elephants knew they were going to die, they all went to this big, secret graveyard to do it — and it was full of ivory! Well, where do checks go when they bounce? To the bounced-check graveyard, of course, and it must be full of rubber!

There are three main repositories of information on your checking-account activity. They contain only *negative* information about your history — banks only report the bad news to them. Each of these repositories has a database of information that its members, retailers, and other subscribers use to help make decisions regarding the acceptance of checks or the opening of accounts. This information helps members reduce their financial losses from returned checks, improve customer service, and safeguard against identity theft and fraud. Three of the repositories are

✔ **Chex Systems** (www.consumerdebit.com/consumerinfo/us/en/
chexsystems/report/index.htm; 800-428-9623)

✔ **Shared Check Authorization Network (SCAN)** (www.consumerdebit.
com/consumerinfo/us/en/index.htm; 800-262-8186)

✔ **TeleCheck** (www.telecheck.com; 800-209-8186)

Maybe working with all that negative information has rubbed off on these
companies, but they aren't as easy to deal with as the other relatively
consumer-friendly credit bureaus. They're regulated under the Fair Credit
Reporting Act, so you can get a free copy of your report and dispute errors as
you can with the other credit bureaus.

But you can't get a report online. You must call a toll-free phone number and
go through a menu before you finally get to a live person, who will then
request lots of information, including the usual identification information such
as your driver's license number, Social Security number, and some check-
specific data such as checking-account routing and account-number address.
After you submit your request, the report follows by mail in 10 to 15 days.

You can look at sample reports from two of the major check-reporting
bureaus online:

✔ **ChexSystems:** Go to www.consumerdebit.com and, under "Consumer
Assistance," click on "Sample Consumer Report." Then, next to
"ChexSystems report," click "View Sample."

✔ **SCAN:** Go to www.consumerdebit.com and, under "Consumer
Assistance," click on "Sample Consumer Report." Then, next to "SCAN
report," click "View Sample."

Gambling with Central Credit Services

When you want credit, usually you want it now. Well, at least one credit
grantor couldn't agree with you more! Every minute you go without credit
can cost them money. Who are these guys? Why, it's none other than your
friendly neighborhood casino or bingo parlor. And — what are the odds? —
there's a credit-reporting agency just to serve their needs!

The gaming industry is thrilled with Central Credit Services (CCS). And why
not? In its own words, "Services from CCS help put more cash on the floor."
Personally, I like cash in my pocket, rather than on the floor, but I'm not fussy.

Need a credit line of $10,000, $50,000, maybe $1 million or more? Have a
credit score of 300? Want the money fast, in cash, with no hassles, fees, or
interest? How about 45 days, interest-free, to repay whatever you draw from

the line of credit with no strings attached? Oh, I almost forgot. How about dinner and a suite at the best hotel in town because you were such a good customer and borrowed lots of money?

Sound like a lender's nightmare? Welcome to the world of Global Cash Access, the parent company of Central Credit Services, and owner of the largest gaming-patron, credit-bureau database in the world. Every day thousands of gaming patrons make just such requests from casinos all over the United States and around the world. Instant financial reports on new and seasoned gamblers have to be available quickly, or the patron (the best patrons are sometimes affectionately called *whales* by the casinos) will migrate to another casino.

Gamblers live in a culture of their own. It's no wonder they have a unique credit-granting system. Central Credit is the big Kahuna of what is called the gaming-patron credit-database industry.

When a gambler needs cash at a casino, he can either go to an ATM and pay through the nose for a cash advance, or he can stroll into the casino credit department and ask for a *marker.* The super-sophisticated modern gaming systems not only give you a card with a unique number — similar to what you get with your garden-variety ATM card — but the card ties into your file that contains your name, picture, birth date, Social Security number, and *casino rating* (how much you bet, how long you play, and if you win or lose) for that day and for your previous trips to the casino. Use this card at an automated cashier's window and be sure to smile for the camera, because it may use face-matching technology to be sure you are who you're supposed to be.

A marker entitles you to interest-free chips or cash with very generous repayment provisions. Gamblers think only a chump would use an ATM or her own money when the free stuff is available and comes along with oodles of customer service, freebies, and, yes, even that most elusive of commodities, respect. *Capisce?* What a deal! (I tried this out myself when I was researching this section at the Atlantis Casino and I almost thought I was Bond, yes, James Bond, when I asked the croupier for a marker in front of some impressed and impressive ladies!)

How does Central Credit Services do it? A worldwide network of casinos accumulates each patron's marker experience and makes it available in much the same way that creditors report your experience to the three credit-reporting bureaus. If you're late paying a marker, have too many markers outstanding at the same time, or have a derogatory notation (for example, you punched a dealer in the nose), it all gets tracked in the Central Credit database. This data, accumulated worldwide from casinos and gaming establishments, along with information from consumer credit bureaus and bank-reporting agencies, is entered into your patron record.

The stakes are high for both you and the casino. We're not talking about the lender losing out on a monthly 1 percent interest income ($500 on a $50,000 cash advance). We're talking about the whole $50,000 as potential income to the casino if you lose it all. These are big numbers with big risks and big rewards. About 80 percent of a casino's profit comes from 20 percent of its customers. And they don't use credit cards — they use markers. So speed and accuracy in making underwriting decisions are critical to successfully doing business with some very particular people, whether you're in Vegas, the Bahamas, or Monte Carlo. In fact, the competition for business is so stiff and so profitable that to minimize the risk the of a patron going next door to gamble, the goal is to offer the patron preapproved credit during the check-in process at the front desk. Now, that's what I call a welcome gift amenity!

You can contact Central Credit Services at its headquarters in — where else? — Las Vegas. Here's CCS's info: 3525 East Post Rd., Suite 120, Las Vegas, NV 89120; phone: 702-855-3000 or 702-262-5000.

Chapter 3

Knowing Whether You Need Help and Where to Get It

* *

In This Chapter

▶ Deciding whether credit counseling is for you

▶ Understanding how credit counselors work

▶ Considering a debt-management plan

▶ Choosing a good credit-counseling agency

▶ Seeing how credit counseling can help your credit

* *

*I*n the United States, money is the last taboo. Bad breath, substance abuse, even erectile dysfunction — no problem. Credit or money issues? Red flag! So much of your self-image is expressed in terms of financial worth that admitting to bad credit is worse than saying that your mother stills buys your clothes. It just isn't what 21st-century U.S. society expects of attractive, robust, successful adults like you.

Getting advice from someone with lots of experience is a smart thing to do. A friend or relative who cares about you and who has been successful with managing money is even better. Yet when it comes to admitting to money or credit problems, otherwise-confident people get nervous.

Why? Because it's embarrassing. When you ask for help with your credit, you have to reveal your vulnerabilities and shortcomings. And to make matters worse, you're probably afraid that the person you go to for help will be wary of being hit up for money to solve your problem.

This is where a professional credit-counseling agency can help. Consider it a "Dutch uncle" without the family guilt trip, or a financial consultant minus the hefty price tag. The best credit counselors can help you understand the roots of your debt problem, what to do to solve it, and how to ensure that it never happens again. And they'll do it for the price of a good lunch (which your Dutch uncle would have wanted anyway).

Sounds great, but there's one catch: You have to find the help that works for you at a price you can afford and with successful results. In this chapter, I show you how.

Figuring Out Whether to Ask for Help

If you've been asking yourself whether you need to turn to a credit counselor for help, you're no doubt feeling some financial pressure — even if it's only a vague pinch. To help sharpen the picture for you, ask yourself — or yourself and your partner if you're not in this alone — some key questions that will lead you to clarity:

- **Are you overwhelmed?** You know you're overwhelmed when:
  - You don't answer the phone because it may be a creditor.
  - You fight with your partner about financial issues.
  - You're having trouble sleeping or getting up in the morning.
- **Are you dealing with multiple problems at the same time?** You know your financial problems are snowballing if:
  - Three or more creditors are hounding you.
  - Three or more situations (for example, financial, medical, and marital) are creating stress in your life.
- **Are you (or you and your partner) in conflict on the solution?** You may be debating over:
  - Increasing income to meet your lifestyle
  - Decreasing expenses to adjust your lifestyle to meet your income
  - Getting a loan to pay off debt
  - Filing for bankruptcy

If you answered yes to any of the preceding questions, you stand to benefit from talking to a professional who will help you see where you stand and what your options are. In the following sections, I walk you through some of these issues in greater depth.

Situations you can handle on your own

In the following sections, I outline three credit situations that you can probably resolve without much help. *Remember:* If you answered yes to any of the questions that I started off this section with, do not pass GO and do not collect $200 — go straight to getting help from someone you can trust (more about that later in this chapter).

Be sure that, if you go it alone, you

- ✔ Identify the cause of the problem and resolve it.
- ✔ Know how much money you have available to work with.
- ✔ Act quickly.

Credit cards

If you can't make this month's payment or if you've missed a month's payment already on your credit card, be proactive. As long as you know what you can afford, and you don't mind explaining your situation over the phone, you can get quick results. Here's what to do: Call the toll-free customer-service number and tell them who you are, what happened, and how you'd like to handle it. If you need a break from having to make payments, say so. If you can make up the missed payments over the next month or two, make an offer (just make sure your offer is something you can make good on).

Usually, if you're proactive and contact the credit-card company before they contact you, this approach will establish you as a good customer who needs and deserves some special consideration — much better than an elusive customer who's behind in payments, doesn't call, and may be a collection risk.

Be careful about asking for a payment to be stretched out for more than a month or two. If you need three months to catch up, you may get it or even qualify for a longer hardship program, but they may close your account, which will hurt your credit.

You may be asked to do more than you think you can. Do *not* agree to anything you don't think you can deliver. Saying that something is not possible, and explaining why, is much better than caving in but not being able to follow through. Ask to talk to a supervisor — they have more authority to bend the rules.

Mortgages

If you're within the grace period allowed in your loan documents, just send the money in if it will make up the shortfall. If you're past the grace period, you have varying amounts of time to make up the deficit, depending on the state you live in. Let's say you're behind on your monthly payment of $1,000. If you can only send in $500 extra with the next month's $1,000 payment, you'll still be short $500, right? Wrong. You may be behind the full $2,000 if the bank did not accept either payment because you didn't catch up in full. So, the gist is, if you aren't far behind and you can catch up in one shot, do it. Otherwise, don't delay, see the "Choosing the Right Credit-Counseling Agency for You" section (later in this chapter), and get help.

Student loans

Getting a short-term waiver is not difficult if you have a good reason. Unemployment, a low-paying job, illness, a return to school — each of these reasons may qualify you for a short-term waiver, but only if you give the lender a call before you get into a default situation. The student-loan people are usually very forgiving as long as they think you're playing it straight with them.

If you don't have enough money to apply to your financial problem, you won't be able to satisfy your creditors. But don't despair: There is a way to find it. The first step in addressing a financial problem is to maximize your sources of income and minimize your expenses. A spending plan or a budget will help you with that. Turn to Chapter 11 for more on budgeting.

Problems you'll need some help with

Certain situations create more financial stress than others. Credit counseling can help with the three main categories of problems that can wreak the most havoc:

- ✔ **Multiple bill collectors:** Most people can handle one or two collectors. But when you get to five, ten, or even more, you're pulled in many directions at once by their conflicting demands. It only takes one unreasonable creditor to make your situation impossible.

- ✔ **Joint credit problems:** Credit problems are exacerbated when you share them with someone who doesn't see things the way you do. Compromising is hard enough in good times; in stressful situations, finding solutions agreeable to everyone can be much more difficult.

- ✔ **Debts that are backed by assets:** If you take out a loan to buy a car, your loan is secured by that car. If you take out a loan to buy a house, your loan is secured by the house. In other words, *security* is what you stand to lose if you don't or can't pay back the money you borrowed. For example, if you don't make your car payment, the lender can take your car. If you don't pay your mortgage, the lender can take your house. If you don't pay your credit-card bill, the lender doesn't have any collateral it can take, because it has no security beyond your word and your willingness to pay as agreed.

As a general rule, the more security that lenders have, the less willing they are to work with you to solve what is clearly "your problem." It's easier than most people think to lose these assets if you're not making payments. Often, the rules are complex and not well-explained by the lender. Because the loans are secured (by the assets, like the car or the house), the lenders tend not to get very excited about deficits. They can't lose — but you can! If you can't come up with the entire deficit quickly, get help before things snowball.

TECHNICAL STUFF

A brief tale of credit counseling in the United States

Imagine if we let 16-year-old kids drive high-performance cars — with no driver's education, no speed limits, and no police except at accident scenes. You wouldn't be surprised if the accident rate soared, would you?

This little scenario is similar to what happened with the credit-card industry in the 1960s. Credit users were not crashing just one card, but as many as five or ten. The only credit professionals were the collection agencies that cleaned up after the ever-increasing number of credit pile-ups. And the collectors made the mess even worse, because each one wanted all the available cash for his company. So the credit user was caught in the middle of competing, aggressive, and often very unpleasant interests.

From this devastation came the development of nonprofit agencies that made it their mission to educate people in the use of credit (driver's education), put together spending plans based on individual goals and resources (speed limits), and helped structure workouts when credit crashes happened (EMT assistance). These nonprofits called themselves *consumer credit-counseling services* or *credit counselors*.

Until recently, credit-counseling agencies were generally community-based groups that specialized in helping local residents through financial-education classes, personal budgeting, and customized plans (often called *debt-management plans*) to get the individual out of debt. Credit counselors were serious and sometimes difficult people to deal with. Filled with the burning spirit often found in small, messianic, nonprofit agencies, they required the debt-shocked people who showed up on their doorsteps to fill out endless forms. Then, even after extensive

counseling, the counselors sent the consumers home to think over their recommendations and be sure they weren't rushing to an inappropriate solution. A less-than-positive customer-service experience, to say the least.

In the mid-1990s, some enterprising people figured out a new and controversial model for delivering credit counseling. It was very easy to use but delivered less in terms of solutions to the consumer's problems, and cost more in terms of fees and service charges. The high fees and low cost of a lower level of service helped launch a new industry. This new industry was made up of ultra-profitable "debt mills," which had the resources to dominate the advertising media while operating on the edge of the nonprofit laws. You've probably seen their ads on TV or heard their messages on your answering machine.

They say that every dark cloud has a silver lining. In response to the debt mills, the legitimate credit-counseling agencies were forced to adapt to a much more competitive marketplace. Most agencies are now open evenings and weekends. They do business over the phone and over the Internet, as well as in person, and they have high standards for customer service. In many ways, they've become more technologically based but have retained their mission and customer-focused values. They're much better organizations than they were even as recently as four years ago. From a consumer credit-counseling service, you can not only get help for your immediate credit problem, but also get information and guidance that will set you in the right direction for a debt-free future.

Working with a Credit-Counseling Agency

A legitimate, certified credit counselor may be just the help you need to begin resolving your financial woes. A credit-counseling agency serves as an objective party to help you sort through your problems, see your situation through the eyes of professional, give you some credit education, offer personalized budgeting advice, and design a customized plan to get you out of debt — all for nothing or next to nothing.

Beware of services that overcharge and underserve the credit-impaired, offering a product based on technology rather than public-service, mission-oriented values. If you're already up to your eyeballs in debt, avoid these debt mills like the plague! You need the maximum help for the minimum cost and you won't find it with them. (I help you differentiate the good guys from the bad guys later in this chapter.)

What credit-counseling agencies do and how they work

A credit-counseling agency analyzes your sources of income and your expenses. The agency will

- ✔ Detail what you owe.
- ✔ Give you an organized picture of your financial situation.
- ✔ Provide options that match your resources, lifestyle, and goals.
- ✔ Tell you the steps you need to take to reach those goals.

Whether you first contact a credit-counseling agency by phone, e-mail, or in person, the counselor will ask you why you're there, what you'd like to accomplish at the meeting, and what your short-term and long-term goals are.

Then some fairly detailed data-gathering will take place. You'll be asked about your income sources and tax deductions, as well as your monthly expenses. Having a good idea about what your monthly expenses are is very helpful, but it isn't a requirement — if you don't know, the credit counselor can help you estimate them. A quick subtraction of expenses from income will tell you how much you have available for monthly debt service, if any. The counselor will suggest ways to adjust your expenses or income, to get you to a *positive cash-flow* position (in which more money is coming into your household than is going out).

Next, you and the counselor will go over all the debts you have to pay. The positive cash flow from the earlier calculation will be applied to the amount you have to pay out. If anything is left over, you're basically done — you'll leave with an action plan and a budget you can follow to keep your expenses in line with your income. If the result is negative (you have more expenses than you have income), you and your counselor will rework the expenses to free up cash flow and he'll tell you what your debt service would be under a *debt-management plan* (see the "Debt-management plans" section, later in this chapter, for more detail).

This process of reducing your expenses and increasing your income will continue until you and the counselor get to a positive cash flow or it becomes apparent that, no matter what you do, the numbers just don't work in your favor. If you can't get to a positive cash flow, the counselor will refer you to an attorney or other community resources for additional help.

Everything I describe in this section can be done through the mail, over the phone, or via e-mail. Often, the process involves more than one of these methods over a series of contacts and days. For example, you might start out on the Internet filling out a contact form and asking questions; then you might follow up with a phone call to clarify and discuss matters further; and you might go into an office or use the mail to finalize your solutions. The method of contact you use is just a matter of what you're most comfortable with — one method isn't better than another.

You get to make all the choices about what happens next, whether it's tightening your belt, cutting out piano lessons to stretch household income, or seeing an attorney to pursue legal remedies. It's your life and it's your money, so you get to pick the approach that works for you.

What a credit-counseling agency can offer you

Alas, there is no magic wand to make all your financial problems disappear, but a good certified credit counselor will always offer solutions. Expect more than one solution, and expect some solutions you don't like. Your counselor will give you a balanced perspective of what you need to do, how long it will take, and what resources are available to help you along the way. Your counselor will probably discuss bankruptcy, as well as other solutions. The key: The counselor will propose solutions not just in the light of your current situation, but in light of your future needs.

Goal setting for the future

A good credit counselor offers solutions with your future goals in focus. A solution that works best for you is one that not only deals with current issues but takes into account how you see your future. For example, if you're planning to buy a house, get a security clearance at work, or send your triplets to college in five years, that future goal will affect the course of action that will best fit your needs.

Improved communication with your family

For about 75 percent of the over 1 million people who bare their souls to credit counselors each year, advice and direction are all they need. An unexpected by-product is improved financial communication. For many couples and families, credit counseling is the first time that goals, spending priorities, and even some secrets such as hidden debts are openly discussed.

An action plan that works for you

Expect to have a customized *action plan* when you're finished with your credit counselor. To be useful, an action plan has to fit you and the way you live. If it doesn't, you won't follow it. You don't wear clothes that are too tight — and you won't follow a poorly fitted financial plan. A comfortable budget designed with your spending and saving style in mind is more likely to be something you'll follow.

If you're struggling toward the abyss of debt, a good credit-counseling agency can help you understand how you landed in your predicament, what you need to do to correct the problem, and how to maintain your good financial reputation. For example, one man I worked with was having trouble making ends meet and didn't know why. When we created a budget, it turned out that, although he thought he was spending less than $100 a month on food, he was really spending over $700 eating out with his girlfriend! A few words with his honey, and he was back on track again.

The credit-counseling process isn't something you can breeze through in 15 minutes, because the plan you'll walk away with is tailor-made for you and your financial situation.

Periodic checkups

Expect some fine-tuning as you go. Although your counselor will anticipate as much as possible when developing your plan, he can't foresee the future. Murphy's Law applies to credit counseling in spades. Not only can things go wrong, but with limited financial resources, every bump in the road will feel much worse. Ongoing involvement with your credit-counseling agency as you navigate this credit-repair journey will help you stay the course. Expect the agency to make this easier for you, by giving you names, e-mail addresses, and phone numbers of people to contact beyond the agency for more help. You should be able to go back to your counselor for additional suggestions and referrals as you go along although most people, when they have a workable plan in hand, are off on their own.

Debt-management plans

For about 25 percent of those who turn to credit counselors, more than advice is prescribed. In these cases, in addition to the action plan (see "An action plan that works for you," earlier in this chapter), a debt-management plan is recommended. A debt-management plan (sometimes called a *debt-repayment plan*) involves the agency as an intermediary (for a small monthly fee it handles both communications and payments on your behalf) and it includes revised payments that:

✔ Are acceptable to all your creditors

✔ Leave you enough money to handle your living expenses

✔ Generally get you out of debt in two to five years

An alternative to bankruptcy. A workout plan. Debt consolidation. An interest-rate-reduction plan. All these descriptions have been attributed to debt-management plans. In fact, debt-management plans offer all these benefits — and perhaps a lot more. Here's how: When creditors realize that you can't meet the original terms of your credit cards or other loan agreements, they also realize that they're better off working with you through your credit counselor. Under a debt-management plan, your creditors are likely to be open to a number of solutions that will be to your advantage. These include:

✔ Stretching out your payments so that the combination of *principal* (the amount you originally borrowed) and interest will pay off your balance in 60 months or less

✔ Changing your monthly payments to an amount you can afford to pay

✔ Reducing your interest rate and/or any fees associated with your loan

✔ Stopping creditors from hounding you day and night

Why would creditors be willing to do all these things for you? Because if they don't do some or all of them, and if you really can't make the payments, you'll file bankruptcy — and your creditors will never get their money.

The critical point here is that the creditor has to believe that you can't make the payments as agreed. But how does the creditor believe that without staking out your house or apartment to verify that you aren't drinking Champagne and driving a new Corvette? The creditor generally takes the word of the nonprofit credit-counseling agency you've gone to for help.

The value of an intermediary

Some people wonder why a credit-counseling agency has to serve as an intermediary as part of the debt-management plan. Why can't the agency just set up a plan and leave you to follow it on your own, without paying them a monthly fee?

The answer is twofold:

✔ **Most people hit a bump or two in the repayment road.** Through its ongoing involvement, your credit-counseling agency can explain your situation to the creditor, dispassionately and professionally. Many plans would blow up at the first misstep without the trusted intermediary to smooth strained communications.

✔ **The creditors want the credit-counseling agencies involved.** Agencies can be easily reached for questions, the agencies' checks don't bounce, and the agencies don't get excited and yell over the phone the way consumers have been known to do.

Sounds like a good deal: lower interest rates, smaller payments, and all. Well, the debt-management plan isn't a free lunch. The minuses may include the following:

✔ A possible negative impact on your credit report (although just being in a debt-management plan does not affect your FICO score)

✔ An increase in interest rates (unless you pay in full and through the credit-counseling agency you originally signed up with)

✔ Restricted access to credit during the term of the plan

✔ Difficulty in changing credit-counseling agencies after you begin a debt-management plan

The bottom line is this: If you're in debt crisis or you're concerned you may be getting close to it, a debt-management plan from a good credit-counseling agency may be just the solution. If you're just shopping for an interest-rate reduction or a consolidation-loan alternative, a debt-management plan may *not* be in your best interest.

Protection for your financial reputation

Think of your credit report as your electronic financial reputation. If you do what you promise, the report is good. If you don't do what you promise, your report gets ugly. A credit-counseling agency can help you, through a debt-management plan, to renegotiate the terms of debt *before* your bad credit behavior hits your credit report and ruins your reputation.

Steering clear of debt-settlement plans

Debt settlement is not the same as credit counseling or a debt-management plan. Debt settlement is, in the opinion of many experts, an unethical approach to solving your financial issue. It is sometimes advertised as a way to save money, but it can be one of the most expensive methods of all!

In a debt-settlement plan, you pay money to a company that holds your money without making any payments until your credit is trashed, the creditor gives up hounding you, and the creditor is supposedly ready to take less than the face value of the debt as a settlement.

This course of action will *severely* damage your credit for years to come. If that's not enough to scare you off, consider this: Often, if you actually get to a settlement, the amount forgiven by the creditor becomes income to you! You guessed it: The IRS wants taxes on the forgiven amount — which can, in some cases, add up to thousands of dollars due on April 15 to Uncle Sam. And those agents at the IRS don't go away! Even if you later decide to go the bankruptcy route, the IRS still gets its money.

Debt settlement is an unsavory business in which the worst players keep all your money if you miss a payment to them. My advice: Don't do it!

A faster repair process

If you already have a bad credit report, credit counseling can help you restore your financial reputation faster. For example, let's say you were five months late on a $200 monthly payment. Your next bill will show $1,200 due, and your credit report will show that you're five months late. Typically, after three on-time payments of the new agreed-upon amount (the amount in your debt-management plan, which may be less than $200 and may be at a reduced interest rate), your account may be reported to the credit bureau as "current." That's a good thing!

To reach the current-account or on-time stage on your credit report without credit-counseling assistance, you would've had to make your current payment of $200 each month, plus a monthly late charge in addition to many more payments above $200 — until the $1,200 deficit was made up. In addition, under the terms of a debt-management plan, creditors often eliminate over-limit and late fees, as well as reducing your interest rate — which you'd be hard-pressed to get them to give you on your own. The net effect is that more of your money goes to reducing your debt load faster.

Choosing the Right Credit-Counseling Agency for You

You've done the hardest part already: Deciding to look for assistance isn't easy. Now all you need to do is follow a few simple guidelines that will help you choose the best agency, and you'll be on the road to credit wellness.

But how do you separate the debt mills (which may exacerbate your credit woes) from the genuine nonprofit services that help people and families regain financial control and credit health? Don't fret — in this section, I help you identify the real community servants and arm you with the right questions to ask to make sure you get the help you need.

What to look for in a credit-counseling agency

The best way to be sure you're working with a legitimate nonprofit organization is to ask if the agency is currently accredited by the Council on Accreditation (COA). COA is the largest third-party accreditor of nonprofits and does a very comprehensive, agency-wide audit of practices, safeguards, and policies before certifying an agency. Perfectly good nonprofits are out there that *aren't* accredited, but there are no dishonest agencies who *are*.

Good questions to ask a credit-counseling agency before you start working with them include the following:

- ✔ **Is your organization not-for-profit?** Some nonprofits are shams, so the fact that an agency is nonprofit doesn't mean it's good. So, be sure to ask about affiliations with organizations you know (like local housing authorities, the United Way, the military, or governmental agencies such as the U.S. Department of Housing and Urban Development [HUD] or the Federal Reserve) or that have been in business for at least ten years.

- ✔ **Are your counselors certified? Who provides the certification?** Certification of credit counselors by an independent third-party organization is a sign that the organization is committed to adhering to quality standards set for the credit-counseling profession. (See "Looking for accreditation," later in this chapter, for more information.)

- ✔ **What fees will I be charged?** Do not, under any circumstance, work with an agency that charges a large up-front fee. Some agencies will promise to allow you to earn the fee back over a period of time — walk away. The conditions and timing may make it unlikely that you'll earn it back. Besides, you need the cash more than the agency does! Many agencies will work with you for free or for a nominal payment. Depending on the agency, you may pay a small amount for the initial counseling session or pay a low monthly fee. If they recommend a debt-management plan, the agency may charge a setup fee. (See "Paying the Piper: The Cost of Credit Counseling," later in this chapter, for more information on counseling fees.)

✔ **How long will the counseling take?** Anything less than 30 to 45 minutes will just deal with surface issues and won't help you to set new goals, understand how you got into debt in the first place, and figure out how to stay out of debt in the future.

✔ **What lifestyle changes will I need to make to be successful?** To be successful in getting out of debt, you probably have to make changes in your spending habits. The agency should help you learn to budget, set financial goals, and begin a savings program.

Any agency that you're considering should be willing to discuss all these issues with you. If the organization is not willing to answer or does not spend the time to give satisfactory responses, find a different agency.

With all the different choices out there, take your time and do your research before choosing a credit-counseling agency. You want to choose an agency that is reputable, works with your interests and needs in mind, and expresses interest in helping you improve your financial situation in both the short- and long-term.

What should you expect when you turn to a credit-counseling agency for help? Check out the following list:

✔ **Agency accreditation and certified counselors:** Insist on independently certified counselors and an independently accredited agency. Mr. Goodwrench who works on your car is certified, Mr. Goodbucks who works on your spending plan and credit should be, too! (See the "Looking for accreditation" section of this chapter for details about two accreditation services.)

✔ **Professional service and basic courtesy:** You should be treated professionally, the same as if you were meeting with a certified public accountant (CPA) or an attorney. The office décor may not meet the standards of a high-powered law firm, but the service level should. Look for friendliness and patience. Following a courteous greeting, you should be given the opportunity to explain in detail what issues brought you to the agency and what help you would like.

✔ **Thoroughness:** You should expect to answer a lot of questions about what deductions come out of your paycheck, what you spend in detail, and what you owe to whom. Expect some questions that you hadn't thought of.

✔ **Multiple written solutions:** Expect to get more than one choice to address your concerns. Expect these solutions in writing. You should also get a written budget or spending plan that is based on your situation, not general guidelines.

✔ **Appropriate fees:** Up-front fees, if any, should be no more than $75. Better yet, the agency will offer low, pay-as-you-go, monthly fees no greater than $50 a month. The agency gets paid as you get help, and it has an incentive to keep you happy. (See "Paying the Piper: The Cost of Credit Counseling," later in this chapter.)

✔ **Willingness to spend time:** A good credit counselor will work efficiently but take the time necessary to understand your problem and to educate you. A ten-minute phone conversation or e-mail exchange is not counseling. The real value of counseling (as opposed to being jammed into a debt-management plan) is understanding how you got where you are. You'll be provided a range of options and come away with a workable plan that includes a detailed analysis of income and expenses.

Making sense of agency claims

What can a credit-counseling agency really do for you? In the blitz of hype, promises, and vaguely misleading ads, the answer is confusing at times. As long as you commit the time, pay the fees, and aren't continuing to run up your credit cards, here are the kinds of valid claims you should expect from an agency:

✔ **Some *interest concessions* (reduction in your interest rates):** One or two of your interest rates may go down a lot; others may go down just a little — your interest rates really depend on your creditors, not on the agency.

The agency will have more clout in persuading the creditor to offer some leeway than you would have on your own. For example, one major creditor I know of reviews each debt-management plan, line by line, and offers interest concessions based on the perception of your need, as well as its corporate policy. An agency that takes the time to explain your situation to that creditor may be able to save you a few percentage points.

✔ **Cessation or reduction of collection calls:** The agency will likely be able to persuade your creditors to stop the haranguing calls from the collection companies. The calls usually stop after you've made payments for about three months, though some creditors will stop calling you as soon as your debt-management plan is in place. Very few, if any, creditors will continue calling you if they're getting paid regularly.

✔ **Waiver of late charges and over-limit fees:** The agency can usually arrange to have these charges waived after a debt-management plan is launched.

✔ **Current-account status on your credit report:** With the help of a credit counselor and a good debt-management plan, your accounts may be brought to a current status on your credit report within three months. The federal regulators allow creditors to re-age your account for good reason once every five years. Every month that your payment is short or missing, your account ages from 30 days late to 60 days late and so on. When an account is *re-aged,* it is brought up to current or pays-as-agreed status in one shot — but only once in a 60-month period. Usually, three successive payments do the trick, even if you're more than three payments behind.

✔ **Halting of court actions for wage garnishment:** If there are pending court actions to garnish your wages, those may still go ahead, but the actions will often stop just before the court order is executed. Your creditors will want to be ready to collect if you fail to pay, but most creditors recognize that, by taking your wages, they're inviting you to file bankruptcy — and if you file bankruptcy, they don't get any of the money you owe.

✔ **Improvement of bad-credit status:** If you have damaged credit when you start the process with your credit counselor, it will improve.

✔ **Referrals to helpful resources:** Your credit counselor is armed to supply you with referrals to community or professional resources to help you with everything from marriage counseling to job placement to substance abuse.

✔ **A personalized budget:** A written plan to help you budget your money and spend it based on your personal priorities is something that will provide benefit for years to come. This last item is, in my opinion, the most important and valuable. If you don't have a budget that allows you to spend your money on the things you decide you need, save some for a rainy day, and learn to resist all the temptations that seduce you every day, nothing else you get from a credit counselor will help.

Some agency claims are just plain ridiculous. Here are samples of what a credit-counseling agency may promise but will *not* be able to do:

✔ Make you debt-free today.

✔ Reduce your debt up to 60 percent in seconds.

✔ Stop embarrassing collection calls as soon as you call an agency.

✔ Give you money in your pocket at the end of the month.

✔ Erase all your debts and save you thousands of dollars.

To add to the confusion, some of the terms used in ads have meanings that are very different from what you may think they mean at first glance. For example if the ad says:

✔ "Not-for-Profit," it doesn't mean inexpensive — or even honest.

✔ "IRS 501 (c) (3) approved," it doesn't mean the agency has been investigated and approved by the IRS. It means the agency *told* the IRS it qualified for tax exemption under the tax code.

✔ "The agency has established relationships with creditors," it doesn't mean it'll get a special deal for you. Creditors take money from anyone who will give it to them and that's an "established relationship."

✔ "You'll get out of debt fast without repayment to your creditors," it doesn't mean you can walk away from all your bills with the agency's settlement program. The agency is ignoring secured creditors (such as mortgage holders, child support, IRS debts, student loans, and others).

The bottom line: Always be sure the agency you work with is legitimate and respected. In the following section, I give you ways to check out an agency.

Seeking referrals

Finding an above-board agency can seem bewildering at times — even with the tips and warnings I provide in the previous sections. Sometimes, the decision can be made a bit easier when you know what reliable sources think of the place you're considering. In the following sections, I give you some places to turn for more information.

Looking for accreditation

Both the Council on Accreditation (COA; www.coanet.org) and the International Standards Organization (ISO; www.iso.org) accredit nonprofit credit-counseling agencies. COA specializes in nonprofit and government agencies in the United States. It requires a more in-depth level of detail in the accreditation process than ISO does. (For example, COA conducts a rigorous review of a board of directors to be sure it effectively promotes the public over its own financial enrichment.) I like that COA sends people who are in the credit-counseling business to audit the agency because the auditors really know what to look for. ISO is best known for standardizing for-profit and manufacturing companies worldwide. It also accredits nonprofits. ISO uses the same standards of quality for both.

Key aspects of accreditation include checking whether:

✔ Client funds are being handled appropriately.

✔ The agency is licensed to conduct business in the state you live in.

✔ The agency has a trained and certified staff.

Being accredited is a feather in an organization's cap and you can expect to see it prominently displayed on its Web site or informational materials.

Just to be safe, ask if the accreditation is current — just because an agency was accredited years ago doesn't mean it is today.

Turning to Uncle Sam

Every state has a consumer-protection office, which can offer references to credit-counseling agencies. In some states, this office is part of the attorney general's office; in other states, it's the responsibility of the local district attorney. Either way, you can use today's equivalent of *The Untouchables* G-Man Elliott Ness to check out the agencies you're investigating. These public servants can tell you about complaints filed and legal action taken against credit-counseling agencies in your area.

While I'm on the topic of helpful civil servants, I always like to mention congressional delegations. Because the best credit-counseling agencies offer local education and information programs, often in conjunction with other community resources, those agencies are likely to have worked with the local congressperson's office in the past. Your elected officials like to refer constituents to organizations that are safe and won't cost them votes. They count votes, you count money — same thing! Explain to your congressperson that you'd like help finding a reputable credit-counseling agency in your area. (You won't be the first one to ask.) Your congressperson may want to contact the agency first, and then get back to you.

You can find the phone numbers for your state's consumer-protection office and congresspeople in the "Government" section of your Yellow Pages or in the Blue Pages of your phone book.

Seeking help from the Better Business Bureau

The Better Business Bureau (BBB) is a good source of information about complaints against companies and organizations in your area. It's not unusual for businesses to have some complaints against them. But you should be on the lookout for the *number* of complaints and whether the complaints have been satisfactorily resolved. You don't want to do business with a dishonest company or even an honest company that's not very good at what it does!

Here's how it works: The BBB will not give you an opinion or legal advice. It will present you with the facts, based on business-reliability reports, dispute-resolution history, and consumer information/advisories. I particularly like that it includes regulatory actions taken or pending against the company. You can call your local BBB or connect online. The Web address is `www.bbb.org`.

Over the years, my experience with the BBB has been great. Although they say they don't, if you ask sometimes the local BBB representative will give you a specific referral or a strong indication of which agencies *not* to call. If it's too late for advice and you have a problem with the credit-counseling agency you chose, the BBB can offer you help to resolve the issue and log your experience to help warn others.

Tracking down information online

For the computer-comfortable, GuideStar provides a great Web site (www.guidestar.org) that puts together and distributes information on more than 1 million nonprofit organizations. The service has been around for over a decade and gets its funding from some of the biggest foundation names in the United States, including the Carnegie Corporation of New York, the Ford Foundation, the W. K. Kellogg Foundation, the Lilly Endowment, and so on — which just means it already has all the money it needs, so I feel comfortable recommending it to you!

At the site, plug in the name of the company in question, sign in, and you'll have access to IRS tax returns, a financial summary, and the names of those on the board of directors. Red flags include excessive salaries for the bosses (a salary for a large company boss can be larger than yours, but it shouldn't be excessive when compared to others in the same-size company in the same business), relatives of the bosses on the payroll, a lot more revenue than expenses, and any for-profit companies receiving big payments or that are owned by the bosses.

Paying the Piper: The Cost of Credit Counseling

Credit counseling does entail a number of costs. Some are financial, others are personal, and some may affect you for years to come. Don't get nervous — *not* getting the help you need has costs, too, some of them devastating (paying more for credit and insurance, losing job opportunities, getting a divorce, dodging phone calls).

Who would ask someone who can't pay his bills or afford groceries to pay a fat counseling fee? No one you want to deal with, that's for sure. Legitimate credit counselors charge *very little* for their services — or nothing at all.

Credit counseling is one of those rare industries in which the more you pay, the worse service you're likely to receive. Why? Because the best agencies understand that you're having trouble paying bills and that every dollar you pay them is a dollar you can't send to your creditors. So the agency keeps its fees as low as possible. But how can they do this and still offer good service and attract qualified staff? Well, they get donations and grants from others, especially creditors, to keep their pricing as low as possible. A little like Robin Hood, the credit-counseling agency gets funding from the rich companies and gives affordable services to you!

For about 75 percent of people who seek credit counseling, the pain and suffering is brief. In the hour or so they spend with the counselor, they arrive at a solution and obtain the information they need to yield a huge change in behavior. And off they go, having paid little or nothing for their brief session with the credit counselor, but wiser for the experience.

The other 25 percent of people who visit a credit counselor benefit from a debt-management plan. Because a debt-management plan is an ongoing program that takes months to work through, a small monthly fee — $10 to $50, depending on the complexity and your ability to pay — may be charged. This fee is affordable and makes more sense than a fat, up-front fee that may cause you to slip farther behind in your bill payments.

Table 3-1 outlines the fees you should expect to pay, as well as fees that you can safely consider unreasonable. If the agency you've approached charges you fees that fall in the "Unreasonable" column, find another agency.

Table 3-1	The Costs of Credit-Counseling Services	
	Reasonable	*Unreasonable*
Counseling *	Free to $50	Your first-month debt-management-plan payment ($100 to $1,000)
One-time setup fee *	Free to $75	More than $100
Monthly fee	$15 to $50	More than $75

* The combination of the counseling fee and the one-time setup fee should not exceed $75. There may be other optional charges for things like getting a copy of your credit report or educational materials (such as books), but you should have the choice to say, "No thanks."

Some agencies try to justify large fees by saying you can earn it all back, plus more, through their incentive programs. If you hear this pitch, walk away — incentive programs don't work for you. In addition, some agencies ask for a percentage of the money you save on interest and fees. If this sounds familiar, walk away. You need the money more than the credit-counseling agency does — and if the agency doesn't understand that, it doesn't understand credit counseling.

I said there were personal costs, too, and I haven't forgotten: Admitting to a stranger that you need help is humbling. Realizing you haven't exactly been communicating with your spouse about money matters — and then having to do so — can be daunting. Lastly, changing behavior is never easy. Yet more than a million individuals and families seek credit counseling each year — and grow a bit because of it.

How are credit counselors compensated?

Offering a quality hour of credit counseling costs a lot — but you won't be paying it. You can't afford to cover what your credit-counseling agency's help, rent, and overhead costs, so the agency accepts donations from your creditors, who *can* afford it. This situation has never bothered me, because creditors understand the risks and costs of lending. They have to take some responsibility for the damage done by generous, risk-based lending rules — or in some cases, the lack thereof — and for not providing much in the way of instruction for the proper use of their products.

Be assured, however, that despite the fact that good credit-counseling agencies are being subsidized by your lender, the agencies will work for you to come up with the best solution acceptable to all parties and, if push comes to shove, will put your interests over those of the creditors every time.

Finally, individual counselors should never be compensated based on the outcome of a counseling session. In reputable agencies, they are paid salaries or hourly rates based on helping you find an appropriate solution, not selling either a product or a debt-management plan.

Part II
Finding Out Where You Stand

The 5th Wave   By Rich Tennant

"I don't know how the heck these credit agencies get this information, but I returned that rake and snow blower to my neighbor 6 months ago!"

In this part . . .

I focus on *you* and how you can determine exactly where your credit stands by accessing and understanding the most important credit tool at your disposal: your credit report. I reveal how to get ahold of your credit report for free, when it's best for you to do so, and what your credit report and credit score really mean to you and your future. I explain the various components that go into building a good credit score. I help you determine whether your credit score measures up and how you can improve it. I tell you about the other credit reporters in the sectors of insurance, medicine, gambling, employment, checking, and even renting. Finally, I help you understand what your credit report contains, how information gets there, and who can get at it besides you.

Chapter 4

Getting Your Hands on Your Credit Report

*R*ecognizing the value of good credit is an important first step in gaining control of your financial life, getting the best interest rates, and even landing that next job or promotion. The next step is getting your hands on the information that others — including businesses you hope to borrow money from, get credit from, or be employed by — use to learn about your credit history.

But how do you get a copy of your credit report so you can be sure it's accurate, up-to-date, and complete? In this chapter, I tell you the who, what, where, when, and — most importantly — the *how* of getting your hands on your credit report. You'll not only find out about the three largest and most well-known of the credit bureaus, but also get familiar with the data repositories that report traditional credit and more. Finally, you'll discover the lesser-known places where data pertaining to you and your life resides.

So come along with me on a trip that will take you from the portals of the big credit bureaus to the bounced-check graveyard and even to the cashiers' cages in Las Vegas! It's all about your information — where it's kept and how you can get at it.

Requesting Copies of Your Credit Reports

Three main sources of credit information dominate the credit industry today. They are Equifax, Experian, and TransUnion. These credit bureaus are basically huge databases of information. Within the databases are hundreds of millions of individual files on folks just like you and me. Where does all that information come from? Lenders, bill collectors, courts, public utilities, and others who provide goods and services to you today and get paid down the road.

Credit-reporting bureaus do not put data in your file. They simply maintain the files that others put the data into.

It's very important to the consumer and the credit grantor that the information in your report be correct — and if the information isn't correct, it can be very costly to you (you may not get the loans you want, or you may have to pay much higher interest than you should have to pay) and to the lender (if they don't get their money back). Each month, all the agencies that report information about you to the credit bureaus have numerous chances to mix up, misreport, or misfile that information. They don't mess up all the time, but they do occasionally, and these errors are why reviewing your credit report at least once a year is so important — even if you've never had credit problems.

Button up your overcoat. Wait an hour after eating before swimming. Stop crossing your eyes or they'll stay that way. These are some of the bits of advice you got while you were growing up. I don't know about you but my mother never told me to get a copy of all three of my credit reports. Well, call me "Mom" but you really should check each of them, at least annually.

Many people assume that if they get a copy of their credit report from one of the bureaus, they've done everything they need to do. But the reality is that the information Equifax has is slightly different from the information Experian has, and the information Experian has is slightly different from the information TransUnion has. You generally won't see major differences from one report to the next. However since not all creditors report to all bureaus, if you're new to credit, the differences may be important enough that a few missing trade lines can have a noticeable impact. Also, you could have a perfectly clean Experian report while your TransUnion report could have some negative items on it in error, or vice versa.

Even though it means a bit more effort and hassle, reviewing copies of all three of your credit reports is absolutely essential. But don't despair! Under the new FACT Act, which went into full effect in 2005, every American is entitled to one free credit report from each of the three bureaus per year. Not since the days of the elusive nickel beer and the free lunch has there been this much excitement in credit reporting. You're also entitled to an additional free report from each of the bureaus if:

✔ You were denied credit within the last 60 days.

✔ You are unemployed and planning to seek employment within the next 60 days.

✔ You're on welfare.

✔ You're a victim of fraud or identity theft and have reported it to the police.

In the following sections, I tell you where to go to get your reports, what kind of information you'll need to provide, and when you should check your reports.

Where to get your reports

The FACT Act now requires each of the credit bureaus to provide you with a free copy of your credit report each year, but don't expect them to come knocking on your door, offering you your free copy. You have to ask.

That said, getting a copy of your credit report from any of the big-three credit bureaus is simple. You can get things started with a phone call, a visit to the bureau's Web site, or through the mail. Here's the contact information for all of the three major credit-reporting bureaus:

✔ **Equifax,** P.O. Box 740241, Atlanta, GA 30374; phone: 800-685-1111; Web site: www.equifax.com

✔ **Experian,** P.O. Box 2104, Allen, TX 75013-2104; phone: 888-397-3742; Web site: www.experian.com

✔ **TransUnion,** 2 Baldwin Place, P.O. Box 1000, Chester, PA 19022; phone: 800-888-4213; Web site: www.transunion.com

The big-three bureaus have set up a central source where you can get your free credit report. If you go to any of the bureau Web sites, they'll redirect you to this central source. So why even go the individual sites? Because each site has some informational and educational features, and they're the places for you to order (at a cost) a credit score in addition to a free credit report. If you want to skip the individual sites and go to the central source that allows you to pick up all three reports, here's the information you need:

Annual Credit Report Request Service
P.O. Box 105281
Atlanta, GA 30348-5281
Phone: 877-322-8228
Web site: www.annualcreditreport.com

I strongly suggest that you get a copy of your report from each of the three bureaus.

Who else can get their hands on your report?

Anyone can get a copy of your credit report if he has *permissible purpose* — in other words, if the person has a valid reason to review your report — *and* if you've given that person your permission to do so. The permission part can often be lost in the fine print of a credit-card application or at the bottom of an employment application.

What counts as a permissible purpose under the law? Here are some examples:

✔ **Credit approval:** When you apply for credit (whether that's filling out a credit-card application or applying for a car loan, student loan, or mortgage), the creditor or lender has the right to get a copy of your credit report. This only makes sense — they need to know whether you're likely to pay them back or whether you have a history of defaulting on loans.

✔ **Renting an apartment:** It only makes sense that a landlord would like to know if you pay your bills on time before giving you the keys to an expensive piece of real estate. Most rental applications contain permission to access your credit file and also any tenant history information that may be available.

✔ **Employment:** When you apply for a job, that prospective employer can get a copy of your credit report. Although this may be less obvious than the applying-for-credit reason, your financial history says a lot about what kind of employee you might turn out to be. If you're irresponsible with money, the logic goes, you may be irresponsible at work as well.

✔ **Insurance underwriting:** When you apply for car, homeowner's, renter's, medical, or any other kind of insurance, the insurance company has the right to get a copy of your credit report. Depending on the type of insurance you apply for and the state in which you live, the insurer may get a copy of your credit report and use the information in it to help predict the likelihood not of a default in premium payments but of your likelihood of filing a claim. Insurers and their actuaries believe there is a strong relationship between past financial performance and future claim experience.

✔ **Issuing a professional license:** Licensing authorities take their responsibilities very seriously. Before allowing you to become licensed — or, in other words, approved to perform a specific job — they want to know all they can about your background and how you've conducted yourself in the past. Let's say you want a license to sell stocks and bonds, and deal with someone else's life savings, it makes sense to see how you handle your own money. Want a gambling license? Same thing applies.

✔ **A court order or subpoena:** If a court orders you to appear before the court or subpoenas information about you, the court can also get access to your credit file.

✔ **Reviewing or collecting an existing account:** When an account is overdue and sent to a collector for action, the collector will want to know who else you owe money to and what kind of payer they're dealing. In some cases, if a person moves a lot, they use the information in the credit report to find a current address or phone number. (The industry term for this is called *skip tracing*.) However, even if you're current in your payments to your credit-card issuers, mortgage company, or other creditors, they can look at your account from time to time to determine if your credit quality is deteriorating or, on the brighter side, to increase your limits.

> ✓ **If you owe the Internal Revenue Service money:** If you owe the tax guys and don't come across with the payment in the time specified, they'll look in your credit report to find out if you have assets to attach. Some examples of things they look for are real estate, cars, bank accounts, and so on.

What you'll need to give in order to get your reports

Whether you contact a credit bureau directly to get a copy of your report, or you go through the central source to get all three at once (see the preceding section), you'll need to provide information that lets them know that you are who you say you are. The information requested will vary from one bureau to the next, but the following is a list of some information you're likely to be asked for:

✓ Your Social Security number

✓ You credit-card account numbers

✓ Your former addresses and the dates you lived there

✓ Your employment history

✓ Your favorite drink (just kidding)

When you order your credit report, they may try to sell you your credit score as well. If you want your credit score, be sure you're buying a real FICO score and not a knockoff. Equifax is the only bureau that can sell you a true FICO score. You want a real FICO score because that's what most lenders use, and you want to be looking at the same number that they're looking at. (See "Getting a Copy of Your Credit Score," later in this chapter, for more information.)

The other two credit-reporting bureaus — Experian and TransUnion — use a slightly different score, although those scores are still developed by Fair Isaac, the company that developed the FICO scoring measures. If this is confusing, let me explain more: Fair Isaac developed what is known as the FICO score. The people at Equifax bought the rights to market the specific FICO formula along with their credit data to their retail consumer customers. Experian and TransUnion did not buy these rights. Fair Isaac, wanting to make three sales rather than just one, developed similar, but different formulas and sold them to the other bureaus.

When you should get copies of your credit reports

The information in your credit report is used for many purposes — from granting a mortgage to getting homeowner's insurance to renting an apartment — so you should get copies of all three of the big-three (Equifax, Experian, TransUnion) at least once a year. If you're planning to make a big purchase, look for a job, or buy insurance, get your report a month or two in advance; this will give you time to dispute any errors (like from your sister's last bankruptcy) that may have ended up on your report before people start checking out your credit.

Don't get your report more than a couple months' in advance, however; if you get the report too soon, new errors may slip into your file between the time you got your report and the time your report was checked by interested parties. Real-estate closings can be delayed, mortgage rates can go up, and job opportunities can be lost if there is incorrect negative information on your credit report. So give yourself time — but not too much time — to get the report, correct it, and then go forward with your plans.

You should get a copy of your report when you're planning to:

- Buy or lease a car
- Buy a house
- Rent an apartment
- Apply for a job
- Apply for a professional license (such as a license for selling securities or insurance)
- Apply for a security clearance
- Join the military
- Be up for a promotion
- Get married
- Get divorced
- Switch insurance companies or buy new insurance

Even if none of the preceding situations applies to you, I still recommend that you get copies of all three of your reports annually. Why? Because people may be making decisions about your future, using your credit information without your knowing it (for example, you may be considered for a promotion at work). Because you can get one copy of each report free once a year, I recommend that, every four months, you order a report from one of the three bureaus, rotating through them so that you'll have three separate chances, at spaced intervals, to see if something unexpected has shown up.

Getting a Copy of Your Credit Score

Getting your hands on your credit report is one thing — but getting a copy of your credit score is not as straightforward as you may think. And a misstep here can cost you more money and give you less-than-accurate information.

A credit score is an additional component used in most credit reviews. When lenders order your credit report, they also order your credit score. A credit score summarizes your risk of default in a three-digit score that ranges from 300 to 850.

Unlike your credit report, which you get for free once a year, you have to request and pay for a copy of your credit score. Not just any credit score will do. You want your FICO score, which is the credit score lenders use.

You can only get your FICO credit score from two places:

- **myFICO.com** (phone: 800-319-4433; Web: www.myfico.com)
- **Equifax** (P.O. Box 740241, Atlanta, GA 30374; phone: 800-685-1111; Web: www.equifax.com)

The other credit-reporting bureaus — Experian and TransUnion — offer credit scores, but not the *FICO* credit score.

Experian and TransUnion supply FICO scores to lenders, but because of a deal Equifax worked out with myFICO, Equifax is the only company that can sell FICO scores to consumers.

You can only get a copy of your FICO score if you're ordering a credit report at the same time. If you want an Experian or TransUnion credit report and your FICO score, you'll need to pay for a report and score package at myFICO.com or get all three reports and your FICO score at Equifax.

The only credit bureau that can provide you the FICO credit score used by most lenders along with its credit report is Equifax.

If your lender uses TransUnion or Experian to make a lending decision (you can find out which bureau they use by asking the lender), you want to get a copy of your TransUnion or Experian credit report, and then get your FICO score (from myFICO.com).

Tracking Down Specialty Reports: From Rental History to Gambling

In addition to the big-three credit-reporting bureaus, there are other, lesser-known, specialty reporting agencies. As the name implies, they specialize in a subset of credit-related data, covering areas such as gambling, checking accounts, medical claims, and insurance. If you're being underwritten for credit or other permissible purposes like auto insurance, renting an apartment or a promotion at work in one of these areas, the person reviewing your application will most likely request a report from them in addition to a traditional credit report from one of the big-three credit bureaus.

The information these specialty credit bureaus collect can have an impact on you. Among the better-known specialty reports are the insurance bureaus, such as Choice Trust, which sells its CLUE products based on your auto and homeowner insurance claims history, as well as information for background employment and rental checks; the Medical Information Bureau (MIB), which accumulates and sells your medical-insurance claims history report; and ChexSystems, SCAN, and TeleCheck, all of which sell various check-verification products. Included in the growing list of companies that report on you are those that specialize in rental history, workers' compensation claims, and gambling history.

You have the right to request and obtain your credit reports from these agencies for free annually, just as you do with the traditional credit bureaus. Some contain only negative information—or they may have absolutely no information about you at all (you've *really* never been to a casino?). Table 4-1 provides the contact information for the major specialty bureaus to get you started — call the number for any bureau you want a report from, and ask how to order a free copy.

Table 4-1	Specialty Credit-Reporting Bureaus	
Category	**Bureau Name**	**Contact Info**
Casinos	Central Credit Services	702-855-3000 or 702-262-5000
Checking accounts	Certegy/Equifax	800-437-5120
	CheckCenter/CrossCheck	800-843-0760
	CheckRite	800-766-2748
	ChexSystems	800-428-9623
	International Check Services	800-526-5380

Category	Bureau Name	Contact Info
	SCAN	800-262-7771
	TeleCheck	800-710-9898
Employment	ChoiceTrust Employment Reports	866-312-8075
Insurance	CLUE Auto History	866-312-8076
	CLUE Homeowners' History	866-312-8076
	ISO's A-Plus Auto and Property Databases	800-709-8842
Medical information	Medical Information Bureau (MIB)	617-426-3660
Rental information	Accufax	800-256-8898
	American Tenant Screen	800-888-1287
	ChoicePoint Tenant History Reports	877-448-5732
	National Tenant Network	800-228-0989
	Tenant Data Services	800-228-1837
	Tenant Screening Services	800-388-2335
	UD Registry	818-785-3905
Mortgage financing	Innovis	800-540-2505

Chapter 5

Making Sense of Your Credit Report

"**I**s this thing in English?" "Okay, what do these terms mean? And where does it say if I'm doing a good job, anyway?" "How do I tell whether I'm passing or flunking"? "Does anyone hear speak credit-ese?"

I confess: At first glance — and for the first-time reader — a credit report, with its huge volume of information and its industry jargon, can be a little overwhelming. All those columns, numbers, terms, and historical information. . . . But trust me — daunting though it may appear, your credit report is no Code of Hammurabi. Although the format and terms may vary by credit bureau or credit-report reseller, the detail in your credit report is in a pretty basic language that I can have you speaking in no time. And you don't need to get an advanced degree, learn a complex code, or pass a secret initiation ritual to do it.

In this chapter, I walk you through the basic outline of a credit report, breaking it down into its various parts and explaining its terms and components. I also shine a light on the credit score, and help you understand and then unmask what I call *credit-score inflation*.

Give me the time it takes to read this chapter, and I'll have you whipping through your credit report, feeling confident that you know where you stand in the eyes of your creditors, insurance company, employer, and anyone else who looks at your report. If you have a copy of your credit report from one or more of the three major credit-reporting agencies — Equifax, Experian, or TransUnion — you can follow along with this chapter. (If you don't yet have a copy of your report, turn to Chapter 4 for information on how to get one.)

What's not in your credit report

With all the information available on the Internet and in data files, you can easily become concerned about what exactly is in your credit report and what is not. In order to set the record straight and put you at ease from the beginning, your credit report from Equifax, Experian, or TransUnion does *not* contain:

✔ Your gender

✔ Your race or ethnicity

✔ Your national origin

✔ Your religious preference

✔ Your political affiliation

✔ Your checking- or savings-account information or major purchases that were paid in full with cash or check

✔ Business accounts (unless you're on record as being personally liable for the debt)

✔ Details about your personal lifestyle or friends

✔ Bankruptcies that are more than ten years old

✔ Charge-offs or debts placed for collection that are more than seven years old

✔ Your credit score (Although your credit score is generated based on information in your credit report, it is not part of the report itself.)

Before you get too comfortable with what's not disclosed in your credit report, be aware of this. *Indirect disclosure* may allow some of your "personal" information to get passed on. Medical information is one example. Even though credit bureaus do not report medical history, detail on your credit report might give away information about your medical condition. Here's how: Say, you're paying off a debt for a hospital stay. The account noted on your credit report names the facility — the Mental Health Center for Individuals with Chronic Fear of Flying. You apply for a job as a flight attendant. As part of its background check, your prospective employer requests a copy of your credit report. They easily deduce that you have (or had) a fear of flying, and they know that this job will require a lot of it. A week later, you get a letter saying the position has been filled.

Okay, so this is a pretty extreme example. But it illustrates that, without disclosing medical reports or particulars about a health condition, the detail on your credit report *can* reveal personal information that is legally restricted from your file. Some other disclosures that can happen include employment history you forgot to mention to a prospective employer, frequent changes of addresses (which might make you look unstable), and multiple inquiries from Central Credit for gambling lines of credit (which could raise a question for a lender or an employer).

But help is at hand! Under a new FACTA provision, consumer credit-reporting agencies may not report the name, address, or telephone number of any medical creditor unless the information is provided in codes that do not identify or imply the provider of care or your medical condition. Another section of FACTA says a creditor may not obtain or use medical information to make credit decisions.

Perusing Your Credit Report

Perhaps the best way to get a handle on how your credit report comes together is to take it apart — starting from the outside and working in. First, I help you to understand the big picture. Then I talk about each part in more detail.

Each credit report contains the following elements:

- ✔ Personal profile
- ✔ Accounts summary
- ✔ Public records (which include public records, negative remarks, collections, and late payments)
- ✔ Credit inquiries
- ✔ Account history
- ✔ Credit score (optional)
- ✔ Your 100-word statement (optional; see Chapter 6 for more information on writing a 100-word statement)

Note: The three credit-reporting agencies use slightly different names for each of these sections.

I cover each of these items in the following sections. For a sample credit report from TransUnion, check out the CD. For information on where to find samples of the Equifax and Experian reports online, turn to Chapter 2.

Personal profile: It's all about you

This section of your credit report may be labeled "Personal Profile" or "Personal Information," depending on which credit bureau issued the report.

Appearing first in the order of credit-report elements, your profile section contains the key components that help you make sure that the report is actually about *you:* your name (and any of your previous names), Social Security number, address(es), and current and previous employers.

Be sure to check this section and make sure all the information is correct. An error could cause someone else's credit history to end up on your report.

Account summary: An overview of your financial history

This section of your credit report may be labeled "Account Summary" or "Credit Summary," and it may follow the "Personal Profile" section or appear later in the report. It may also be the first part of the "Account History" section (covered later in this chapter), depending on which bureau's report you're looking at.

This information illustrates your history in broad terms. It includes summaries of open and closed accounts, credit limits, total balance of all accounts, payment history, and number of credit inquiries. Why a summary? Well, lenders are people, too (sort of), and they'd rather read one page and go to lunch than read 60-plus pages of eye-glazing detail (my longest personal credit report was 66 pages). But don't worry: If you're hungry for painstaking detail of your payment past, you're certain to find it in the "Account History" section of the credit report.

 If something in the summary section looks like it's not yours, if it's too old (see the "Knowing how long items stay on your credit report" sidebar, later in this chapter), or if a paid loan still shows a balance, make a note to check it out in the "Account History" section.

Public records: Tallying up your days in court

This section is one you'd probably rather skip if you had the choice. No wonder some reports title this section "Negative Remarks"! Public records are only negative items that came from — you guessed it — a public record (for example, from a court proceeding). If you're lucky, this section will be empty. Some examples include bankruptcy, tax liens, judgments, and, in some states, child-support information.

Credit inquiries: Tracking who wants your credit report

Knock, knock. Who's there? This section shows who's been knocking on the credit bureau's door, asking if you were home. They may have been given your credit report or perhaps only your name during the recent past, as allowed by law. According to the Fair Credit Reporting Act, those with a permissible purpose specifically listed in the law may receive credit information. This includes businesses and individuals you've given permission to, such as your employer, insurance company, or lender, as well as yourself.

This section includes the date of the inquiry and how long the inquiry will remain on your report. An inquiry that you initiated, say, to shop for or obtain credit, stays on your report for two years.

On the credit report that you request, information about those who inquired for the purposes of extending a preapproved credit offer are included for your information only. These inquiries are not revealed to creditors and do not affect your ability to obtain credit.

Account history: Lock, stock, and barrel

Your "Account History" section, sometimes titled "Account Information," is the heart of your credit report. It shows all open and closed accounts with excruciating detail about payment history, balances, and account status over the last seven years.

How is this section different from the "Account Summary" section (earlier in this chapter)? Well, if the summary is like that ounce of wine you taste before accepting a bottle in a nice restaurant, this is the barrel it came from. Take a deep breath and dive in!

Each credit-reporting bureau displays this detail in its own unique way, using some different terms. I'll take them one-by-one, and then I'll make a fourth stop and show you the version of the reports you get from myFICO.com when you request your credit score.

Equifax's version

Equifax reports its "Account History" by type of account. These include mortgages, installment accounts, revolving accounts, and so on. Account numbers are shortened for protection of account information.

Here's a list of the information that Equifax reports in its "Account History" section:

- **Balance:** The amount owed to a creditor on an account.
- **Date Reported:** The date on which information was last updated.
- **Past Due:** The amount of money owed that should have been paid by now but hasn't been paid.
- **Account Status:** Indicates if you've paid as agreed or are late (and if so, how late).
- **Account Owner:** Indicates whether the account is an individual or joint account.
- **Term Duration:** The total number of payments you're expected to make on your loan (for example, 60 payments for a 5-year car loan).

✔ **Type:** The account type. Here are the account types you may find:

- **Installment account:** Installment accounts are loans that are for a set amount of money and often a set period of time. Your mortgage and car payment, for example, are on installment — you may have a set amount to pay at the same time each month, until the debt is paid off.

- **Revolving account:** Unlike installment accounts, balances of revolving accounts don't have to be paid off in a set amount of time and as you pay off a part of the balance, the amount available for new purchases increases. Your credit cards fall into this category.

- **Other account:** This category might include personal loans — for example, if you've gone to your local bank and taken out a loan to cover something like a computer or a vacation.

- **Collections account:** These are accounts that have been sold or turned over to a collection agency, usually when the account is more than 180 days past due.

✔ **Date Open:** The date on which you opened the account.

✔ **Date Reported:** The latest report from the lender, whether provided monthly, quarterly, or less frequently.

✔ **Date of Last Payment:** The date listed here may be different from the date reported. If you're in arrears, your last payment may be September 2005 and the last date reported may be December 2005. If you had no activity on a credit-card account for six months, the last payment date could be June 2005 and the last reported date could be December 2005.

✔ **Scheduled Payment Amount:** This information only applies to installment accounts, in which a set amount of money is due at a set time every month.

✔ **Creditor Classification:** The type of creditor.

✔ **Charge-off Amount:** Debt or portions of debt that were written off by the creditor because of nonpayment and inability to get the money from you. You want this amount to be *zero*. Any amount — no matter how small — is not a good thing to have on your record.

✔ **Balloon-Payment Amount:** The big lump-sum payment at the end of some loans. Your loan may or may not have one.

✔ **Date Closed:** The date you or the lender terminated an active account.

✔ **Comments:** Additional information about the closed account. Some examples can be "Account Transferred or Sold," "Paid," "Zero Balance," "Account Closed at Consumer's Request," and so on.

✔ **Current Status:** Provides the payment status and refers to whether you've paid or are paying as you said you would. You may see terms such as "Pays" or "Paid as Agreed", or "X Days Past Due"

✔ **High Credit:** The highest amount of credit extended to you by the creditor.

✔ **Term's Frequency:** How often your payment is due (weekly, monthly, and so on).

✔ **84-Month Payment History:** Equifax will show each month's status for the last seven years of payment history. Terms used in reporting the status include the following:

- Pays as Agreed
- 30 (30 to 59 days past due)
- 60 (60 to 89 days past due)
- 90 (90 to 119 days past due)
- 120 (120 to 149 days past due)
- 150 (150 to 179 days past due)
- 180 (180 or more days past due)
- CA (collection account)
- F (foreclosure)
- VS (voluntary surrender)
- R (repossession)
- CO (charge-off)

Experian's version

On Experian's credit report, all accounts — satisfactory or adverse — are grouped together in the "Account History" section. For security, the complete number does not appear.

Here's a list of the information that Experian reports in its "Account History" section:

✔ **Account Type:** Refers to whether the account is installment, revolving, open, and so on (see "Equifax's version" for definitions of these terms).

✔ **Account Status:** Indicates whether the account is open or closed. Your department-store credit card with a balance of $1,000 is open. So is the card you've had for eight years but haven't used since the day you opened it. The credit card you canceled last year is closed.

✔ **Monthly Payment:** The last reported minimum payment that you owe(d). This is typically applicable for installment loans such as auto loans or mortgages, if reported at all.

✔ **Date Open:** The date on which you opened the account.

✔ **Balance Information:** The amount you owe. Balance information is sometimes on the report, and sometimes it's not — this is not because the credit bureau wants to save trees, but because some creditors don't want their competition to know what a big spender and great customer you really are.

✔ **Terms:** The total number of payments you're expected to make on your loan (a 30-year mortgage would be 360, for example).

✔ **High Balance:** The most you ever owed on the account.

✔ **Limit:** The highest dollar credit limit you've ever been approved for.

✔ **Past Due:** The amount of *money* overdue rather than the amount of *time* (30 or 60 days) it is or was late. Say your payment on your credit card was $50, but you didn't make it. Now you would owe $100 — $50 is due for the current month, and $50 is due from last month. If you're late enough with a lender, the entire balance can be due — now. This can even apply to your mortgage!

✔ **Remarks:** Comments that either you or the creditor may have sent to the bureau about this account. For example, you may contest that you received services for an account that shows that you haven't paid as agreed. This is where you tell your side of the story.

✔ **Payment Status:** Indicates whether you've paid as agreed. "Current" is good, as is "No Data." Any other labels are not good signs.

TransUnion's version

TransUnion reports its account history in groupings, including "Adverse Accounts" and "Satisfactory Accounts." Account numbers may be displayed in full. Contact information for the creditor, including mailing address and maybe a phone number, are also included (handy, if you don't have quick access to this information).

Here's a list of the information that TransUnion reports in its "Account History" section:

✔ **Loan Type:** This refers to whether the account is a credit card, line of credit, conventional real-estate mortgage, home-equity loan, charge account (retail account), or other designation. In the case of mortgages, the information includes the name and address of the loan servicer.

✔ **Late Payments:** These are grouped under three headings of 30, 60, or 90 days old.

✔ **Remark:** Indicates whether the account is open or closed.

✔ **Balance:** Your current balance at the time the account was last reported.

✔ **Date Updated:** The date of the latest report from the lender. Some lenders report every month, some report quarterly, others report less frequently.

✔ **High Balance:** The most you ever owed on the account.

✔ **Collateral:** The security (such as a house) pledged for the payment of a loan. Collateral is typically listed for mortgages; the listing shows the property address of the collateral securing the loan.

✔ **Credit Limit:** The maximum amount you've been approved to borrow.

✔ **Past Due:** The amount of money overdue on an account.

✔ **Terms:** The total number of payments you're expected to make on your loan (180 for a 15-year mortgage, for example).

✔ **Payment Status:** Indicates whether you've paid what you owe as you promised. Typical positive descriptions include "Paid," "Paying as Agreed," and "Unrated."

✔ **Account Type:** May be different from the loan type; further defines the loan type (for example, a conventional real-estate mortgage [loan type] may be a mortgage account [account type]).

✔ **Responsibility:** Lists individuals who are named on the debt — and indicates whether the account is individual or joint. It is *not* a reflection of how responsible you are.

✔ **Date Opened:** The date on which you opened the account.

✔ **Date Closed:** The date on which the account was closed.

✔ **Date Paid:** The date the loan was paid off; may be different from the date closed depending on the circumstances (for example, if you opted out of a rate increase and closed your account, you would still have time to pay it off over the original terms).

myFICO.com's version

When you order your credit reports from myFICO.com, the comprehensive history is in the "Accounts Summary" section, which begins with an overview and then rolls right into the detail. Like the Equifax and Experian reports, only a portion of the account number is revealed.

Here's a list of the information that myFICO.com reports:

✔ **Account Number:** A shortened or crossed-out version of the real thing.

✔ **Account Type:** The type of account, such as overdraft checking account (the line of credit you have associated with your checking account to keep from bouncing checks), revolving account, open account, and so on.

✔ **Credit Limit:** The maximum amount you can borrow in this account.

✔ **High Credit:** The maximum amount of money you've borrowed.

✔ **Min. Monthly Payment (Terms):** The minimum payment due or the installment amount followed by the term of the loan (for example, 360 monthly payments for a 30-year mortgage).

✔ **Date Opened:** The date on which you first opened the account.

✔ **Date of Last Activity:** The most recent lender report.

✔ **Date Paid Out:** The date you made your final payment.

✔ **Date Closed:** The month and year you closed the account; may be different from "Date Paid Out" or "Date of Last Activity."

✔ **Loan Type:** The type of loan, such as charge account, conventional real-estate mortgage, line of credit, credit card, and so on.

✔ **Collateral:** The security (such as a house) given or promised for payment of a loan. Collateral is typically listed for mortgages; the listing shows the property address of the collateral securing the loan.

✔ **Description:** Overall status of the account. It may be described as "Closed," "Account Closed by Consumer," "Account Closed Due to Transfer," and so on.

At the end of this information for each account, a box contains more detail important to the creditor — and to you. Within the box, you'll find:

✔ The balance

✔ The current status of the loan (such as "Paid as Agreed")

✔ The amount past due, if any

This information is followed by the monthly payment history and a seven-year payment-history summary box showing any late payments by age of delinquency (30, 60, or 90 or more days late).

Credit score

Depending on which report you order, your credit score may be indicated as "FICO Score," "Plus Score," or "Score Power."

Your *credit score* is a three-digit number that considers more than 20 variables in a complex calculation and provides an indication of your overall creditworthiness. Many scores are marketed today and they can be very confusing — each giving different numbers based on different scales. (See Table 5-1, later in this chapter, to help makes sense of it all.)

The most important score for you to get your hands on is the FICO score — the one that your prospective lenders, employers, and other business and personal partners are looking at. You'll get a FICO score if you order any of the credit bureau reports from myFICO.com or if you order the Equifax report from the credit bureau directly.

Counting down the years: How long items stay on your report

A garden-variety delinquency — you're 30 days late on a bill payment, for example — drops off seven years from the date the delinquency was first reported.

If the delinquency becomes 180 days old or goes to a *charged-off status* (accounting-speak for a worthless debt that is written off the books, but still owed), the Fair Credit Reporting Act states that the seven-year reporting period begins upon the expiration of the 180-day period of the date the account first became delinquent. So, for more-serious negative items, the seven-year clock starts from the date the account was either sent to collections, charged off, or had any other similar action that caused it to be reported under a new category. This means, then, seven-and-a-half years from the first delinquency. Chapter 7 bankruptcy stays on for ten years, and Chapter 13 bankruptcy stays on for seven years from the *date of discharge* (the date you finish paying — typically either three or five years from when you start).

Even though information is out there for a long time, as the months and years roll by, the information becomes less important to your credit profile. The fact that you were late on a bill one time three years ago will not concern most creditors. They're typically more interested in your recent history (that is, the past two years or so). Why? Because people and their situations change over time. I always like to think that I learn from my experiences (don't ask my wife) — and most people do, too. That's why recent information is much more valuable in decision-making. Plus, as more credit usage accumulates in your files, any negatives become a smaller and smaller percentage of your history, thereby literally getting buried in the past.

The credit score appears in different places, depending on the source you order from. Although it may be in the front or back of the report, it's prominently featured with an explanation based on the reason codes I cover later in this chapter.

Your optional 100-word statement: Getting the last word

You have the right to add a statement to your credit report of up to 100 words — the credit bureaus are required to include this statement whenever your credit report is accessed by anyone. This statement is helpful in explaining any extenuating circumstances, and it allows you an opportunity to document any disagreement with data provided by creditors.

Use this privilege with some care. Your statement may draw attention to an event that is far enough in the past that a lender would not have cared about it or noticed it otherwise. Your comments stay on the report as long as the account does — and that may be too long. You can get the statement taken off, however, by notifying the bureau.

Examining Your Credit Score

Just as you would fuss a bit to get ready for a date or special occasion, when you're being courted by a lender, you want to be sure all your data is buttoned, neat and pretty. Let's take a minute to look at *you* from a lender's point of view. How do you look in their eyes? Along with your credit report, lenders can also buy a credit score based on the information in the report. How many times have you heard someone say, she's a perfect ten! High praise indeed. Well, lenders think of you based on your credit-score number; specifically how you measure up to the perfect score of 850.

Your credit score is a three-digit number that speaks volumes about your financial life. The pages of information contained in your credit report are boiled down to a number that gives those who want it fast a quick snapshot of your creditworthiness. The credit score used by the vast majority of lenders is called the FICO score. Your credit history can earn you a FICO score ranging from 300 (the lowest; in other words, the *worst* score you can get) to 850 (meaning, if credit scores were IQ assessments, you'd be Einstein!).

Credit scores can have a huge impact on your financial status. A high score can deliver you great rewards — including easy access to credit, good terms on loans, and the best insurance rates — and it can even help you get a job. *Remember:* Prospective employers often request your credit report and score.

If you want to make sense of your credit report, understanding the role of the credit score in lending makes sense. Score usage has grown from occasional to essential in modern lending. Because of the volume of transactions and the rapid response consumers are accustomed to — especially those who use online tools — credit scores have become a virtual necessity for busy lenders who can size up a prospective borrower in the time it takes to glance at the one three-digit number.

Understanding the main credit-score models

More than one credit score exists, and understanding the differences between them is important. Why? Because you want to be sure that you receive the same score that your lender sees.

Is credit scoring fair to minorities?

Scoring does not consider your gender, race, nationality, or marital status. The Equal Credit Opportunity Act does not allow lenders to consider gender, race, nationality, or marital status when underwriting credit. Independent studies have shown that credit scoring is not unfair to minorities or people with little credit history. In fact, FICO developed expansion scoring to better address the needs of just such groups. In other words, it is an accurate and consistent measure of repayment potential for everyone with some credit history.

The big daddy of credit scores is what I call the "true" or trademarked FICO score developed by Fair Isaac. Although each of the three credit bureaus has a proprietary score also developed by Fair Isaac, it is not the same "true" trademarked FICO score that most lenders use. Because the bureaus make money selling *their* proprietary scores, they push these scores on their Web sites. As a result, you'll see multiple names, including "Score Power," "Score Plus," and others.

Not all credit scores are the same. For the sake of illustration, I pulled all three of my own credit reports and scores online within a 24-hour period so there wouldn't be time for any variation based on new information. Here's what I found: My scores varied from 793 to 899. My score was better than — take your pick — 80 to 98.9 percent of all U.S. consumers. It's easy for this to be confusing, in fact they confused me a bit. But when you consider that the underlying information each bureau has is different and the scoring formulas are different also, I guess you can somewhat understand there might be some differences. Table 5-1 spells it all out.

Table 5-1	Credit-Score Comparisons		
Source	*Range of Scores Available*	*My Score*	*Percentage of U.S. Consumers below My Score*
Equifax Score Power	300–850	806	91
Experian Plus Score	330–830	793	98.9
TransUnion Personal Credit Score	400–925	899	95+
FICO Score Using Equifax Data (from myFICO.com)	300–850	806	91

(continued)

Table 5-1 *(continued)*

Source	Range of Scores Available	My Score	Percentage of U.S. Consumers below My Score
FICO Score Using Experian Data (from myFICO.com)	300–850	806	83
FICO Score Using TransUnion Data (from myFICO.com)	300–850	788	80

Are you seeing the pattern here? Notice how, with the Experian Plus Score and the TransUnion Personal Credit Score, the score looks a lot better than the Equifax Score Power? (This is kind of like switching the "Size 10" label on a dress with a "Size 6.") The Experian Plus Score and the TransUnion Personal Credit Score appears to have overstated the percentile of the U.S. population that my fabulous credit rises above by as much as 15 percent. Could it be to appeal to my male credit-score ego? Sure! Maybe bigger does make a difference? Or maybe it's what the marketing people thought would sell more reports. Also note that when they apply the same "true" FICO score to all three databases, the percentile of scores below me is very different.

The message is clear. Don't get hung up on a number. Be as good as you can be, but don't get excited and kick the dog over a 790 instead of an 800. The most important thing is to know what your *lenders* know about your credit score. On this topic, you want to be on the same page with them.

In Chapter 2, I go into more detail about the credit scores. The main points to keep in mind are:

- ✓ Your FICO score is different for each credit bureau report, if only because each bureau has different data about you in its files.
- ✓ Be sure you're getting a FICO score, not a proprietary bureau score.
- ✓ You can get the lender-used FICO score from myFICO.com or Equifax.
- ✓ Because credit reports commonly have errors, you're likely to have a faulty credit score. Dispute errors and outdated items to get the most accurate score possible.

If you're in a rush and cannot wait the 30 or so days a credit bureau takes to resolve a dispute, thereby giving you a more accurate score, consider a *rapid rescorer*. These are credit-score and credit-report resellers who will add verifiable corrections to your report quickly and give you a new report and score, as the name suggests, rapidly. They can often get your lender a new, updated score in a few days.

TIP

Getting a FICO Expansion score

The FICO Expansion score is a new credit score from the elves at the Fair Isaac workshop, designed for consumers in new (sometimes called *nontraditional* or *emerging*) markets. It uses nontraditional credit-bureau data to predict risk for a growing number of U.S. consumers who would otherwise not have a FICO score because of their nonexistent credit histories. An expansion score may be helpful for:

✔ Younger people who haven't had the time to develop a long credit record

✔ New arrivals to the United States

✔ Women or men who may be recently widowed or divorced and didn't have much credit in their own name

✔ People who get a thrill out of pulling out a wad of bills to buy things and traditionally operate on a "cash basis" (thereby not developing a credit history)

If you fall in one of these categories, without a FICO Expansion score you'd need to provide documents such as rent and utility bills, verification of employment history and home address, and more, in order to get a loan or conduct other business that typically requires a credit check. If you don't have a standardized score, you may end up paying higher interest rates because, with little or no credit history to consider, lenders would tend to be more conservative in assessing your credit risk.

In today's fast-paced credit environment, a quick, objective assessment using a FICO Expansion score can take the place of the community banker who used to know all his borrowers personally. The elves at Fair Isaac believe that about 50 million consumers fall into this thin or no-credit profile. Bless that FICO Expansion score's cold and calculating little heart.

Telling a good score from a bad one

True FICO scores — you know, the ones available from myFICO.com (or from Equifax — just be sure you're getting a "FICO score" and not someone else's "Gigundo Score") — range from 300 to 850. The higher the number, the better the score. Looking at the spread of scores in 20 percent groupings, the general population falls as follows:

✔ Twenty percent have scores above 780.

✔ Twenty percent have scores in the range of 745 to 780.

✔ Twenty percent have scores in the range of 690 to 744.

✔ Twenty percent have scores in the range of 620 to 689.

✔ Twenty percent have scores below 620 or below.

Connecting risk-based pricing to your credit score

Most lending today is done on *risk-based pricing*. This simply means that rather than saying "no" to a bad-risk customer, lenders can say "yes" and still make money on the risky loan because they're charging a high interest rate and fees. This allows more people to get more loans — if at a higher cost — and it relies heavily on credit scoring to accurately predict losses. Using an industry-accepted measure like a score helps the lender in many ways. One is that they can better predict losses in a portfolio. Another is the lender has a new answer to those embarrassing questions, like "What were you thinking of when you made that loan?" (The correct answer of course was "lunch," but citing a credit score sounds so much better to the boss.)

But who's complaining? You get the loan, the lender gets more business, and everybody is happy.

Or are they?

Overpaying for a loan may be unnecessary if the loan pricing was driven by a credit score that was not as accurate at it should have been or if you didn't know how to do your homework to get the best score you deserve.

Another factor, besides your personal risk profile, that sets the rate at which you will be lent money is that most loans are packaged together and sold to investors through markets like the New York Stock Exchange. The packages that loans are put into have similar *quality levels*. In other words, a person must have a certain credit score to be considered for a loan in that particular loan package. A package of loans with a quality of, say, a credit score above 619 is a different animal from one below 620. The point groupings will vary with time and economic conditions.

What do credit-score groupings look like in today's market? As an example, let's take a $150,000 30-year, fixed-rate mortgage with one point in fees and a down payment of 20 percent. The rates would look like this:

Score	Rate	Monthly Payment	Total Interest Paid
500–559	9.289 percent	$1,238	$295,772
560–619	8.531 percent	$1,157	$266,400
620–674	7.595 percent	$1,059	$231,095
675–699	6.445 percent	$943	$189,366
700–719	5.907 percent	$890	$170,536
720–850	5.782 percent	$878	$166,228

As you can see from the chart, maintaining the highest credit score possible can save you tens of thousands of dollars in interest charges for a mortgage loan. The dollar amounts aren't as high as with a mortgage loan, but a high credit score will save you money in interest charges for any amount of money you plan to borrow.

In the current environment, the difference in loan terms between 745 and 820 (the top two groups) may be small, but the difference between 619 — which is in a lower group than 620 — is very large. Moving *between* groups (say, from 730 to 760) is more important than moving *within* them (say, from 700 to 730). And most of the lending risk, as well as the high pricing to offset it, is seen in the lower groups.

So how high is high enough? In a time of relatively easy credit, such as we had in 2005, the saying is that all you need is a pulse to get a loan. Although this may not be totally true, getting a loan in 2005 was certainly easier than it was several years ago.

What we don't know is whether the future will hold the same, easier, or tighter credit requirements. Over time, the standard for lending has swung in a pendulum from easy to tight and back again. So, keeping your credit as clean as you can is all the more important, because today's record will be there for seven years, while tomorrow's credit market will surely change one way or the other.

Knowing the reason for reason statements

Along with your credit score, you get up to four reason statements on your credit-score report. What's the reason for reason statements? Well, a lender can't make money turning down business, so if your score is getting in the way of commerce, knowing the reason why can help identify how to correct the situation and get those fees and loans flowing once again!

The creditors get what is called a *reason code,* and you get the interpreted version of that called the *reason statement.* For example, if a reason code revealed that your lower-than-desired score was because of an inordinate number of open accounts used to the max and not because you never pay on time, the lender might be more willing to take you on.

Some 60 different codes give you and your lender a "hint" about what caused your credit troubles. Additionally, they may be helpful in allowing you to determine whether your credit report contains errors and where the errors exist, because they highlight areas that lowered your score.

The reason codes are interpreted by the bureaus. Typically, following whatever section your credit score is in, these reasons may list both positive and negative reasons for your score, with tips to help increase your score muscle. According to Fair Isaac, among the ten most frequently given score reasons (your lender's specific wording may vary) are

- ✔ Serious delinquency
- ✔ Serious delinquency, and public record or collection filed
- ✔ Derogatory public record or collection filed
- ✔ Time since delinquency is too recent or unknown
- ✔ Level of delinquency on accounts
- ✔ Number of accounts with delinquency
- ✔ Amount owed on accounts
- ✔ Proportion of balances to credit limits on revolving accounts is too high
- ✔ Length of time accounts have been established
- ✔ Too many accounts with balances

Part III
Doing Damage Control

The 5th Wave   By Rich Tennant

"Coming out of bankruptcy, I can say I learned my lesson—don't spend what your relatives don't have."

In this part . . .

If credit problems are creating an ugly credit image, consider this part your "tips to a more beautiful credit report." I promise results — whether we're talking minor blemishes or major reconstructive surgery. First, I cover your rights under the new FACT Act — how it entitles you to an accurate, up-to-date report, and provides clout in getting the bureaus and creditors to correct your credit information. If you have bad credit, I show you how to stop it from deteriorating further and begin to build a positive report and credit score as quickly as possible. You discover what collectors can and can't do, and how to keep them from hounding you. Finally, I help you sort out whether you're eligible for or should consider bankruptcy.

Chapter 6

Cleaning Up Your Credit Report

*I*f you're like most Americans, you value your privacy. Despite the plethora of daytime talk shows in which guests air the most intimate details of their lives, we as a culture typically keep our private lives to ourselves. This extends to our financial lives as well. You don't broadcast your salary to your neighbors or tell all your relatives how much money you have in the bank. And if you have some credit skeletons in your closet, you certainly don't share that history — possibly not even with your own family members.

Despite your desire to restrict access to the more-intimate details of your personal financial history, your credit report is accessible to much of the world. In this environment of full financial nudity and disclosure, the best you can ask for is that your credit profile be as accurate as possible. At the very least, you should demand that your financial record is your own and not someone else's.

The detail in your credit report is used to determine much more than a loan approval or a low interest rate. People who make decisions about you try to find acceptable social, political, and business reasons for making those decisions. They look for independent and valid data — void of discrimination, favoritism, or prejudice — to help come to a conclusion.

And the best and biggest sources of data available today are the credit-reporting databases. The information in your credit report is a good predictor of future behavior in non-financial areas of your life. Among the kinds of decisions being made about you based at least in part on what's in your credit report are

✔ Decisions about whether to give you credit

✔ Decisions about whether to hire you

✔ Decisions about whether to give you a promotion at work

✔ Decisions about whether to give you an insurance policy

✔ Decisions about whether to grant you a professional license in your line of work

✔ Decisions about whether to grant you security clearance for your job

So, if you're borrowing, looking for work, seeking career advancement, renewing insurance, or getting licensed, to get the most you can from the 21st-century American financial system, you want to make sure that your credit information is accurate, current, and, yes, about *you*.

In 2003, the Federal Trade Commission estimated that more than 10 million Americans had been the victims of identity theft. That's a huge number. Some people think consumers are getting better at protecting their information, and others think the hackers will keep finding new ways to get at it. Whichever one you think is right — and recent research says the consumer may be winning — this is something to guard against.

Aside from ID theft, just based on human error and sheer volume, you may have errors on your report.

Congress has done its part by tightening up the laws around personal data and giving you sweeping rights through an update to the Fair Credit Reporting Act called the Fair and Accurate Credit Transaction Act (FACTA or FACT Act for short). All you need to do is exercise the rights granted by this law — and that is exactly what this chapter will help you do. So, come along with me and you'll discover the ins and outs of cleaning up your credit report.

How the FACT Act Helps Keep Your Credit Record Clean

The FACT Act is about getting the facts about you straight. Its full name, the Fair and Accurate Credit Transaction Act of 2003, actually creates the acronym FACTA, and you'll find me referring to it as both FACTA and the FACT Act throughout this chapter and this book.

Basically, the FACT Act is an updated version of the Fair Credit Reporting Act (FCRA) and includes new sections intended to help consumers fight the growing crime of identity theft. How so? By defining and setting credit-reporting standards for:

✔ Accuracy

✔ Privacy

✔ Limits on information sharing

✔ Consumer rights to disclosure

What does that mean to you as a consumer? Plenty. The FACT Act goes way beyond ensuring that you get free access to your credit report. Under the new law:

✔ You're entitled to a free copy of your credit information once a year (see Chapter 4 for information on how to get a copy of each of your reports).

✔ You can get additional free reports if you believe your identity has been stolen.

✔ If your identity is stolen, you just have to make one phone call to report it to the credit bureaus and initiate a fraud alert (as opposed to having to contact each one of the three credit bureaus individually).

✔ Your local police force now plays a role in helping you block fraudulent information from appearing on your credit report.

✔ When a suspected identity theft is reported to them, credit bureaus must take steps to ensure that all credit transactions with your name on them are actually from you.

✔ Creditors are required to give you an early-warning notice if any negative information is placed on your credit report.

✔ When deployed overseas, active-duty military personnel may place a special alert on their files to protect their credit.

✔ Credit- and debit-card receipts can no longer show your entire account number — only the last five digits.

I cover the FACT Act in more detail in Chapter 13, where I also discuss the details of combating identity theft.

Requiring lenders to help you

It's nice to have willing helpers — especially when their willingness is backed up by the force of law! In the past, the credit bureaus and the companies that exchange information with them were less than forthcoming about sharing your information with you. The FACT Act has changed that. Lenders have a new obligation to make sure your information is correct and to give you the help you need to keep your identity safe, spot problems early, and stop them after they start if your identity has been compromised.

Predicting identity theft before it happens

The FACT Act demands that financial institutions establish procedures to attempt to spot identity theft *before* it occurs. To predict an identity theft before it happens may seem as far-flung as calling in a psychic on a murder case. But like our trusty weather forecasters who look to the skies for clues to tomorrow's weather, financial prognosticators are writing programs to look for specific activity in your financial records that may indicate a problem. In fact, several credit-card companies are now touting their own programs to fight identity theft.

Certain events — such as a change of address, a request for a replacement credit card, or efforts to reactivate a dormant credit-card account — may signal a potential fraud.

That said, you can only do so much to protect yourself from identity theft, and in most cases you won't know about a problem until after it has happened.

Instituting an early-warning alert

The FACT Act requires that creditors give you what might be called an early-warning notice, which can serve as your first sign that something is amiss with an account and give you the opportunity to halt devastating abuse of your credit in its early stages.

The FACT Act doesn't dictate how *big* of a notice the creditors must give you. You may have to look closely to even see it, so be sure you do your part by closely monitoring your credit reports, bank accounts, and credit-card statements. Anyone who extends credit to you must send you a one-time notice no later than 30 days after negative information — including late payments, missed payments, partial payments, or any other form of default — is furnished to a credit bureau. This includes collection agencies as long as they report to a credit bureau.

Before negative information is reported, the early-warning notice may look something like this:

> We may report information about your account to credit bureaus. Late payments, missed payments, or other defaults on your account may be reflected in your credit report.

This notice means something bad is in your account history and if it is reported to the credit bureau, it will be negative. Whether it's reported or not, it's lurking out there.

After negative information has been reported, the early-warning notice may look like this:

> We have told a credit bureau about a late payment, missed payment, or other default on your account. This information may be reflected in your credit report.

The wording makes it sound as though the bad information may not show up. It will — and probably already has.

Protecting your credit-card number from identity thieves

If you're of a certain age, you probably remember the carbon paper that lay between the copy of your credit-card receipt that you kept and the copy kept by the business where you made the purchase. In those old days before electricity (okay, I'm exaggerating), thieves could rifle through trashcans and Dumpsters to gather the carbon paper slips and capture credit-card information so they could buy all sorts of things on your account. Savvy consumers always made a point of asking for the sheet of carbon paper and tearing it up.

Carbon paper has practically gone the way of the dinosaurs, but credit-card account numbers remain vulnerable. Receipts that include full account numbers and expiration dates are a goldmine for identity thieves. The FACT Act sets a national standard for truncation of card information.

The FACT Act says receipts for credit- and debit-card transactions may not include the card's expiration date or more than the last five digits of the card number. However, fully implementing this rule will take some time. If you receive a receipt that has your full account number on it, bring it to the attention of the business, and insist that they get with the program — now!

Note: Another FACT Act section allows consumers who request a copy of their credit file to also request that the first five digits of their Social Security number (or similar identification number) not be included in the file.

Getting help from the police

It shouldn't be a big surprise that if FACTA requires credit bureaus and creditors to take actions to protect your credit, the law may dictate that *you* follow some directives as well. Here's the deal: If you claim that your identity has been stolen or another fraud has been committed, you're required to report the crime to your local police. This rule is meant to deter unscrupulous people from making false claims in order to "clean up" their credit reports —

when they have, indeed, made some poor financial moves — just before they apply for credit or a loan.

Here's how the police reporting process works: Let's say you discover an account and/or activity on your credit report that isn't yours, and you suspect someone is using your identity. You don't need legally acceptable proof or a smoking gun — it's your identity, and your suspicion is enough to file a police report. So, you go down to your local police station and file the report, giving them all the facts and circumstances. There is no standard form or procedure; each police department has its own.

Just make sure you get the police-report number with the date, time, police department, location, and name of the person taking the report. You're likely to have to provide this information if you deal with insurance claims or work with credit-card companies and other lenders to clear your account.

The police may or may not investigate your claim. Regardless, you must have the formal police report to submit to the credit bureaus in order to clear the fraudulent information from your report. (See Chapter 13 for more on identity theft.) The police report will also help cover you against liability in case someone assumes your identity and is arrested for criminal activity using your name and personal data.

Providing help for military personnel overseas

Just in time for what seems to be an increasingly active period of military action in the world, FACTA has also creates another new alert. The *active-duty alert* allows active-duty military personnel to place a notation on their credit report as a way to alert potential creditors to possible fraud.

While on duty outside the country, military personnel — as well as their families at home in the United States — are particularly vulnerable to identity theft and may lack the means to monitor their credit activity. (Calling TransUnion isn't exactly a high priority when you're being shot at.) It seems only fair that, while soldiers are protecting their country, their country should protect them from credit problems.

An active-duty alert stays in your credit report for at least one year. Under active-duty status, any business that is asked to extend credit to you must contact you at a telephone number you provide, or take other "reasonable steps" to ensure that the credit application was generated by you or someone in your family whom you've authorized to do so.

The FACTA rules are in addition to a rewrite of the Soldiers and Sailors Civil Relief Act (SSCRA), which was enacted in late 2003. Protections under the SSCRA include the following:

✔ **Any court hearings for which you must be present can be held off by at least a 90-day stay (if you request it), if your military service will keep you from being able to defend your interests.** The judge can grant additional delays as the case warrants.

✔ **You can get your interest rate on pre-service loans and obligations reduced to 6 percent; interest in excess of 6 percent per year must be forgiven, not just deferred.** But you have to ask the lender for the reduction in writing and include a copy of your military orders.

✔ **You cannot be evicted from rental property for not paying the rent (if the monthly rent is $1,200 or less) without proper court action.** The law gives you other special protections if the rent is between $1,200 and $2,400.

✔ **Your housing leases entered into before you started active duty may be terminated if you're under orders for a permanent change of station or deployed for at least 90 days.** You don't need a military termination clause in your lease.

✔ **You can cancel automobile leases if your orders are for 180 days or more, whether the auto is for the serviceperson or the serviceperson's family members.** If you sign up for an auto lease while you're on active duty, you can terminate it if you receive orders to go to a location outside the continental United States or deployment orders for a period of 180 days or more.

✔ **You can keep your state of residence for tax purposes if the military moves you to another state.**

Summarizing your rights under the FACT Act

The FACT Act offers you, the consumer and credit-user, expanded rights regarding your credit report, granting you more empowerment than perhaps at any time in our modern history of credit. In addition to requiring lenders and credit bureaus to play a greater role in protecting you, FACTA offers a host of consumer rights. In summary, you have the right to:

✔ **Limit access to your credit report.** Only people and institutions with a need recognized by the FCRA and further limited by FACTA — usually generated by an application with a creditor, insurer, employer, landlord, or other business — are permitted access to your credit report.

✔ **Require your consent before anyone is provided with your credit reports or specialty reports that contain medical information.** Your employer, prospective employers, creditors, insurers — anyone — needs your permission before he can access your private information.

✔ **Have access to all information in your file.** Ask and you shall receive. You must be given the information in your file, as well as a list of everyone who has recently requested access to it.

✔ **Be informed if your report has been used against you.** Anyone who uses information in your credit file and takes action against you — such as denying an application for credit, insurance, or employment — must reveal that the information in your credit report was used to make the decision. Recently, this rule was expanded to require that you be notified if you're approved for credit at a higher interest rate than first offered.

✔ **Dispute inaccurate information.** After you say that your report contains inaccurate information, the credit bureau must investigate the items — usually within 30 days — and give you a written report of the investigation and a copy of the revisions made to your report if the investigation results in any change.

✔ **Place a statement on your report.** You may include a single, 100-word statement in your report, explaining extenuating circumstances or noting your disagreement with items on your report.

✔ **Have inaccurate information corrected or deleted.** Inaccurate or unverified information has to be removed from your file, usually within 30 days after you dispute it. If the reported information is later found to be valid, it can be reinserted into your report, in which case you must be given a written notice telling you of the reinsertion. The notice must include the name, address, and phone number of the information source.

✔ **Have outdated information removed.** In most cases, information more than seven years old — ten years for bankruptcies — should be deleted from your credit report. If it is not, you may demand that it be dropped.

✔ **Exclude your name from lists for unsolicited credit and insurance offers.** Although creditors and insurers may use file information as the basis for sending you unsolicited offers of credit or insurance, they must also include a toll-free phone number for you to call if you want your name and address removed from future lists. The opt-out toll-free number for all national credit-reporting agencies is 888-567-8688.

✔ **Receive damages from violators.** If those who report information to the credit bureaus don't follow the law, you can sue them in state or federal court. Some people have, and they've collected millions of dollars!

For the complete story on FCRA

If you just can't get enough of this stuff, the complete text of the FCRA, 15 U.S.C. 1681-1681u, is at the Federal Trade Commission's Web site (www.ftc.gov). You can also contact the FTC at:

Federal Trade Commission
Consumer Response Center, FCRA

Washington, DC 20580
Phone: 877-382-4367

If that doesn't satisfy you, contact your state or local consumer-protection agency or your state attorney general to find out more about your rights.

Examining Your Credit Report for Problems

The task of repairing your credit is a lot easier than it was in the world before FACTA. Arm yourself with the information in your credit report (one from each of the three major bureaus), as well as your FICO score from myFICO.com. (Chapter 4 shows you how to get these reports.)

When you have your credit report, you're poised to take the necessary steps to clean up the information that's there — removing outdated or inaccurate details, adding positive information, and even increasing your credit score. By doing all this, you can put yourself in a better position to receive credit and earn the most attractive interest rates when you do borrow.

As you study your credit report, you may be surprised by how many accounts you find. Because your credit report includes negative information for the past seven years and positive information for much longer, you're likely to see accounts you've forgotten about and perhaps even some you didn't realize you still had. Many creditors don't close accounts — even if you haven't used them in years. Retailers in particular are famous for this. Still, your task is to weed through the data — current and ancient alike — and identify errors and inaccuracies. (For a rundown on all the different sections of your credit report, turn to Chapter 5.)

Here's what you should look for in particular:

✔ **Make sure your name is spelled correctly and your Social Security number is correct.** With all the data moving through the financial reporting system, it is easy for a "Jr." or a "Sr." to be missed, as well as for confusion over a "II" or "III" designation to occur.

✔ **Check to see which of your accounts are shown on your credit report.** Remember that your credit report may not show all your accounts, because creditors are only required to supply information to one of the three major credit bureaus.

✔ **Look to see if accounts are showing the activity they ought to.** If you see accounts that are familiar but activity that isn't — such as a late-payment notation, when you're certain you've never been late — you'll want to report that error to the credit bureau. Also, if you see accounts you don't recognize, it be a simple mix-up or something more serious, like identity theft. Again, call the bureau and find out.

✔ **Look for accounts from a bank or store with which you have never done business.** This may have been added to your credit report because of a misspelled name or incorrect Social Security number.

✔ **Identify which accounts are showing negative activity.** Negative activity can include things like missed payments or late payments.

✔ **Bank and store mergers can result in multiple entries for the same account, so be sure that an account that moved from one source to another is listed only once.**

✔ **Look for any overdraft protection lines of credit.** These lines of credit often outlive the account they're protecting. Closing these lines of credit can be helpful if you have a lot of credit available.

✔ **Check out all the addresses the reports list for you.** Incorrect addresses can lead to incorrect information.

If an account is not listed and you believe it would be a positive addition to your credit report, ask the credit bureau to add this information to your report. Although the bureau is not required to do so, they'll probably add verifiable accounts for a fee. After you add the account to your report, keep in mind that the account may not be updated if the creditor does not generally report to that credit bureau.

Disputing Inaccurate Information

You can't legally remove accurate and timely information from your credit report — whether it's good or bad. But the law does allow you to request an investigation of any information in your file that you believe is out of date, inaccurate, or incomplete. You won't be charged for this, and you can do it yourself at little or no cost.

Inaccurate data serves no purpose for anyone in the credit-report chain. The credit bureaus, the lenders, and you all want the information in your report to be accurate.

The process for disputing and correcting inaccurate information has been made as easy as possible by the credit bureaus. Your role is to check your reports at least once a year and, if you see information that looks unfamiliar or wrong, file a dispute.

Here's what happens when you dispute information: After a dispute is received, the bureau contacts the source that provided the data. That source has 30 days in which to respond. If the source cannot verify the data within the time allowed, the information must be removed from your report. If, on the other hand, the information is verified, it stays on your report. In either case, you're notified in writing of any actions that occur as a result of your dispute. If you disagree with the findings, you can ask how the investigation was conducted and who was contacted, as well as add a statement to your report saying why you disagree.

Under the Fair Credit Reporting Act (FCRA), both the credit bureau and the organization that provided the information to the credit bureau — such as a bank or credit-card company — have responsibilities for correcting inaccurate or incomplete information in your credit report.

In the following sections, I let you know how to file a dispute with the credit bureaus, as well as with the creditor in question.

With the credit bureaus

Not all the bureaus have the same information in their files. So, if you look at your Experian credit report, see an inaccuracy, follow the dispute process, and have it corrected, you might not be out of the woods. TransUnion or Equifax might have *different* inaccurate information. So, you need to get all three reports to see which contain *which* false data.

If the same error appears on two or all three reports, you only need to dispute it once; if the information is inaccurate, the credit bureau will report this finding to the other two bureaus on your behalf.

Correcting all three reports is important, because some lenders or business-people purchase the three-in-one report that includes a credit score and credit-history information from each of the three bureaus.

Each of the three credit bureaus has slightly different procedures for consumers to file disputes, but all three allow you to dispute by phone, online, or by mail:

✔ **Equifax:** Call 800 685-1111, and be sure to have your 10-digit credit-report confirmation number (on your report) available. You can also dispute by mail at Equifax Information Services LLC, P.O. Box 740256, Atlanta, GA 30374 (no confirmation number is required on written correspondence) or online at www.equifax.com.

✔ **Experian:** You can dispute by phone at 888-397-3742; online at www.experian.com; or by mail at P.O. Box 2104, Allen, TX 75013-2104.

✔ **TransUnion:** You can dispute any information by phone at 800-916-8800; online at www.transunion.com; or by mail at TransUnion Consumer Solutions, P.O. Box 2000, Chester, PA 19022-2000 (be sure to include your TransUnion file number, available on your TransUnion credit report).

You can initiate a dispute concerning inaccurate or out-of-date information by phone, online, or in writing. The phone route may be a little easier, but most experts suggest that you do everything in writing or online to create a trail of documentation you can point to if things go wrong or get lost.

If you choose to dispute items on your credit report via mail, write a letter stating which item(s) you're disputing. Include any facts that support and explain your case, and include copies (not originals) of documents that support your position. Enclose a copy of your credit report with the items in question circled. Be sure to provide your complete name and address, and tell them what your desired action is (correction or deletion).

Figure 6-1 is a sample letter disputing information on your report. (It's also available on the CD, along with other letters you may find useful.)

If you're contacting the credit bureau by mail, send your letter by certified mail, return-receipt requested, so you can document the fact that your dispute letter was mailed and received. Keep copies of your dispute letter and enclosures.

The credit-reporting agency must forward all relevant data you provide to the company that originally provided the information. When the company receives the request for verification from the credit bureau, it must investigate, review all relevant information provided, and report the results to the credit bureau:

✔ **If the information is found to be inaccurate,** all nationwide bureaus are notified so they can correct this information in your file.

✔ **If the company cannot verify the accuracy of the information you're disputing,** the information must be deleted from your file.

✔ **If the disputed information is incomplete,** the credit bureau must update it. For example, if you were once late in making payments, but your file didn't show that you had caught up, the bureau must show that you're now current in your payments.

✔ **If the disputed information in your file shows an account that belongs to another person,** the bureau must delete it.

June 1, 2006

Complaint Department
Name of Credit Reporting Agency
Address
City, State, ZIP

Dear Sir or Madam:

I am writing to dispute the following
information in my credit report:
*[Identify item(s) disputed by name of source, such as creditors or
tax court, and identify type of item, such as credit account,
judgment, and so on]*

The items I am disputing are also circled on the
attached copy of the report I received.

This item is *[inaccurate or incomplete]* because *[describe
what is inaccurate or incomplete and why]*. I am requesting
that the item be deleted *[or request another specific
change]* to correct the information.

Enclosed are copies of *[describe any enclosed
documentation, such as payment records, court documents]*
supporting my position. Please reinvestigate
this matter and *[delete or correct]* the disputed
item(s) as soon as possible.

Sincerely,

Your Name
Your Address
Your City, State, ZIP

Enclosures: *[List what you are enclosing]*

Figure 6-1:
A sample
letter to a
credit
bureau
disputing
information
on your
report.

TIP

Avoiding a frivolous dispute

The credit bureau must investigate the items in question — usually within 30 days — unless it considers your dispute frivolous. If the bureau considers your request frivolous, they're required to notify you within five business days; the bureau must tell you why it considers your dispute frivolous and explain what you must do to convert the dispute into one that will start a reinvestigation.

So how can you make sure your dispute isn't seen as frivolous? If you send a long list of disputes — for example, all the negative information on your credit report — you may give the appearance of trying to overwhelm the credit-reporting agency with requests and they may refuse to honor your request. For this reason, you're better off sending only a few disputes in a single letter.

When the investigation is complete, the credit bureau must give you the written results and a free copy of your updated credit report if the dispute results in a change of information. If an item is changed or removed, the bureau cannot put the disputed information back in your report unless the company providing that information verifies its accuracy and completeness. Then the credit bureau must give you written notice that includes the name, address, and phone number of the company that provided the verification.

You can request that the bureau send notices of corrections to anyone who received your report in the past six months. If you've applied for a job, you can have a corrected copy of your report sent to anyone who received a copy during the past *two years* for employment purposes.

If you aren't satisfied with the results of your dispute, you can dispute the item directly with the creditor (see "With the creditor," later in this chapter). Be sure to include copies of all the information you have. You also have the right to include a 100-word statement of the dispute in your report and in future reports. Submit the written statement to the credit-reporting agencies, which are required to include it in your report (see "Adding a 100-word statement," later in this chapter).

REMEMBER

When the negative information in your report is accurate, only the passage of time can assure its removal. Most accurate negative information stays on your report for seven years, but certain exceptions to the seven-year rule exist:

- Criminal convictions may be reported without any time limitation.
- Chapter 7 bankruptcy information may be kept on your report for ten years.

- ✔ IRS liens remain on your credit report indefinitely, until removed by the IRS.

- ✔ An inquiry in response to an application for a job with a salary of more than $75,000 has no time limit.

- ✔ An inquiry because of an application for more than $150,000 worth of credit or life insurance has no time limit.

- ✔ A lawsuit or an unpaid judgment against you can be reported for seven years or until the statute of limitations runs out, whichever is longer.

If you're unhappy with the results of your dispute and think you have been treated unfairly or have not been taken seriously, contact the Federal Trade Commission (FTC). The FTC works to prevent fraudulent, deceptive, and unfair business practices in the marketplace and to provide information to help consumers spot, stop, and avoid them. To file a complaint or to get free information on consumer issues, visit www.ftc.gov or call 877-382-4357 (TTY 866-653-4261).

With the creditor

Before the FACT Act, there was no provision that allowed you to dispute inaccurate information directly with the lender or provider of the credit information. You had to go through the credit bureaus.

Another piece of good news from FACTA is that any financial institution that submits negative information about you to a national credit-reporting agency has to tell you so. This gives you a heads-up to jump on errors earlier than under the old laws.

The new FACT Act allows you direct access to the furnisher of the disputed information. The actual contact process varies and can be as simple as walking into the credit department and explaining the problem or calling the company's toll-free number or visiting its Web site (many companies' Web sites have information on reporting fraud).

After you've contacted the creditor, it must investigate the dispute and report the results back to you following the same guidelines that the credit bureaus have to follow (see the preceding section), including responding in the same time frame as the credit-reporting agencies.

Best of all, the creditor cannot continue to report the negative information without noting that it is in dispute. And if the information that's been disputed was reported as the result of a possible identity theft, then it can't be reported at all while the investigation is pending.

Challenging data you aren't sure about

The dispute process is protected from abuse by the law. You don't want to dispute information that you know is accurate or claim that an account listing is the result of identity theft when you know that is not the case. However, you can dispute any listing in good faith if you're uncertain of its validity — in other words, if you can't find records that confirm the item, you don't recall the status, or you're simply uncertain that the information has been reported correctly.

Follow the dispute processes outlined in this chapter, and explain why you believe the item is questionable. Just as you might challenge a word that you aren't familiar with in a game of Scrabble with friends, disputing information about which you aren't completely sure is okay. Disputing information that you know is correct is *not* okay.

Again, as with the credit bureaus, the creditor must respond to your request within 30 days. If there is no response, the item in dispute is removed or corrected. If the creditor finds the information to be inaccurate, it must be corrected. If the information is outdated or someone else's, it must be removed. In either case, the result must be submitted to each credit-reporting agency with which the creditor has shared the incorrect information. If your dispute is not found to be valid, you can add a 100-word statement to your report, explaining why you dispute the claim.

Keeping it in the family

Unfortunately, I've seen some cases of identity theft where one family member has opened an account in the name of another family member, which is easy to do because family members often have access to each other's personal information. I knew of a situation in which a father opened a credit-card account in his son's name without the son — a minor at the time — knowing or authorizing it. It was easy enough — the dad had all the boy's personal information (Social Security number, name, date of birth, and so on). The son was left with a large debt when he turned 18.

Under federal law and in most states, the son in this situation would be considered a victim of identity theft. Using your own child's or parent's credit is still considered identity theft because the information was used to open a credit account without authorization. The son has the right to report the crime to the police, who would issue a report that can be submitted to the creditor along with a request that the account be removed from the son's credit report. The creditor then would collect the debt from the father.

Such cases often pose a difficult choice for family members whose loved ones have betrayed them. Call the relative or call the police — it's up to you.

Adding Information to Your Credit Report

The best way to get positive information inserted into your credit report is to make payments to your creditors on time and in the full amount each month. Do so for a year or more, and you'll have made great strides in improving your credit history and your credit score.

You can also add some information to your credit report. I cover a few of your options in the following sections.

Getting good accounts added to your report

If you have good accounts that aren't showing up on your credit reports, you can request that they be added. For example, if you have a loan through your credit union and the credit union does not report to the major credit bureaus, you can request that the bureaus verify the account and add it to your report. You may be charged a fee to do this, but it may be worth the cost if the account will improve your credit standing.

Opening new credit accounts

Another way to insert information is to open new credit accounts. Opening types of accounts that are not already on your credit report is particularly helpful. For example, you may have several credit cards, so you could add an installment account — which might increase your "Type of Credit Used" profile (see Chapter 2 for more information).

Be careful when using this to tactic to improve your credit score. You may do more harm than good if you open an account with a large amount of available credit — this is likely to push your available credit over the limit of what is acceptable by lenders.

Adding a 100-word statement

Don't like what others are saying about you? You can add a 100-word statement to certain items on your credit report. Although a statement won't change your credit score, it may help answer questions that a lender or underwriter may have when reviewing your report. Yes, the score is important, but so is the underwriter's review. This statement can be used to accomplish several things:

- ✔ **Explain a series of late payments, collections, or charge-offs due to a life event such as a job loss, divorce, or illness.**

- ✔ **Dispute information that you believe is incorrect, but that the credit-reporting agency will not remove from your report.**

- ✔ **Tell your side of a negative report.** For example, you may have ordered a product that was not delivered on time or was unsatisfactory to you and you refused to pay for it. Although the situation was not resolved in your favor, you might be able to explain it more clearly in your 100-word note.

Do these 100-word statements really help? It depends on who is reviewing your credit report. The statement will stay on your report as long as the disputed item does, and at least one credit-reporting agency — TransUnion — thinks it's important enough to offer you help in writing it (call 800-916-8800 for help from TransUnion).

If you decide to put a statement on your report, be sure that your statement doesn't outlive its usefulness. As old information becomes less of a factor in your score, or even drops off your report, statements can highlight past payment problems better forgotten, especially if the credit report shows no recent delinquencies. Your outdated statement could call attention to past situations that no longer apply, and it may hurt more than it helps.

Cleaning Up Your Check-Registry Reports

As if tracking your use of credit isn't enough, some-credit reporting companies track your use of checking accounts. These companies are part of the specialty national credit-reporting bureaus, and they're covered by the FCRA and the FACTA.

The check registries, as they are known, are repositories of information on your checking-account activity. They contain only *negative* information about your history. It doesn't seem fair that all those good checks go unnoticed, but life can be cruel sometimes, and these bad-news boys only report bounced check information.

Each registry has a database similar to those maintained by the credit bureaus. The check registries' information is used to help make decisions regarding check acceptance or account opening. The main check registries are TeleCheck, SCAN, and ChexSystems. For information on how to get copies of your check-registry reports, turn to Chapter 4. Review your report carefully and make sure that all the information included is yours.

Steering clear of credit-repair companies

If you're desperate for ways to speed up the recovery process, you may suddenly be looking at credit-repair companies as your last hope (even though you can repair your credit on your own). You may be asking yourself, "Why not?" Well, the answer to "Why not?" is this:

✔ **Credit-repair companies can get you into a lot of trouble.** Most credit-repair companies use one of two strategies. Their first strategy is to challenge everything on your credit report, or at least such a large portion of it that the credit bureau and the creditors will not be able to respond to their disputes within the legal time frame allowed. As a result, the items not verified will come off your credit report in 30 days. Sounds good, right? Not really. Although credit bureaus may be slow, they're tireless machines. So at some point in the near future, the information that was removed will be verified and it will reappear on your credit report. If you're thinking, "Yeah, but I can get a loan while the information is deleted," consider this: When the information comes back on your report, you can be considered to have committed fraud. Ouch!

Their other strategy is to establish a new identity for you, using an employer identification number (EIN). The idea is that, with your new identification, you'll begin to develop a good credit report and leave behind all the bad stuff. But savvy creditors usually see through this ploy when a credit report shows very limited or no activity. Some credit-repair agencies suggest that you use the EIN as a Social Security number. If you're able to pull this off, you'll get into trouble and find yourself facing all sorts of legal unpleasantness. Why? Because you've essentially established a false identity and gotten credit under false pretenses. Nice.

Remember: If you do what the credit-repair company tells you to do, and if any of it turns out to be against the law, you — yes you, your mother's favorite child — can be prosecuted!

✔ **Credit-repair companies have a terrible track record of delivering what they promise.** Unlike credit counseling, which has also come under fire for having disreputable elements, credit repair is a much more recent phenomenon and the industry has not adopted independent standards of conduct. In fact, the industry has such a poor reputation that it has a very restrictive federal law named after it. The Credit Repair Organizations Act has as one of its two objectives "to protect the public from unfair or deceptive advertising and business practices by credit repair organizations." Need I say more?

✔ **Credit-repair companies are expensive.** And if you are someone like me, famous for frugality, this is not a small objection. Typically, the cost is at least $400. Chances are, if you're in a situation where you need help repairing your credit report, that money can serve you better by paying off some debt. If you're short on time and long on money with bad credit, why not hire someone to improve your credit for you? Certainly you could ask an attorney or accountant to help you through the process of improving your credit, but it will not be cheap and unless you have other business with these professionals, I would question why anyone with their credentials would apply their considerable talents and egos to such a mundane task. If you were to ask your lawyer to wash your car, chances are you'd get a big "no thanks," even of you were willing to pay the attorney her hourly rate. The same should be true of your request to repair your credit. But the hidden

answer to this question is that it's very difficult to know with whom you're sharing all
the information on your credit and financial
histories. When you consider the damage
they might cause you, I'm sure you can see
that it's not worth the price — in any sense
of the word.

Cleaning up your credit report is not as difficult
as you may have heard. Erase the past? No. But
you can make sure all the good stuff that may
have been missed is added to your reports, that
the old bad stuff is removed, and that no one
else's information is on your report.

If you get your check-registry reports and you disagree with something you
see, you can file a dispute just as you can with the three major credit bureaus.
The dispute process works very much the same for the check registries as it
does for the credit-reporting agencies although you can only dispute in writing and through the mail.

Submit a dispute by mail to the address listed here:

- **ChexSystems,** Attention: Consumer Relations, 7805 Hudson Rd., Suite
  100, Woodbury, MN 55125 (Phone: 800-428-9623; Fax: 602-659-2197)

- **SCAN,** Attention: Consumer Referral Services, 7805 Hudson Rd., Suite
  100, Woodbury, MN 55125 (Phone: 800-262-8186; Fax 800-358-4506)

- **TeleCheck,** 5251 Westheimer, Suite 1000, Houston, TX 77210 (Phone:
  800-209-8186)

The agency has 30 days in which to investigate the item on your report and
verify its accuracy or the item must be removed. And just as with the big-
three credit bureaus, the check registries have to clean up, correct, and
remove outdated information.

Here is a summary of the rules they have to live by:

- **Remove old information.** Information cannot be reported for more than
  seven years. After five years from the date reported, however, the
  provider can initiate the removal of information.

- **Update records.** A paid non-sufficient fund check does not have to be
  removed from your report. It does, however, have to be marked paid.

- **Get free reports for declines.** Just as with your credit report, if you're
  turned down for a bank account or have your check declined, you're
  entitled to a free report from the check registry that provided the report
  to the bank or establishment that refused you.

- **Add statements.** If your dispute doesn't result in a change to your
  report, you have the right to add a 100-word statement to your report.

Chapter 7

Keeping Bad Credit from Getting Worse

. . . .

In This Chapter

▶ Being open with your creditors

▶ Cutting your expenses

▶ Organizing your bill paying

▶ Dealing with joint debt

▶ Working with potential lenders

▶ Building a savings account

. . . .

A credit counselor I knew, a young woman about 5 feet tall and maybe 100 pounds on a heavy day, had a meeting with a female client to help her resolve her debt issues. The client, a guard from the women's state prison, was 6 feet tall and looked to be about 180 pounds. The guard, wearing her uniform — you know, the one with the badge, wide belt, and big boots — entered my colleague's office, looked down at her, and asked, "You're not going to yell at me, are you?"

I tell you this story to illustrate the fact that credit trouble can scare people silly — even people capable of dealing with dangerous criminals. And no wonder: Bad credit can threaten your economic safety in ways that rival the damage done by a thief who breaks into your home. A poor credit record can rob you of a good home, an affordable car, and an income. So it's understandable that the corrections officer trembled before the tiny woman who was there to help her put a stop to her credit woes.

Trouble is, when most people confront credit trouble, they tend to let their fear lead to panic, which leads to bad decisions. For instance, they might run to a credit-repair service (see Chapter 6 if you want to know what I think of that!), shuffle around their debt, or get pulled into some debt-consolidation schemes that make matters worse. I've even known people who've been in such despair about their debt mess that they've stopped opening their mail for months at a time because they couldn't face their bills!

Credit problems may be no big deal to you — all you need to know is what to do, what to say, or what to ask for. Or, like the correctional officer, this may be the stuff your nightmares are made of.

If you believe you're in credit trouble and you feel your anxiety level spiraling, this chapter's for you. Relax, take a calming breath, and read on. In this chapter, I reveal how to put the brakes on runaway spending and park your pocketbook until you regain control of your financial situation. I show you how to communicate to your creditors to gain their support instead of putting them on the defensive. I also offer some simple but very effective steps to make sure that you don't ever find yourself in credit trouble again.

If you think your credit isn't bad enough to warrant a panic attack, good for you. Panic is never a good thing. But keep reading: Bad credit doesn't always mean you're behind in your bills! You may be defined as a bad credit risk because credit-scoring programs predict that you're approaching the edge of a financial cliff. In other words, because of your borrowing patterns rather than your paying patterns, you may look like someone who's bound for a credit crash. So, read on to see what you can do to get yourself back on solid ground.

Taking Actions That Help Instead of Hurt

Let me just remind you of that infamous credit score I explain at length in Chapter 5 — you know, the one that prospective lenders, employers, insurers, and life partners may use to evaluate your worthiness, credit and otherwise. The big-daddy of credit scores, FICO, is calculated based on massive amounts of data grouped into five categories. Three of the five have nothing to do with late payments. Like an iceberg floating in the sea, 50 percent of your score comes from items below the surface. These three are

- **How much money you owe:** This category takes into account the amount you owe in various types of accounts, the number of accounts that have balances, and how close you are to the maximum. This is 30 percent of your score.

- **How many new credit lines you have:** The scoring considers when you opened them, how many older accounts you have, and the number and timing of applications for credit. Count this category as 10 percent of your score.

- **What types of credit you use:** This part tallies your credit cards, retail accounts, installment loans, mortgage, consumer finance accounts, and so on. It makes up 10 percent of your score.

In other words, you may never have made a late payment in your life — and still may have a credit score that causes businesses to think twice about lending you money. What can you do to get yourself in better financial shape without triggering any of these scoring factors? Read on.

Putting the brakes on your charging

First and foremost, if you see yourself getting in credit trouble, stop charging until you can get back on solid ground. How much you owe is 30 percent of your credit score. Some tips to remember:

- ✔ **Keep balances on your credit cards below 50 percent of their limits if possible.** High outstanding debt near a card's max can affect your score.

- ✔ **Pay off debt rather than move it around if you can.** The most effective way to improve your score in this category is by reducing your outstanding credit balances.

- ✔ **Don't close unused credit cards.** Closing unused credit cards messes with your ratio of credit card debt to available credit.

- ✔ **Don't open a lot of new credit cards just to increase your available credit.** Opening a lot of new cards in a short period of time could backfire and actually lower your score.

Note that even if you pay off your credit cards in full every month, your credit report may still show a balance on those cards. The total balance on your last statement is generally the amount that will show in your credit report.

Leveraging new credit lines to your advantage

Keeping your debt load the same but spreading it over existing credit lines can help keep monthly payments manageable and avoid missed payments. One strategy is to transfer balances to new lines with attractive rates. This can be a temporary help, but it will result in some inquiries on your report that could possibly affect your credit score. An *inquiry* is the credit event that you initiate when you apply for credit and the lender pulls your credit report to inquire about your credit.

One additional credit inquiry may not affect your credit score at all. Or one additional inquiry may take less than five points off your score. But opening several new credit accounts in a short period of time may not be helpful for people who have a short credit history. Multiple credit requests can represent greater credit risk. You want to avoid large numbers of inquiries on your credit report, particularly if you have few accounts or a short credit history. For example, industry statistics show that six inquiries or more on your credit report mean that you may be eight times more likely to declare bankruptcy than if you had no inquiries on your report.

Your FICO score does not take into account any inquiries from businesses with whom you did not apply for credit (like all those unsolicited preapproved offers that come in the mail), inquiries from prospective or current employers, or your own requests to see your credit report.

This may sound like a catch-22. How can you look for a better deal and improve your credit situation if *looking* counts against you? Don't despair—help is at hand. The solution is *rate shopping*. When looking for a mortgage or auto loan, people — I mean those who are not concerned about their imminent credit demise — may cause multiple lenders to request their credit report, even though they're only looking for one loan. The folks behind the credit-score model realize this and show mercy to loan shoppers by counting multiple auto or mortgage inquiries in any 14-day period as just one inquiry. In addition, the score ignores all mortgage and auto inquiries made in the 30 days prior to scoring.

If you want to shop around for the *best* credit line or loan opportunity, confine your shopping excursion to 14-day chunks — or find a loan within 30 days — and the inquiries won't affect your score.

Inquiries remain on your credit report for two years, although FICO scores only consider inquiries from the last 12 months.

Working for the right credit mix

Having a mix of credit from different sources is a good thing. Each type of credit (credit cards, retail accounts, installment loans, mortgage, consumer finance accounts, and so on) shows that you can handle different repayment obligations, such as a minimum payment on a credit card or a set payment on an installment loan. Also, retail cards (such as Sears or Macy's) are different from bankcards (such as MasterCard or Visa), and finance companies are different from mortgage companies.

Watch out for having too many high-interest, high-fee, high-risk lenders (like payday loans) if you're trying to get the most mileage out of your credit score.

Your score takes into account your mix of credit cards, retail accounts, installment loans, finance-company accounts, and mortgage loans. You do *not* need to have one of each, and opening credit accounts you don't intend to use isn't a good idea. Overall, installment accounts (mortgage, auto) will help your score the most.

The credit mix usually isn't a huge factor in determining your score — but it is more important for those with shorter credit histories or less-than-average information on which to base a score.

Closing an account you wish you never met doesn't make it go away. A closed account will still show up on your credit report and may be considered in computing the score. Say you have a credit card with a negative mark on it. It will still be reported and scored after it is closed.

Communicating with Your Creditors

For many people, communication isn't easy. Men can have a hard time communicating with women, parents with children, adults with teenagers. If you compound this apparently widespread communication disability with emotion, guilt, and maybe even some anger, you have a recipe for conflict and communication breakdown. Yet this is the very situation that thousands of people find themselves in when they're trying to put a stop to their credit crises. People just like you pick up the phone, call their creditors, and find themselves in a yelling match with a representative who seems to have the sensitivity of a robot.

Alas, there are two sides to every story. From your end of the phone line, it looks like this: You're a responsible adult who has been a good customer for a long time. A series of unfortunate, unexpected, and undeserved events has descended upon you like a flock of unwanted relatives. You've tried for months to overcome your payment problems before asking for help. You can't seem to catch up. You're at the end of your rope — dangling at the edge of a cliff. But with some help, you know you can pull yourself out.

From the creditor's end of the phone line, the scenario looks like this: You made an agreement and broke it. Everyone else pays their bills on time — why shouldn't you? You may be overspending and living it up beyond your means. You need to catch up on payments as fast as possible. If you don't come through with your payments, their business will be hurt and they'll be calling their own creditors.

See how the same scenario can be seen so completely differently? And before you accuse me of being soft on the creditor, let me just reassure you — I *am* on your side! I just know that you'll be more successful in getting the outcome you want if you're able to see the situation from your creditor's perspective. For whatever reason, you haven't been able to keep all the promises you made to your creditors. Although this doesn't mean you're a bad person, it does indicate that doing business with you may have a higher risk associated with it than doing business with someone else.

So now it's *your* job to assure your creditor otherwise. Is resolution possible here? Yes — if you do your homework, offer a solution, and follow through with what you promise. Where do you start? What do you say?

To minimize negative perceptions, be proactive from the start and follow the steps in this section.

Contacting your creditor promptly

Early inquiries for solutions are much more productive and much less upsetting for everyone. From the creditor's point of view, there are three types of customers:

- ✔ Good customers who pay as agreed
- ✔ Good customers with a temporary problem who are willing to work things out
- ✔ Bad customers who have to be chased

If you can't be the first type, you want to be the second.

The best time to let your creditors know you're in trouble is as soon as you *know* a negative situation is on the horizon. Don't wait until you've missed a payment — or more — on that credit card or auto loan. Don't wait for the phone to ring — or the letter to come — and *then* give your story. Get in touch *before* the payment is late.

I don't tell you this just because I'm a moral and upstanding guy (although my mother thinks I am). Sure, it's the right thing to do. But my motives are practical, too. By preempting the bad-news announcement, you increase the odds that your negative event won't show up on your credit report!

Don't call if you only *think* you may miss the payment. This used to be a good thing to do before the policy of universal default came on the scene. *Universal default* is a risk-management practice that got started after a rash of bankruptcy filings in the mid to late 1990s surprised some of the financial guys in the credit business. Not wanting to be surprised a second time, they developed a type of early-warning system that not only tries to predict when something bad is going to happen, but tries to offset the risk with higher rates (also before the bad event happens). If you're perceived as a higher risk — whether you miss a payment or not — you can get whacked with a very high interest rate on this and any other loan or card that has that feature buried in the fine print.

Explaining your situation

Depending on your own preference, you may choose to contact the creditor by phone, in writing, via e-mail, or through the creditor's Web site. In some cases, communication can even be handled through intermediaries.

Whatever method you use, you need explain your situation as clearly and effectively as possible, assuring the creditor that, despite your temporary difficulties, you intend to resolve them and get back on financial track as quickly as possible.

But what do you want to say? How can you get the help you need and deserve? Here are some elements you want to communicate (using a phone conversation as an example):

- ✔ **Begin the conversation on a positive note.** Say something nice about the company and your relationship to it — for example, "I've always loved your product/service."

- ✔ **Get the person's name.** Call him by name. Don't say "you" or "you people."

- ✔ **Briefly (in a couple minutes or so) explain your circumstances.** For example you lost your job and only have unemployment for income and no savings.

- ✔ **Stick to the facts.** Skip all the gory details that may bias the listener in ways you can't anticipate. For example, you can simply say, "My company was recently downsized and they laid off a lot of us in the accounting division." In this day and age, such circumstances are all too common — and understandable. Don't digress with detail or emotional commentary such as, "Of course, they only laid off those of us who refused to kiss up to the supervisor — funny how they kept that hot little intern who spent a lot of time behind closed doors with him."

Offering a solution

After you've effectively given your side of the story, are you ready to throw yourself on the mercy of your creditor? Not a chance!

Now you're ready to provide a resolution to this unpleasant situation. Yes, this is a critical and very positive step in the communication process. Your lender will be relieved that you've taken the responsibility to come up with a workable plan that makes you look like a person in control. Plus, you'll have *more* control over the outcome if you present a repayment plan that works for you.

Whatever your proposed plan, be sure to cover these bases:

- ✔ **Assure the creditor that you're already taking steps to resolve the problem** *now*.

- ✔ **Offer an estimate of how long you realistically need to rectify the situation.** Not "soon" or "I don't know." Even if you don't know, estimate in round numbers: six weeks, three months, one year. You can always call back and update the timeframe if events warrant and you need to.

- ✔ **Propose a specific payment figure and plan that you can manage.** Don't ask the creditor to suggest a payment. You won't like the answer. It has no bearing on your ability to make the payment and will set a barrier to get over.

- ✔ **Offer specifics.** Avoid saying, "I can't afford the $300-a-month payment right now. You're going to have to accept less." That's not a plan. "Could we reduce the monthly payment to $150 for the next three months? I would even be able to pay $75 twice a month. Then in six months, I believe I can return to $300, which will only extend the length of the loan by six months." Now, *that's* a plan. It shows that you're sensitive to the creditor's situation and you're making a fair effort to make good.

- ✔ **Don't overpromise.** You may want to please the person on the phone. You may feel intimidated or embarrassed. But in the end, the creditor will not be happy if you promise a certain payment and fail to deliver.

If you prefer to handle things in writing, check out Figure 7-1 for an example of a letter you might send. The same letter is on the CD, along with other letters you might find useful as starting points.

Covering all the bases

After you've proposed your plan, your contact will probably have to get someone else's approval and take it through the "proper channels." Don't worry: The company has been through this before and may follow a preapproved policy that may be called a *forbearance program* or a *hardship program* (the names vary from one company to the next, but they're all the same basic thing).

After the terms have been agreed upon, ask for a letter with the new agreement to be mailed or e-mailed to you so there is no misunderstanding. If that doesn't seem to be forthcoming from your contact, or if you don't receive written documentation of the new terms in a few days, follow up yourself in writing.

```
Date


Creditor Name
Creditor Address
City, State ZIP

RE:    Account #:
       Name on Account:
       Balance:
       Regular Monthly Payment:

To Whom It May Concern:

To date I have remained current with the monthly
payment on the account listed above. My financial
situation has recently changed and I am unable to
continue to pay this amount. Briefly describe financial
hardship (for example, I have been laid off and my current income covers
only my basic living expenses).

My intent is to honor my obligation with you and
propose paying $XXX per month for the time being.
I will contact you when my financial situation
improves and I am able to increase this amount.

Thank you for your patience and assistance with
this matter. Please contact me in writing at the
address below by Insert Date 2 Weeks from Date of Letter with
your response.

Sincerely,



Your Name
Your Address
City, State ZIP
Your Phone
```

Figure 7-1:
Proposing
something is
always
better than
hiding out
and hoping
the creditor
will forget
you owe.

Reducing Expenses to Clear Credit Woes

I'm not going to lie to you: Cutting expenses is no fun! But after you've done it successfully, you'll feel much better. So, if you can reduce or even eliminate your credit challenge by doing without for a while, not having any fun will turn out to be worth the effort.

Coming up with a spending plan

The best way I know to cut expenses and set yourself on the road to credit recovery is to develop a detailed spending plan. Don't throw down this book and run out of the room. Believe me, I'm not proposing anything that will leave scars or hurt you permanently. A spending plan will tell you just how much available cash you have to meet your obligations — and have some fun, too. It will allow you to say with certainty that you can afford $50 and not $60 on your monthly entertainment expenses, unless you're willing to reduce your spending on something else.

Creating a spending plan is easy — but putting it in writing is critical! The CD includes forms that will help you. And if you still feel overwhelmed, Chapter 3 offers advice on choosing a good credit counselor who can help you with this process. (Believe it or not, there *are* people who love putting together budgets.)

By writing down where your money goes, you'll have an easier time determining what you need to change — if anything — in your spending habits. After you know how much income you have each month and how much you're spending on what, you'll have a clearer idea what you can promise and deliver on.

Cutting the fat from your budget

The simplest way to cut expenses is much like cutting calories when you're on a diet. When slimming down, you eat the stuff that's low in calories and skip the cake. When cutting expenses, do things that have a low cost (shop at the bargain grocery store with coupons in hand) and lay off the expensive stuff (cancel that reservation to your town's hot new restaurant).

Speaking of calories and entertainment, one of the biggest entertainment expenses in American families is eating out. If you add up your monthly expense for restaurant food, you may be shocked. Cut that expense and eat in. Pack your lunches for work. Make eating at home fun by involving the entire family in preparing some of the dishes you'd order at that fancy restaurant. You'll be surprised to see your monthly food budget shrink by as much as 25 to 50 percent.

Next on the chopping block are other forms of costly entertainment. Eliminating these will free up cash that could be put to better use clearing up your credit problem. Among them might be

- ✔ **Shopping as entertainment:** Cruising the mall often leads to unplanned purchases of clothes, shoes, home accessories, or other nonessential items. Yes, I know clothes and shoes are essential. You and I know, however, that most entertainment shopping is for *wants* not needs.

- ✔ **Movies, theater, sports events, and concerts:** You know how much even a night at the movies can cost — especially after you add up the cost of the ticket, popcorn, and drink. Let's not even talk about season tickets to a major sporting event. If you're afraid you'll become uncultured or uncool, look for free concerts and plays in your community. Use the television or video rentals at home for your sports and movie fixes.

- ✔ **Hobbies:** If your favorite pastimes come with a high price tag — golf, jewelry-making, gambling, or hunting, for example — consider switching to something that demands a little less of an investment — such as bike-riding (if you already own the bike) or bird-watching (as long as it doesn't mean a trip to Costa Rica). *Remember:* You won't have to give it up forever — just until you resolve your current financial situation.

Finally, take a look at your monthly expenses and determine whether you can trim back anywhere. Some places to look are

- ✔ **Cellphone expenses:** Perhaps you could combine several phones onto one plan or switch providers or to a less-expensive plan.

- ✔ **Cable TV:** Turn off the cable and spend more time reading, talking, or otherwise enjoying different pursuits.

- ✔ **Transportation:** Sell any extra vehicles that you could do without in the short term. Walk more and drive less.

- ✔ **Utilities:** Reduce water usage, turn up or down your thermostat (depending on the time of year), and adjust the temperature on your water heater downward.

Cutting back? Look to your paycheck for help

If you're still looking for ways to increase cash flow to divert toward your debt, consider taking a look at your payroll deductions. First, see if you have room to increase your tax withholding deductions. If you get a tax refund each April, then you have room to increase; if you end up writing a check to the IRS, don't do it.

Another place to look to free up some money is your 401(k). I'm not suggesting you take money out of the plan — that would result in some ugly penalties! But you might temporarily reduce or stop your contributions if you're desperate.

The savings from cutting back on expenses may not seem like much at first, but they'll add up quicker than you may realize. And before you believe you can't go another day without a Grande latte from Starbucks, you'll have reached your goal of regaining control of your finances and stabilizing your credit situation.

Paying Your Bills on Time — and in Full

I recognize that if you're reading this chapter, there is at least a chance that not paying your bills on time may be what got you into a bad-credit situation in the first place. So, I'm telling you the way out of your credit problems is to pay your bills on time? Well, you may be on time but have a low credit score for other reasons — like a thin credit file or a negative credit report from things like co-signing for you ex-brother-in-law's motorcycle loan. So whether you've been on time with your bill paying or not, paying your bills on time and in full — beginning *now* — can keep bad credit from getting worse.

Getting organized

Nothing is quite so frustrating as getting hit with a $35 late-payment fee on your credit-card statement because you missed the due date by one or two days. Worse is when you're more than 30 days late because you misplaced a statement and totally forgot the bill until the next statement arrived. And the absolute *worst,* is when all seven of your credit-card issuers notice and — using the latest policy of the trade — bring all your accounts to the default rate of 30 percent!

Getting organized is a surefire way to avoid unnecessary late payments. Here's how:

- ✔ **Pay bills as soon as you receive them.** Make a pact with yourself to get the mail, sit down immediately (or at least when you get back inside your house), and write checks or pay online any bills *that day.*

- ✔ **Mark a calendar with due dates for all bills.** Allow at least a week for bills that are mailed and a few days for bills that are paid online. Place the calendar where you'll see it every day, so you won't miss any due dates.

- ✔ **If you want to wait until the due dates are a little closer to help your cash flow, set up a filing system.** Place bills in folders marked with the day of the month that they need to be paid. The trick is remembering to place the bills in the folders and to check the folders on a daily or weekly basis.

Experiment, find a solution that works for you, and get those bills paid.

Avoiding the paycheck-to-paycheck syndrome

If you're among the many Americans who live paycheck to paycheck, you may find it difficult to pay all bills on time and in full every month because money is so tight. Consider these tips:

- ✔ **If you're consistently paying late or less than the full amount because your payday and the bill due date miss each other by a few days, ask your creditor to change the due date.** You can request that it fall when you have the money to pay the bill in full and on time.

- ✔ **Start a savings account.** Wait, what does this have to do with living paycheck to paycheck? Plenty. If you're living paycheck to paycheck, having some savings is even more critical. How else do you have money to replace the muffler or pay that doctor bill for your child? (Later in this chapter, I delve further into the importance of savings.)

- ✔ **Follow the advice in the "Reducing Expenses" section, earlier in this chapter, to loosen up the money flow so you have more flexibility making payments.**

Yours, Mine, and Ours: Dealing with Joint Debt

The joining of two people in marriage usually means the joining of finances as well, particularly if you live in a community-property state. Community-property states generally treat any property and debt that has been acquired *after* you were wed as owned (or owed) by both of you equally (other than a gift or inheritance) no matter who earned the money or incurred the debt. That means *your* financial habits and/or mishaps are not the only ones that can affect your credit report and your credit score.

Currently there are nine community-property states:

- ✔ Arizona
- ✔ California
- ✔ Idaho
- ✔ Louisiana
- ✔ Nevada
- ✔ New Mexico
- ✔ Texas

- ✓ Washington

- ✓ Wisconsin

For example, say you live in California. If your spouse takes out a credit-card account at that fancy boutique on Rodeo Drive and charges a wardrobe that will cover Oscar parties and vacations on Maui for the next five years, you're as responsible for that debt as she is. I know, the card doesn't have your name on it. Heck, you may even hate the dress. Doesn't matter. If your sweetie doesn't pay up, the owners of Chez Chi-Chi can chase you down to your poolside lounge chair in Malibu and demand payment.

Talking to your creditors is hard, but talking to your life partner about money may be even more daunting. Dealing with joint debt isn't necessarily twice as difficult as dealing with debt alone — it can easily be 20 times harder! If you're trying to keep your bad credit from getting worse and you have some joint debt involved, you may well feel as though your situation is out of control. And it may be. Adding a spouse, co-signer, or ex-spouse to the mix of decision-making and priority-setting is a big challenge, but you can accomplish it with the right approach.

The best tool at your disposal is communication. Talking about money is not the most pleasant subject, but neither is getting calls from bill collectors. To help avoid the one, you have to do the other. Here's what you and your partner need to discuss:

- ✓ **Setting financial goals:** Starting here is important. This conversation is about the future (where all your problems are solved), and setting financial goals gives you a shared positive future that you both buy into, as the impetus to make some changes in your lives. Goals may include saving for college tuitions, saving for retirement, or saving for vacations. Keep in mind that your goals may change over time. Refer back to these shared goals as you continue talking ("If we're going to go to the Caribbean for our anniversary, then we need to . . ."). In the goal setting process you don't have to be specific the first time around. After you get through all the steps that follow, I suggest you go back to the goals and put a price tag and date on each. Then rework the savings and spending plan to see how many you can fit in or what needs to be cut or delayed.

- ✓ **Eliminating debt:** Keep in mind you're trying to keep bad credit from getting worse here, so determining the best way to eliminate and avoid adding to debt is a priority. Come to an agreement about how much you and your partner will allot each month for paying off debt. You also need to agree that neither one of you will add to credit-card balances.

- ✓ **Paying bills:** If possible, pay bills together so you both know how much you owe each month and where your money is going. Decisions that need to be made, such as how much to pay on a particular credit-card balance, can be determined together. This bill-paying time also gives you an opportunity to talk about other financial issues.

✔ **Keeping track of check-writing:** If you have a joint checking account, make sure that checks written by each of you are recorded in one place so that you can keep up with your balance. The same goes for using your ATM or debit card — if you're both drawing from the account this way, you both need to be recording the expenses. If you have two separate accounts, decide who pays what and let each other know how things are going with your respective bills.

✔ **Saving:** Come to an agreement as to how much you can afford to put aside in savings each month. At an early point in your financial life, it may only be $5 or $10 a month. But no matter how small the amount, save it. It *will* add up with time.

Financial surprises are no fun — other than those in the windfall category (a $15,000 lottery ticket, say). Now that you have the good feelings flowing and a plan in place, make a commitment with your spouse to communicate regularly about your finances and avoid making large purchases or other major financial decisions without discussing it with each other first.

Explaining Your Story to New Lenders

Lenders are interested in more than what's in your credit report. Think of the lending process as one that uses one of those old-fashioned balance-type scales with a pan on each end. The negatives from your credit report go on one side of the scale; the positives on the other. If you have enough positives to fill the other side and bring the scale into balance, you may still qualify for that attractive loan or line of credit.

At the end of the day, lenders are concerned with the *likelihood* of your repaying the debt. There are three Cs of credit:

✔ **Capacity:** Is your income sufficient and stable enough to cover the repayment amount?

✔ **Character:** Are you likely to come through with the payment even when it isn't easy?

✔ **Collateral:** If all else fails, do you have assets of great enough value that they could be used to pay the loan balance?

So thinking of the three Cs, positives may include

✔ A recent pay raise (capacity)

✔ Longevity at your company (character)

✔ Home ownership (collateral)

So don't fret if your car stops running and you have to apply for a loan while your credit is still on the mend. You just need to persuade the lender that you're a good credit risk, regardless of what your credit report indicates. How will you do that? Point out the positives. For example, maybe you:

- Have paid your mortgage payment on time for the past two years

- Have consistently paid your utilities bills on time and in full (Bring or mail copies of bills as evidence.)

- Earn a reasonable salary (Show copies of pay stubs.)

- Recently received a pay increase or have accumulated overtime pay or bonuses (Pay stubs serve as proof.)

- Have taken steps to turn around your credit problems, such as starting a savings account (show your balance), paying off loans (show your current statement), or making good on a judgment against you (show your court order)

Saving Money for a Rainy Day

One of the best ways to keep credit from getting worse is to have a savings cushion on which to draw when life's unexpected events come to call. Your goal should be to save three to six months of living expenses in a savings account that allows you access to the funds when you need them.

I can hear you now: "I'm having problems paying *yesterday's* bills — now you want me to save six months' worth of expenses for tomorrow?" Yes, that is exactly what I want you to do. However, and this is a big however, you don't have to do it all at one time. Saving even as little as $10 a month will start the ball rolling.

Get in the habit of saving *some* of your income every month. At first it may be very, very little of your income, but if you establish the *habit* of saving, the amount you're able to save will grow with time, as will your balance. If you open that account, the next time you get a raise, you'll have a place to put that extra money you haven't been used to receiving. Have at least half of your raise direct-deposited into your savings account every month.

Saving money that you aren't already spending is the easiest way to do it. Whenever a bunch of money shows up, half of it goes to the bank. IRS refunds, birthday cash, overtime, or that $10 bill you found on the street. Half for you, half for the piggy in the bank. Even saving a few dollars at a time will get you going and will gain momentum over time. Soon, you won't be living for that next paycheck!

One of the frustrations of clearing up your credit is that life goes on — even while you're trying your hardest to recover. You may be faced with unexpected medical bills, a job loss, or any other number of events that can affect your finances when you can least afford it. If you have even two weeks of expenses in the bank, you're vastly better off than if you had nothing. And this will be invaluable in keeping your bad credit from getting worse.

Chapter 8

Taking Charge of the Collection Process

. . . .

In This Chapter

▶ Getting a handle on the collection process

▶ Understanding your consumer rights

▶ Combating harassment from collectors

▶ Dealing with charge-offs, settlements, and judgments

▶ Avoiding garnishments, liens, and repossessions

. . . .

"*L*et's not make a federal case out of this!" My father used to say that to me if I was getting to be a pain and making matters more complex than they really were. Why? Because everybody knew that if the feds got involved, things would become such a big deal that, well, you just didn't want to go there.

In the case of the collections process, someone has, indeed, gone there — and they've made a *huge* federal case of it. The Fair Debt Collection Practices Act (FDCPA) was enacted to amend the Consumer Credit Protection Act to prohibit abusive practices by debt collectors. That's right, our stalwart elected protectors in Washington, D.C., responded to what they termed the "abundant evidence of the use of abusive, deceptive, and unfair debt collection practices by many debt collectors" in the United States. Hey, they're talking about the *collector,* not you! This law can be your friend.

And it's a good thing, too, because people you don't know and don't *want* to know are writing and calling you for overdue bills. You've always paid on time and sometimes even more than you had to, but no one wants to hear that now. It's not your fault that circumstances beyond your control have kept you from keeping your promises. It happens to everyone sometimes, doesn't it?

Well, you aren't far off track. It happens often enough that debt collection has become a multibillion-dollar industry and over a million of your friends and neighbors opt out of the process and declare bankruptcy each year. In this chapter, I explain how the collection process works, how to get through the process with as little pain and damage as possible, and how to minimize the impact on your credit report.

This chapter is not a legal course on the FDCPA itself. A lot of Web sites and publications offer information about the act. If you're interested in the details, go to the source: the Federal Trade Commission Web site (www.ftc.gov).

In the meantime, I'll give you the lowdown on these collection guys, what you should say and do when dealing with them, and what you have to put up with and what you don't. You can take charge of the collection process, and in this chapter, I show you how.

Knowing What Collectors Can and Can't Do

Let me begin by demystifying the power of collectors. I'm told that collectors are people just like you and me, but with a tough job to do. My personal experience over some 15 years of helping people who are dealing with debt is that this is not always the case. Although some professionals in the debt-collection field see collections as no more than an extension of customer service to customers in trouble, others see collections as a license to bully and intimidate, using unfair and abusive collection practices.

The FDCPA law does not apply to what are called *in-house collectors,* the people working for the original creditor to whom the debt is owed. In-house collectors are governed by individual state laws. Most, however, use the federal rules as benchmarks for their procedures to be on the safe side in case they're called to task for their actions.

The FDCPA outlines procedures and restrictions that govern the practices of outside collections agencies and prevent abuse and intimidation of individuals in debt. Very strict regulations exist governing what a collector may and may not do, as well as what a collector *must* do.

First for the *must:* After you're contacted about a debt by phone, the collector has five working days to send you a written notification of the amount of debt owed and the name of the creditor who referred the debt to the collector. The notice has to indicate that this is an attempt to collect a debt and that any information obtained will be used for that purpose. The written notice also must disclose that you have the right to dispute the debt within 30 days of receiving it.

Post-dated checks: Good for the collector, bad for you

At some point in the collection process, you may be asked to send post-dated checks to the creditor. The logic here is that, with the post-dated checks in hand, the collector will not have to call you to remind you to send in any payments you may have agreed to. It also covers the collector in case you "forget" to send a check at the appointed time.

This practice is akin to putting a piece of bacon on your dog's nose and telling him not to eat it.

Giving a collector a post-dated check is almost always a bad idea, because there is a tremendous temptation on the part of the collector to cash the check too early, even though they aren't supposed to. If they cash the check early and the money isn't in the account yet, the check will bounce, and the collector will be upset. If they cash the check early and the money is there but the collector gets it before you were planning, all your other checks may start to bounce.

A debt collector is *not* allowed to

- ✔ **Use threats.** Whether in writing or over the phone, a collector must use businesslike language. Any threatening, abusive, or obscene language is not allowed.

- ✔ **Annoy you.** An annoying collector — isn't that a redundancy? The rule means that the collector is not allowed to make repetitive or excessively frequent phone calls to annoy or harass you.

- ✔ **Deceive you.** No trick or treat. The collector cannot pretend to be taking a survey or pose as a long-lost school friend or anyone else in order to get you on the phone.

- ✔ **Lie about the consequences.** They can't say you've committed a crime or that you'll be arrested if you don't send payment. In the United States, you cannot be jailed for failing to pay your bills.

- ✔ **Make idle threats.** You can't be threatened with illegal actions or actions that they have no intention of taking. If they have no intention of taking you to court, they can't threaten to.

The debt collector *is* allowed to

- ✔ **Contact you directly unless you tell them to contact your attorney and give them the attorney's contact information.** You can also declare that you don't want to be contacted again about this matter. In this case, the file will usually go straight to a collection attorney.

- ✔ **Contact you by phone between 8 a.m. and 9 p.m.** The collector can only contact you outside those hours if you offer permission.

✔ **Call you at work.** If you tell the collector that your employer prohibits it, the collector must not call you at work.

✔ **Contact you by mail.** The collector cannot put information on the outside of the envelope that indicates a collection attempt. And collectors can't use postcards!

✔ **Contact others to get information on where you live and work.** The collector can't say anything about the debt, though. The sticky part is that if the collector calls your mother and *she* asks who they are, they can state their name and the name of their employer.

✔ **Boost your bill.** The addition of any charges to your bill agreed to under the original terms of your loan is allowed. That's the fine print — that few people read — in all new accounts. This includes endless fees and the costs of collection.

✔ **Ask for a post-dated check.** Depending on the state in which you live, the collector may be entitled to ask for post-dated checks. Check your state guidelines — although it may be permitted, providing a post-dated check is not in your best interest (see the nearby sidebar for more information).

✔ **Report your delinquency to the credit bureaus.** A delinquency showing up on your credit report as a negative will lower your credit score. A charge-off will hurt significantly more.

✔ **Raise your interest rate.** Depending on what your original agreement says, you may be hit with a penalty rate. Doesn't make sense? You can't pay the current bill, so why would they increase your interest rate to 20 to 30 percent (making your bill even higher)? Because you're a higher risk than they thought — and because they can.

✔ **Repossess your purchase.** Some people don't realize that their loan or credit line is secured by their purchase. If this is the case, you may lose that diamond ring, flat-screen TV, or boat as partial payment for the debt. This is almost always a bad deal for you, because the creditor determines the value of the repossessed item — and the creditor can charge you for costs incurred in reselling it, too.

✔ **Take you to court.** The collector may decide to obtain a judgment against you in a court of law. A judge's order is sometimes better than collateral to ensure that a loan is repaid. Depending on your state laws, this can be a prelude to garnishing your wages or placing a lien on your home. At the very least, it further damages your credit report.

✔ **Revise the terms of the contract.** Some collectors can offer to allow you to make up your shortfall over time by adding an amount to future payments. Some, to their credit, offer hardship programs, but usually you have to ask for one. Be sure to get any revisions or agreements in writing, particularly if communications are at best strained — you'll need documentation to ensure the agreement is honored.

✔ **Accept or offer a settlement for less than the full amount.** The terms of any final settlement are based on your negotiation skills and the collector's confidence (or lack thereof) of getting paid. When the new amount is agreed upon, the collector usually wants the settlement at once and in a single payment. This will generally be reported as "settled" on your credit report — and it has a negative impact on your standing. Depending on the amount of the write-off (usually a $600 threshold), you may get a 1099C in the mail at tax time. This means the forgiven portion of the debt is considered income to you, and taxes are due on it.

TIP

Fighting harassment

Getting harassed by a collections agency? You aren't the first. If you complain to the Federal Trade Commission (FTC), which watches over the collection industry, you'll be among 25,000 others who lodge collection complaints annually. Some consumers have even taken collectors who overstep the law to court, where some of the consumers won very large settlements.

To file a complaint against a collector who is harassing you, contact the FTC at www.ftc.gov or 877-382-4357. The FTC won't follow up for you on your specific case, but your complaint will help others by allowing for patterns of possible law violations to surface.

Other things you can do about harassment or abuse include the following:

✔ **Take a deep breath.** Always be professional and as calm as you can manage, and never raise your voice. Take notes during each call. Be prepared with facts and dates, and know what you're going to say before you say it. After all, the collectors do!

✔ **Ask for a name.** Always get the name of the person calling you, and ask for full contact information including the name of the company and the manager of the office making the call. Do this before things get out of hand, at which time they may be less likely to cooperate.

✔ **Just say no.** If the collector goes over the top or breaks a rule (threatens, yells, uses obscene language), you can tell him to stop it and call back when he can act in a businesslike manner. Keep a record of the call and behavior.

✔ **Contact the original creditor.** Even though you aren't in good graces at the moment, a complaint here can get action. No business wants past or future customers scared away by an abusive collector. The original debt holder can always take the debt back and deal with you directly if you make a good case. Plus, the original creditor may save some collection expenses!

✔ **Contact the collection manager.** Remember, you were smart enough to ask for the manager's name when you were first contacted, so use it. Your complaint may be the one that gets the abuser canned. No collection agency wants to be sued because of a bully who can't be professional.

✔ **Tell them to tell it to your lawyer.** This is a double-edged sword. After you tell a collector to contact your attorney, she must cease all contact with you. Usually, the collection agency sends the debt to its own lawyer and either contacts your lawyer or sends you a court summons. The billing meter is running on both sides, so you don't want to do this lightly — if you lose, you'll have an even bigger bill to pay. That said, being summoned before a judge can be a lot less intimidating and may have a better result than putting up with an over-enthusiastic collector.

Taking Charge of the Collection Process

The best way to deal with the collection process is to take positive action as early in the game as possible. Debts do not improve with age, and they certainly don't go away if you ignore them. In fact, as debts age, they get bigger and uglier and harder to satisfy. So getting control as early as possible makes a lot of sense.

The collection folks don't care why you fell behind in your payments. They care about what you're going to do about your debt — and when. Accounts that are 30 to 90 days *delinquent* (overdue) are usually handled by people working for the company to which you owe the money. If you're contacted by a third-party collector early in the process, chances are the company hired them because of their tact and effectiveness rather than their skill at offending people.

Outside or third-party collectors are covered by the FDCPA and must abide by those rules (see "Knowing What Collectors Can and Can't Do," earlier in this chapter). Even in-house collection departments tend to follow the federal rules, simply because they set a good standard for defensible policies.

The biggest difference with an in-house or inside collector is that these guys may want to keep you as a customer as well as collect the money due. This situation may give you the opportunity to work things out amicably. However, if the business determines it's unlikely to get payment from you, then your customer status will become less and less of a factor in working things out (that is, they won't really care how nice they are).

Calling the creditors before they call you is always better. Calling a creditor when you can't make a payment places you in a much different category than you'll find yourself in if they do the dialing. Good faith will be on your side, but even that will fade if you don't deliver on your commitments.

Asking for verification

You get a call or a letter claiming you have a past-due financial obligation. Even if you're sure you owe the money, asking for detail — which account, what the bill was for, the age of the debt, when the statement was mailed to you — never hurts. Why? I'll give you two good reasons:

- ✔ **The collector may be wrong.** Creditors make mistakes — asking for a little proof is reasonable. You're not denying you owe the debt; you just need to be sure they have the right customer and the right account.

✔ **You may be the victim of a scam.** There are people out there who will call or write and say you owe money — and maybe you do, just not to them. These crooks typically use the telephone or e-mail to contact you and convince you that you'll be in serious trouble if you don't repay your debt immediately. They may even have proprietary information that persuades you that they must be legitimate. They aren't. The message here: Get the facts before you act.

In fact, the FDCPA rules say that you have 30 days to respond to a collection attempt, and you're well within your rights to dispute the debt. To do so, I suggest that you use certified mail with a return receipt. All you need to do is ask that they provide proof of the debt. Keep copies of everything you send. When you dispute the debt, the collector must stop all activity and provide you the proof of your obligation before reinitiating contact. Meanwhile, the clock is running during the dispute period, and your credit is still aging — time spent here will count as additional time past due if the debt is verified. If the verification process takes two weeks when all is said and done, that time may push your account into the 60-day delinquency category on your credit report. So try to resolve matters as quickly as possible when you're sure the debt is yours.

Negotiating a payback arrangement

When you and the collector are in agreement that all the particulars of the debt are legitimate, it's time for you to make an offer to resolve the obligation — whether the cause of the delinquency was an unintended error or unfortunate circumstance.

You want to convey your concern and reassure the collector that you're sincere in your commitment. But that doesn't mean you shouldn't negotiate for an arrangement that favors you. As you're discussing the repayment terms, think of some concessions you'd like to have. For example, you may want the creditor to:

✔ **Keep it from the credit bureaus.** If, for example, you're able to pay off your obligation and you're just 30 to 60 days past due, ask that your oversight not be reported to the credit bureau.

✔ **Waive late fees.** It doesn't hurt to ask the creditor if they'll waive the late fees. Be sure to tell them that, if they do, you'd be happy to get off the phone so you can run to the post office to mail your check. Most — not all — will agree.

✔ **Give you a lower interest rate.** Not the ideal time to try to get a better interest rate? Actually, it is. The lender feels some sense of urgency to resolve your situation. So ask for a break on the interest rate in order to help you become current faster. On a delinquent credit-card account, for example, you may be looking at a 30 percent default interest rate. The lender knows that adding this much to a strained budget will increase the chances of a larger and more costly default, or even a bankruptcy if you feel hopeless. The bottom line is that lenders will often help if you're sincere.

If you're 90 days or more past due, you're on thinner ice because you're more seriously late and three months of fees will probably be in the $100 vicinity. You may just ask for bureau-reporting forgiveness (that costs them nothing). If, on the other hand, your situation is such that you can't pay back the money right now, you may not have a leg to stand on when it comes to asking for favors. You may just have to set your sights on a reasonable repayment plan that you can live with.

If you're under extreme financial duress, go a step farther and ask if the creditor has a hardship program. You may have to meet some qualifications, but if you do, you could see your interest rate drop dramatically, perhaps even to zero, and have your payments lowered for six months to a year.

Keeping your promise

Following through with whatever promise you make to with the collector is essential. From the collector's perspective, you've already broken your agreement with them to make payments as agreed. Breaking a second agreement will place you squarely in the not-to-be-trusted category. People in this category are only believed when their checks clear the collector's bank account.

To make sure you and the collector are clear on what you promised, make sure you get or put the particulars in writing. Get names, addresses, and phone numbers of everyone you've talked to, and include a written copy of your agreement with the payment. Asking for an e-mail confirming the arrangement is a reasonable request. A letter is a little more challenging, because the delivery time may cause you to delay your acting on your promise for another five days or so. The collector wants you to act today. So if this is the case, confirm all the agreements in a quick note with names and times (don't forget to keep your copy), and send it off with your payment.

If you're in such dire straits that any payment plan may push you over the financial edge, work on a *spending plan* (see Chapter 11 for more information). After you've established your goals, identified your sources of income, and tackled your living expenses, you can discover what you can afford for debt service.

Collecting on a mortgage

An overdue mortgage payment is definitely a different animal from other types of overdue accounts. The rules for mortgages are very different, because the debt is secured by a piece of collateral — namely, your home. The result: Mortgage collections are very low-key and no one gets excited. Most correspondence is done in writing, although some phone calls may be included, particularly if you have a local lender.

A mortgage payment 90 days past due is a serious problem, and you must correct any deficiency as soon as possible. The reason? After your payment is 90 days overdue, you have to pay all the money past due — three months, plus the regular payment — or the foreclosure process begins. Yes, it's true: If you're over the 90-day mark and send in a double payment, there's an excellent chance that it will be returned to you as not enough. So,

for example, let's say your mortgage is $1,000 a month. At 90 days past due, you need to send $4,000 plus any late fees. Send in less and you'll get it back, while the clock ticks on.

And that's not all. After you're late on the first payment, the 15-day grace period does not apply any longer to successive payments until you completely clear up the entire past due and currently due amounts. The bottom line: Be careful not to cross the 90-day mark by mistake, thinking you still have 15 days to go.

Contact a good HUD-certified counseling agency and get help before you get to the 90-day-late mark. You can find listings of approved housing counseling agencies by state at www. hud.gov or by calling 800-569-4287.

If this topic is too intimidating, if two or more of you are involved and you just can't seem to communicate on money matters, or you just want help with getting started, a reputable credit-counseling agency can help you with a spending plan. (See Chapter 3 for help finding an agency.)

Saving your credit score by using a credit-counseling agency

If you're seriously past due and you're having trouble catching up to a "current" or "paid as agreed" status, consider the credit-counseling route. Using a credit-counseling agency can get you current faster. Often, many national creditors will bring your account to a current status after three on-time payments of the agreed-upon payment, and a credit counselor can help you do this. This concession on the part of many lenders normally does not require making up the past-due amount, and it can also be at a lower interest rate.

Fair Isaac's FICO score does not take points away for using a credit-counseling agency.

For an entire chapter on finding a credit counselor, head to Chapter 3.

If you're in the military: Drop and give me your debt

In Chapter 6, I discuss the rules of engagement between the financial system and military personnel. Generally speaking, there are some significant safeguards built into the FACT Act and a rewrite of the Soldiers and Sailors Civil Relief Act (SSCRA), both of which took place in late 2003. Here's what you need to know when it comes to debt collection:

✔ If your military service defending the United States keeps you from defending yourself in court, you can get at least a 90-day stay and the judge can grant additional time, depending on the situation.

✔ Your interest rates can't exceed 6 percent (see Chapter 6 for the details).

✔ Under certain circumstances, you can cancel automobile leases without penalty.

The car dealer you're leasing from may not know this and may try to collect the balance from you.

Write to anyone attempting to contact you for the purposes of collecting a debt, let them know your situation, and specifically ask for their cooperation according to the SSCRA. If you have a spouse at home, you might have him or her follow up on your behalf — be sure to mention that in your initial letter.

Most military units have a financial specialist that may be able to help further. If that fails, contact a lawyer or an accredited credit-counseling agency and ask them to act on your behalf. The lawyer may be expensive, but he should be worth it. The credit counselors will be free or low-cost and most will communicate with you by e-mail.

Explaining your collection status to a new lender

Okay, so you're dealing with the collectors and making progress on getting your accounts current. Life still goes on, and so does the need to access credit. But how can you do this on the best terms possible? You'll have an easier time getting new credit if you explain to potential creditors your past delinquencies before they get your credit report and learn for themselves.

The three Cs of credit-granting are *capacity* (how much debt you can handle), *collateral* (what security you may be able to pledge in return for the loan), and *character*. Here is where you get to boost the "character" part: Be up front about the problem and the solution you found. This will defuse the situation and make you look like the standup person you are, without putting the lender on the spot. One last reason to do this is that it will give the lender an opportunity to suggest a more appropriate product for you that may still serve your needs while making it easier for you be approved.

Handling Those Collection Phone Calls

You're late on one or more bills. You're starting to receive calls about making payments. You may find yourself in the middle of a recurring nightmare of insatiable callers who will not go away, but who seem to take strength from your inability to give them what they want.

This does not have to be the case. The FDCPA protects debtors from harassment from collectors — particularly where it involves the use and abuse of the telephone. Armed with your knowledge of the rules and a plan of action, you can handle those calls before they handle you.

Deciding whether to answer the phone

If a collector has been pursuing you, you may find yourself reluctant to answer the phone, for any number of reasons. You may have had a hard day at work, you may be overtired, or you may not be feeling in control of your emotions at the moment. Or if you've been contacted by the collector and you've already explained that you're doing your best and that's all you can do, having the same conversation again and again may feel frustrating and unproductive, especially if the collector is on the overbearing side.

You don't have to pick up the phone. But keep in mind that, although answering machines or caller ID can help you screen calls (and may help you with your sanity), they won't help you avoid or solve your debt. If the collector can't reach you by phone, he'll find another way to contact you.

Don't answer the phone if you know you won't be able to have an effective conversation. (For tips on what to say, see the following section.)

Scripting an effective conversation

In Chapter 7, I go into detail about how to handle creditor phone calls. My key advice, though, is to have a plan in mind before you promise anything, don't overpromise and underdeliver, never lose your temper, and don't stand for any abuse. Lastly, if you start to feel overwhelmed or backed into a corner, get outside professional help.

Even though it may not feel this way, you aren't the first or only person to have gone through debt collections. It happens all the time, and you *will* get through it.

If you're late on some bills, expect that sooner or later you'll get a call from a collector. If you've decided to pick up the phone, here's what you need to do:

- ✔ **Get the caller's name and contact information.** Be polite but firm. Ask the following questions:

  - What's your name?

  - Who do you work for?

  - What is your supervisor's name?

  - If I have to write to you, what is your mailing address?

  These questions will set the tone for your dealings with the collector. You'll come across as direct and no-nonsense. And you'll know who to communicate with if you have a complaint. If the collector balks at giving you the information, let them know that the Fair Debt Collection Practices Act requires that a collector identify himself and, if expressly requested, identify his employer.

- ✔ **Use the collector's name.** When you have the collector's name — and by law, collectors have to use their real names — use it. Refer to the individual by name, not "you" or "you people." Why? Because this puts a human dimension on the dialogue and may soften the collector's response to you.

- ✔ **Ask for proof of the debt.** Mistakes happen, and crooks call to get money from people all the time. So to be safe and correct, have the caller send you evidence that shows you owe the money (see "Asking for verification," earlier in this chapter, for more information).

- ✔ **Explain your situation.** After you've established that the debt is yours, the next time the collector contacts you, explain your very short story of why you're behind and what you're able do, if anything, about the debt.

- ✔ **Make an offer.** You can make an offer for a period of time. Say you owe $1,000. If you offer to pay $50 per pay period for the next 20 weeks, that may do it. Or you may offer to pay $25 per pay period until your next raise in three months, at which time you'll pay them $75 per pay period. Offering the amount you're able to pay is always better than waiting for the collector to demand a certain amount. (See "Negotiating a payback arrangement," earlier in this chapter.)

- ✔ **Don't agree to a commitment you can't keep.** Whether the collector pressures you into promising the full payment *now* or you just want to get the caller off the phone, you may find yourself agreeing to something you know you can't follow through on. Being honest — with the collector *and* yourself — is always better. Yes, an unreasonable collector may end up taking you to court. But you'll have a much better case if you show a genuine effort to offer a workable payment plan. And the judge may side with you. (See "Keeping your promise," earlier in this chapter.)

✔ **Get it in writing.** If you come to an agreement, ask for it to be put in writing so it's clear to both parties. If they won't do that, or if you're going to send in money on your own, write the letter yourself (keeping a copy for your records) and send it to the collector by certified mail so you have proof that the collector received it.

Knowing what not to say

Saying the *wrong* thing in a conversation with a collector not only may be unproductive, it can also elevate the conversation into a hostile confrontation that could end up causing you more harm. No matter how adversarial your caller seems, here are some definite don'ts:

✔ Don't let yourself get drawn into a shouting match.

✔ Don't make threats.

✔ Don't say you're getting a lawyer if you don't intend to.

✔ Don't say you're going to file bankruptcy if you don't plan to.

✔ Don't lie for sympathy (for example, "My mother's in the hospital," when your mother's kicking up her heels by the pool in Boca). When you're caught in a falsehood once, you'll have a hard time being believed again.

Identifying Escalation Options That Help

When you're dealing with a debt collector, you may arrive at a sticking point and recognize that she doesn't have the authority to do what you're asking. Instead of stopping at that frustrating dead end, you're better off tactfully suggesting that you'd like to take your situation to a higher authority — one who is empowered to make decisions. This is known as *escalating* the issue. In this section, I show you how to do this, as well as how to contact other people who may be able to help you when the manager doesn't do the trick.

Asking to speak to the manager

Collection representatives who just won't warm to your proposed payment plan may have one of several reasons. They may:

✔ Not believe you're offering your best effort to repay

✔ Have a quota to fill and your offer won't do it

✔ Have strict rules regarding permissible payment options

✔ Be having a bad day and just not feel helpful

✔ Have just been yelled at for coming in late

In short, your best offer to work things out may be rejected not because of the offer itself, but because of other circumstances.

A manager has more flexibility and may even see the bigger picture of a best offer. By asking to speak to the manager, you take the pressure off the little guy and free him to attack another customer while you and the boss work things out. If you look at it as though you're helping everyone, you may have an easier time escalating the problem to management.

It might go something like this:

> I understand that you've done your best to try to resolve this issue satisfactorily. But I'd like to speak to someone who has the authority to make exceptions/waive policy/take my offer to a higher level. It's not fair of me to ask you to go against company policy and take the payment I'm offering. So, please let me speak to a manager.

If the collector doesn't want to let you go, tell her you'll call back on your own and ask someone else. Thank her for trying and say good-bye, nicely. Going over the same ground with the same person will quickly wear thin on one of you.

Approaching the creditor

Surprise! Your original creditor may still talk to you even after sending your bill to a collector. A lot will depend on how you left them. If there were bad feelings or you lost it with a customer-service rep, chances are you won't be welcomed back. But if the transition from inside collections to an outside agency was more a matter of an old delinquency, they may be willing to talk with you.

So why would you want to approach the creditor directly? If you're not getting anywhere with the debt collector, the creditor may be willing to work something out with you. After all, they just want their money, and if the collector isn't any good, the creditor won't get what they want either.

Creditors either place a debt for collection (and pay a commission based on results) or they sell the debt outright. The former is the more common, and the creditor may be okay with taking back the debt, especially if they save a fat commission and regain a loyal customer. If your debt has been sold, Calling the lender won't do any good. But you may well have more room to negotiate because debts are not sold at full value. So a smaller-than-owed payment, may still be a profit for the collector.

Calling in a credit counselor

On your own, you can get to a manager. But the manager can't change policy that was set in the corporate headquarters. Very often, the "big guys" at HQ have already set a special collection policy that applies only to the legitimate credit-counseling agencies with whom they've established a working relationship. So, when a credit counselor gets involved, she may be able to deal with a special department that handles only credit-counseling accounts — and is much more sympathetic than the line collector or manager. So in one leap, you've escalated to high-level corporate policymakers.

Talk to a credit counselor from an accredited agency. Chapter 3 explains how to pick one from a crowded field. The cost is lower than an attorney and the advice is practical rather than legal. The professional analysis of your financial dilemma and its options is valuable. As an intermediary, the credit counselor can deal with your creditors on your behalf and may be able to administer a favorable workout plan (often referred to as a *debt-management plan*) while you follow a fairly strict budget.

Referring it to your lawyer

A good lawyer can work wonders with the more complex legal situations people face from time to time. Like showing up to a gunfight with the second-fastest gun, hiring a so-so lawyer isn't worth the effort. The best attorney for you is one who specializes in debt law. The drawbacks: Lawyers are expensive, and after *you* start down a legal path, so do the collectors.

Get an attorney who specializes in representing debtors. She knows the routine, has the letters on file, and may even know the collection agency or company. Besides sheltering you from having to deal directly with the collectors, the attorney helps slow down the freight train of events heading your way. She'll know what will be acceptable to the collector, collection lawyer, or judge (if things get that far). An attorney may also help you decide whether to play the bankruptcy card. ***Remember:*** Information is valuable and if you use an attorney, you'll be paying for it.

Dealing with Charge-Offs and Settlements

Along the collections road, you come to some significant stopping points. They aren't the end of your financial journey, but you need to know what they are, how important they may be, and what lies around the next corner. Unpaid charge-offs, settlements, and paid charge-offs can hit your credit report like an 18-wheeler with no brakes. Understanding the differences may save you points and money in the long run. If the collector or creditor chooses to *charge off* your account, this does not cancel the debt or even stop the interest from accruing. It only means that, for tax purposes, the creditor considers your account a loss. You still owe the bill and fees, and interest continues to accrue.

Understanding unpaid charge-offs

A debt *charges off* when it gets so old that the accountants won't let the lender count it as an asset, because its value (your paying it) is very doubtful. This usually occurs at 180 days past due, but sometimes a conservative auditor will charge it off earlier.

A charge-off does not mean that you no longer owe the debt — only that the creditor can't count it as an asset for tax purposes.

If you have a charge-off on your credit report, it's a big negative — especially the longer it remains unpaid. Collectors will continue to try to collect the money due, and the account may be sold many times for decreasing dollars to increasingly hungry bottom-feeders who you really don't want to deal with. An unpaid charge-off often makes its way to a legal department sooner or later, and that may result in a judgment being entered against you, a day lost to court, additional legal expenses, and maybe — if it's just not your day — a wage garnishment of up to 25 percent of your take-home pay. This one is uglier than Cinderella's sister.

Paying for charge-offs

When you manage to pay the charge-off debt, it turns into a *paid charge-off* on your credit report. A paid charge-off is not nearly as bad as its predecessor, the unpaid charge-off. You had a problem — perhaps a serious one — but you paid the bill. Hallelujah! Now you can get a little boost on your credit report, and you're on the way to obtaining credit at a more reasonable rate. Why? Simple: You've established that, although you may be a high-risk borrower, you do pay your bills in the end. And some lenders just love people who pay late. You're now better-looking to most lenders than Cinderella's sister, but it's still not time for the ball yet.

Settling your debt

When your creditor allows you to pay off your debt for less than you origi-nally borrowed, this is referred to as *settling a debt*. Your debt may or may not have been charged off. And although you didn't stiff the lender completely, your actions did result in a loss of profit for the company — not a positive incentive to do business with you in the future. This will also have a negative impact on your credit report, so you may want to consider what is more important to you — the money or the credit report?

Many businesses and borrowers accept this route — the businesses at least get *something* rather than nothing, and the borrowers get the collectors off their backs and the debt does go away. In seven years, it will go away from your credit report, too.

If you accept debt settlement as a resolution, get the terms in writing before you send a penny.

If an outside debt-settlement firm — one that you haven't previously dealt with regarding the debt — suddenly shows up as a knight in shining armor to save you with a settlement offer, run away. A number of scams involve "debt-settlement companies" taking payments and never paying the creditor. You're then out the money and still owe the bill. Forget the knight — these guys are more like Cinderella's evil stepmother.

One last consideration regarding settlements: The IRS considers the difference between the amount owed and the amount paid as income. Depending on the size of your debt, the collector reports to the IRS how much money was forgiven in the settlement, and you're responsible for paying income taxes on that amount. For example, if you owe $5,000 and you work out a settlement where you pay only $3,000, then the $2,000 that was forgiven becomes taxable income on your next tax return. As the saying goes, only two things in life are certain — and one of them is taxes!

Obtaining a paid-as-agreed notation

When you find yourself in the world of charge-offs and settlements, you'll discover a lot of moving parts, many not exactly fair to you. So, if you still have the energy — and maybe a good lawyer — ask for the holy grail of concessions in return for paying the bill: a *paid-as-agreed notation* on your credit report. This means that despite the fact that you did not pay your debt *when* you agreed, you did pay the *amount* agreed. If you don't get a paid-as-agreed notation, your credit report will show extra negatives and your score will be lowered.

Getting a paid-as-agreed notation when you haven't paid the full amount you originally owed isn't exactly kosher. But if you have the money and can pay off the debt, you can use the small amount of leverage you have (the payment) to ask the creditor to report the debt to the credit-reporting bureaus as "paid as agreed." This is easy enough for the creditor to do.

This falls under the it-never-hurts-to-try category, so go for it — but get any agreement in writing from the creditor before making the payment. After the creditor has your money, you have no leverage.

Understanding Judgments and What They Mean to You

When a court issues an order telling you that you owe money and commands you to pay it, you have received a *judgment.* Sure, others along the way have pressured you to pay — everyone from the creditor to the collection agency — but now a court is involved. This means legal fees, public-record information on your credit report, and dealing with a system that has absolutely no sense of humor. (Your debt collector will look like Chris Rock in comparison to the court system.) In fact, in many states, a judgment can be renewed indefinitely — which means a big negative on your credit report that might never go away (not in seven years, not in ten years) — at least not until it's cleared up to the collector's satisfaction (including paying reasonable attorney fees and interest, of course).

The judgment itself doesn't put any money in the pocket of the lender or collector. It does, however, set you up for execution — not execution as in the electric chair (although you may feel as though you've received a death sentence), but a *judgment execution.* In essence, if after you've received a judgment and you still don't pay, the lender can go back to the judge and get an execution order. Depending on the laws in your state, the order allows the creditor to:

- Garnish your wages, up to 25 percent.

- Place a lien on your home or other property for the amount owed. The lien is like having another mortgage on the property. Before the property can be sold free and clear, the lien has to be paid off.

- Repossess any property involved with the debt you owe (for example, your car if it's a car loan, or your house if it's a home loan).

A judgment is about the worst thing that can happen in the whole collection process. At this point, many people pull the bankruptcy card out of the deck and ask for a fresh deal. Unfortunately for many people who earn above the median income in their states, bankruptcy is no longer an option. This is one of the reasons why consulting a professional early on in the game makes a lot of sense. If you know that the option to file bankruptcy is not there, you want to know it up front.

Why some lenders don't mind your judgments — and why you should

Some lenders won't consider you for a loan unless you have great credit. Others don't care if you have judgments or a bankruptcy against you. You may consider them saints to overlook a proven risk. Fact is, they probably don't mind the risk because they charge enough interest to still make money. Or they expect you to default and are ready to eat your lunch when you do.

Groucho Marx said it best when he quipped, "I don't care to belong to a club that accepts people like me as members." You really don't want a loan from a company that would lend money to a person with active unpaid judgments against him.

Dealing with IRS Debts, Student Loans, and Unpaid Child Support: Bankruptcy Won't Help

IRS debts, student loans, and unpaid child support are among the more popular of a class of debts that are not dischargeable in a bankruptcy and must be addressed to the creditor's satisfaction. That puts them in a special category, and I cover them in the following sections.

Slow and steady: Paying off an IRS debt

An IRS debt can be one of the easiest debt situations to deal with. First, the IRS knows *you* know who's in control, so they won't use the same high-pressure, strong-arm tactics that other collectors might. Besides, it's not their money they're chasing down — it's taxpayer money. So, you'll probably be able to negotiate a reasonable repayment plan that you can manage over time. They'll even help you out by pulling any tax refunds you have coming straight into the treasury until the debt is paid — just what you wanted to hear, huh?

The slow-moving nature of the IRS can work against you, however. After you pay off the bill, the T-men at the IRS are off to the next taxpayer and have little time or energy to let the credit bureaus or (if they put a lien on your property to make the property security for the repayment) your town-hall clerk who takes liens off your property know that you've cleared the debt.

Keep good records of payments and discharges and follow up by checking your credit report and if appropriate the property records at your local town hall to make sure the records are updated, or you may miss an opportunity to sell your home or property because it has a big fat lien on it that shouldn't be there.

Educating yourself: Student loans

It used to be that student-loan collections were all but nonexistent. Not so any longer. They've been granted non-dischargeable status in the bankruptcy law and they want their money for real. Depending on how many loans are involved — and you may have as many as one per semester you were in school — the effect on your credit of being in default on your student loans will vary.

If you're in default on your student loans, what you assume to be one loan may be as many as eight or ten. Each loan, be it on a semester or yearly basis is reported as a separate loan for each enrollment period. So four or five years of student loans may show up as eight or even ten separate trade lines in your credit report. If you end up in default, you may get a lot of negative information on your credit report, and your credit score may crash from all those negative individual loan entries.

A student loan is not secured with collateral in the normal sense of the word. Following graduation or when you leave school, whether you graduate or not, there are certain situations under which you may be able to defer the payment of loans until another time. Some situations include economic hardship or unemployment. When you're in default with a student loan, you can't defer payment of the loan and you may have to pay it all at once unless you come up with an acceptable repayment scheme. You also won't be eligible for further student aid, your school may withhold your transcripts, state and federal income tax refunds may be used to offset the loan amounts, and your wages may be *attached* or *garnished.* (The loan people can go to court and have a judge order your employer to send them some of your wages each pay period until the loan is paid off. See "Avoiding Wage Garnishments," later in this chapter.)

Working with a student-loan creditor is essential to moving on with a normal life. Dealing with these folks is very much like dealing with the IRS: You need to get in contact, have a plan, make an offer to repay the loan, and follow through.

Kids first: Making child support a priority

Unpaid child support is another category of debt that lives as long as you do. Under the new bankruptcy law, child-support obligations cannot be discharged. And now the courts provide custodial parents the names of collection agencies that specialize in child-support debt — so your ex may work with a collection agency to come after you for what you owe.

Child support is one of the only debts I know of that will get you sent up the river if you continue not to pay it. Remember those courts and their limited sense of humor? Well, they have absolutely none in this sort of case. Not only will you have the collectors to deal with, but you might end up with contempt-of-court charges filed against you, and then it's off to the hooskow for you. This debt is not one you want to carry around. Make it your number-one priority to pay.

Avoiding Wage Garnishments

Little is more essential to the working person than a source of income. It provides for your family, makes the American dream possible, and strongly influences your feelings of self-worth. Take it away, or take away *enough* of it, and life may begin to seem impossible.

Before anyone can garnish your wages, a judgment from a court of law is necessary. You'll get a summons to appear in court for this. If the judgment is not satisfied (that is, you don't pay what you owe), the lender can go back to court and execute the judgment they already have and get your wages garnished. You'll receive another summons if this happens.

In many cases, you can avoid wage garnishments if you've kept good records of the collection process and show up in court when they tell you to. So for the love of Mike, go to the hearings and speak up! If you have a reasonable story to tell the judge, and a reasonable offer to make, you may be surprised at the result. The judge won't be happy that a collector is using up his valuable time with a case that should have already been settled out of court.

The Consumer Credit Protection Act (CCPA) limits the amount of earnings that may be garnished. Here are the rules:

✔ If your *disposable-income earnings* (what is left of your wages or salary after all "legally required withholdings," such as Social Security taxes and federal and state income tax withholdings, are taken out) are $206 per week or more, they can garnish 25 percent of your weekly income.

✔ If your disposable earnings are between $154.50 and $205.99 per week, the entire amount above $154.50 but less than $206 can be garnished. (Subtract your weekly income from $206, and that's how much they can take.)

✔ If your disposable-income earnings are less than $154.50 per week, there can be no garnishment.

Note: The preceding figures are based on the minimum wage of $5.15 per hour, which is current as of this book's publication. If minimum wage is higher than $5.15 per hour when you're reading this book, the figures will be slightly higher.

Your state law may be lower than the federal maximum. Also your boss can't fire you for having a garnishment, but the CCPA does not provide this protection for subsequent wage garnishments. You can find much more information on minimum wages and wage garnishments at the Department of Labor Web site (www.dol.gov/dol/topic/wages/index.htm).

If you owe money for the non-dischargeable debts like child support, the CCPA does not apply. For example, the garnishment law allows up to a total of 50 percent of your disposable earnings to be garnished for child support if you're supporting another spouse or child, or up to 60 percent if you're not. An additional 5 percent may be garnished for support payments more than 12 weeks in arrears. Unpaid debts to federal agencies may be garnished at up to 15 percent of disposable earnings. The Higher Education Act authorizes student-loan guaranty agencies to garnish up to 10 percent of disposable earnings to repay defaulted federal student loans. If you'd like to ask someone about the details and formulas, you can call the Department of Labor at their special toll-free garnishment number: 866-487-9243.

Each state has its own debt-collection laws. Some states permit a lender to garnish your wages, others don't. Some states exempt large amounts or categories of assets from attachment or seizure by a creditor to pay your debt. Others may force you to sell things to satisfy a judgment. The best source for up-to-date information is your state's consumer-protection office. You can find a list of these offices at http://consumeraction.gov/state.shtml.

Taking Your Case to Court

I know how intimidating, embarrassing, and expensive it may be to take time off from work and drag yourself down to a courthouse that probably has no parking anyway. So does you creditor. Most of them count on this. They know that if you don't show up, they'll get just about anything they want from the judge.

So to keep this from happening, I strongly suggest you show up and tell it to the judge. Be sure to bring:

✔ Statements from the account in question

✔ Records of phone calls and written correspondence with the creditor

✔ A payment plan you can afford

You can represent yourself, but you'll be at a significant disadvantage if you do. Trust me, your creditor is intimate with the ins and outs of the court process. If you can afford it, get an attorney. If you can't, go anyway — your presence and your genuine commitment to coming up with a workable way to repay your debt may just be all that you need.

You can show the court that you've made a good-faith effort to propose the best settlement you could afford and be sure to back up what you're saying by your records and a reasonable payment plan that you offered but that was refused. If you went to a credit counselor along the way, mention it; if you can say that they thought your proposed settlement was reasonable, all the better. Of course, none of this reasonable stuff applies to back child support; unless your income has changed for the worse, you have to pay as agreed.

Chapter 9

When All Else Fails: Declaring Bankruptcy

*T*he first time I heard the word *bankruptcy,* I was a kid playing Monopoly. After scooping up Connecticut, Vermont, and Oriental avenues, I found myself without an orange, beige, blue, pink, yellow, white, or green bill left when I landed on my uncle's Boardwalk — with a hotel. My only recourse was bankruptcy. Even then it was bad news.

But not as bad as "Go directly to jail. Do not pass Go. Do not collect $200." Here in the United States, people don't go to prison if they can't pay their bills — except in Monopoly. Instead, they file for bankruptcy.

Why does the United States, one of the most avowed capitalist countries in the world, even have a bankruptcy law? Because in the best capitalist tradition, we recognize that sometimes a person has to take a big financial risk to get ahead or start a new business, and if that new business fails and that person is protected from imprisonment, there needs to be an escape clause that will keep creditors from hounding him for the rest of his life. Without this protection from harassment, the risk of using borrowed capital would be so high that few people would use it and the economy would be the loser. So bankruptcy is good for the economy. Makes me feel patriotic just thinking of it.

Even though the everyday reality may be very different, this is still a land of hope and fresh starts. So when hope runs out and the creditors close in, bankruptcy offers that fresh start for those who need it and for anyone who can qualify.

The year 2005 saw a major rewrite of the bankruptcy statute, raising the bar for those who seek protection. In this chapter, my goal is not so much to explain how the law works — the law is subject to change, interpretation, and litigation, as new laws always are — but to help you figure out whether bankruptcy makes sense for you and to determine the cost in terms of your credit report.

I've seen too many people use bankruptcy for the wrong reasons — instead of providing them with a fresh start, it only locked them into a financial nightmare. So, if you're thinking about bankruptcy, or know someone who is, this is an opportunity to look past the legal fine print and consider what may be the most important financial decision you'll make in the next ten years.

Go directly to the next section. Do not pass Go. Do not collect $200.

Understanding Bankruptcy, Chapter and Verse

The bankruptcy law in this country may seem like a secret code. It *is,* after all, referred to as the Bankruptcy Code, and it contains all those mysterious chapters with numbers — 7, 11, 13 — rather than names. What do they really mean and how do you choose the right one? You came to the right place. But before you pick which one may be right for you, you first have to understand if *bankruptcy* is right for you.

My friends at Webster's define *bankrupt* in several ways, none of them in words your mother would like to hear:

> **Noun:** One who is destitute
>
> **Verb:** To impoverish
>
> **Adjective:** Reduced to a state of financial ruin

So who in his right mind would want a piece of this thing? More than 1 million American families a year. Why? Because they have no other choice. Even though you won't go to prison for debt in the United States, if your debt is truly horrific, you may have days when prison doesn't seem like such a bad trade-off. At least it would stop the endless collection process. So a large emotional component is involved in deciding whether bankruptcy is for you.

A financial or quality-of-life component factors in as well. If your wages are about to be garnished because of your inability to pay a bill — perhaps a totally unexpected and unasked-for medical bill — do you allow your family to suffer the financial consequences? Recent studies have shown that if you are:

> ✔ A divorced female
>
> ✔ A divorced female raising children, or
>
> ✔ A divorced female raising children while trying to collect child support

your chances of filing for bankruptcy are three to five times greater than if you don't fall into these categories. More than half of all those filing bankruptcy have sudden, uninsured medical expenses.

In a real sense, the reason for filing bankruptcy is to seek the protection of the court from your creditors. It's that simple. If you can't deal with the collectors on your own, call in the judge — and the judge will.

Defining bankruptcy types, chapter by chapter

The bankruptcy court allows for many kinds of bankruptcy, identified as chapters with numbers. A Chapter 9 bankruptcy, for example, is reserved for municipalities (cities and such). Chapter 12 allows farmers to reorganize their debt and keep their farms. Most people are familiar with Chapter 11 bankruptcy, because of all the airlines and other companies taking advantage of it to reorganize and keep creditors off their backs until they can turn around. Actually, individuals sometimes file for Chapter 11 bankruptcy, too.

But among all the various chapters, two are most commonly used by consumers who find themselves unable to fend off or satisfy the creditors:

> ✔ **Chapter 7:** Also known as *liquidation,* this is the most popular form of bankruptcy. It requires you to give up some assets (the liquidation part) and gets you out of almost all your liabilities.
>
> ✔ **Chapter 13:** Often referred to as *wage-earner bankruptcy,* this form of bankruptcy allows you to keep most of your assets and pay back what you can over a period of time, usually three to five years, under court supervision and protection.

The new bankruptcy law: Tightening up on consumers

Bankruptcy law comes under the jurisdiction of the federal courts. States, however, can pass laws that deal with what is called the *debtor-creditor relationship* and, as a result, some property and other exemptions vary by state.

The Bankruptcy Abuse Prevention and Consumer Protection Act of 2005 is a federal law that has had a wide-ranging impact on bankruptcy in the United States. It was enacted because Congress recognized that some people have abused bankruptcy protection over the years; the act establishes restrictions to prevent such abuse in the future.

Here is a brief summary of the new provisions if you pursue bankruptcy:

- ✔ **You have to pass a means test to be eligible for Chapter 7.** You must prove that you can't afford to pay your bills — even a part of them.

- ✔ **You're required to get credit counseling from an "approved nonprofit budget and credit-counseling agency" before you can file.** The U.S. Trustee provides a master list of approved agencies you have to choose from. You can find out who is on the list by contacting the clerk of the court where your bankruptcy is to be filed. Also you can contact the two largest networks of credit-counseling organizations:

  - National Foundation for Credit Counseling (www.nfcc.org; 800-388-2227)

  - Association of Independent Consumer Credit Counseling Agencies (www.aiccca.org; 800-450-1794)

- ✔ **After you file but before you're discharged from the bankruptcy, you must complete a course in financial management.** Again, the U.S. Trustee must approve the providers.

- ✔ **You're limited in what you can buy immediately before filing.** Having made the decision to file, you can't go out and spend up a storm or take cash advances and then not have to pay. Generally, the limits apply to the 90 days preceding your filing.

- ✔ **You have to wait a set amount of time after filing for bankruptcy before you can file again.** The law says

  - Eight years between Chapter 7 bankruptcies

  - Two years between Chapter 13 bankruptcies

  - Four years between Chapter 7 and Chapter 13 bankruptcies

- ✔ **Your *homestead exemption* (how much equity in your home you can keep out of your filing and keep for yourself) is limited by state law.** In addition, if you acquired your home less than 40 months before filing, you're allowed a maximum exemption of $125,000 — regardless of your state's exemption allowance.

- ✔ **Under Chapter 13 bankruptcy, all your disposable income must be included in the plan and every year you have to document your income and expenses to see if you can pay more (or less).**

- ✔ **Your attorney must certify that what you say in the documents you use in court is true.**

✔ **You cannot get rid of debts for taxes, domestic support, student loans, or drunk-driving injuries.**

✔ **Domestic-support obligations are a priority debt that must be paid.** (A *priority debt* take precedence over other debts you owe and is paid completely.) However, the *bankruptcy trustee* (the person appointed by the court to administer your Chapter 13 plan) receives administrative fees before your spouse, ex-spouse, or kids get their money. What a country.

✔ **You may be evicted if you don't pay your rent after you've filed for bankruptcy.**

✔ **You must provide your latest tax return to your creditors if they ask for it.** Before you can finalize your bankruptcy, you'll need to give information about your financial status to your creditors so they can see that you can't afford to pay what you owe. If you're filing for Chapter 13, you must provide your tax returns for the last four years.

Determining Whether Bankruptcy Is Right for You

Declaring bankruptcy is no small decision. It's a change that can stay with you in some form for up to ten years. It's a decision that will affect your self-image. It's a condition that will redefine your credit report and certainly lower your credit score.

In other words, bankruptcy is a major life event, so it's something you want to consider very seriously. Don't get me wrong — it may just be the best alternative you have if you've suffered some serious financial setbacks. But before you take the plunge, invest time in carefully weighing all your options.

Making the bankruptcy decision

As you consider bankruptcy, ask yourself this: Can you do anything more to help meet your obligations? Do you have hope of finding a solution to this mess? If you answered no to both questions, you're on the right track in considering bankruptcy.

I've known people who've answered no to both questions but still vowed they'd eat peanut butter for the rest of their lives before they would declare bankruptcy. (Most of them were from Sicily; I have some uncles from Sicily, and let me tell you, they hate peanut butter.) In the end, though, the decision is really only about money, not your honor, and money just isn't as important as your life (unless you're one of my Sicilian uncles).

Before you make the final decision to throw your credit and creditors off that financial cliff, look into the following to help you make your decision:

✔ **Make sure bankruptcy will solve your financial crisis.** Making all your debts and collectors go away may solve one problem. But will it solve *the* problem? If the problem is overspending, declaring bankruptcy won't help you in the long run. If you've been using credit to supplement your income for basic living expenses, bankruptcy won't help either.

A good credit counselor should be able to help you consider this issue, as well as help you get your spending habits, expenses, and income level on track (see Chapter 3 for more on credit counselors).

✔ **Review and prioritize your goals.** Bankruptcy is a big step and its consequences will linger for years. To make the decision based only on immediate events would be a mistake. How will this decision affect your chances of buying a home, getting married, getting divorced, getting a job? Describe your world as you would like to see it in the next five years, and ask yourself what impact a bankruptcy will have on that goal.

✔ **Consider your options.** Make a list of other ways to deal with your debts. Can you increase your income? Reduce your expenses? Stretch out your payments? Use your home equity to pay your bills for a while until things improve?

✔ **Get a professional, non-legal opinion.** Talk to a good credit counselor (see Chapter 3). You'll have to meet with a credit counselor anyway within six months before filing for bankruptcy. Expect this visit to give you options, an analysis of your spending and income, and an action plan. Make sure the credit counselor gives you a written budget or spending plan. This will go a long way toward answering the question of whether bankruptcy will help.

✔ **Get a professional legal opinion.** Find a lawyer who specializes in bankruptcies. Find out if you qualify for bankruptcy and, if so, which chapter. Make sure you understand what bankruptcy will and won't do for you. Ask about alternatives, including settlements or other options. While you're there, ask about the pluses and minuses of filing for bankruptcy on your own. Called *pro se,* the law allows you to represent yourself — and in some courts with sympathetic judges, this can be a moneysaver (in other courts, it can be a disaster). Your lawyer is the best one to guide you here.

✔ **Talk to your creditors.** Seriously. If you're considering a bankruptcy, let your lenders know and ask if they can offer any repayment plans you may not have heard about. This is a courtesy your creditor may appreciate. Don't expect too much, but talking to your creditors is always worth a shot. If you want, have your lawyer handle this task.

- ✔ **Talk to someone who cares about you.** Yes, even though this person is not a professional, he or she knows you and may have an important perspective. Avoid asking someone who would be personally affected by your choice (such as a person you owe money to, someone who owes you money, or a dependent).

- ✔ **Look in the mirror.** Given your current financial state, how do you see yourself. Consider your goals; weigh the options offered by your creditors, the credit counselor, and the lawyer; and be sure to consider the advice of others who care about you. Now you're ready to decide what is best for your future and your peace of mind. If you don't like what you see, go through the process until you do. Then do what you think is in your best interest.

Adding up the pluses and minuses

Like anything in life, bankruptcy is neither all good nor all bad. In the following sections, I let you know the good part about bankruptcy, as well as the harsh reality of the consequences.

The silver lining of filing bankruptcy

I'm always in favor of hearing the good news first. With bankruptcy, it's no different. Here are some of the positives of filing bankruptcy

You get a fresh start

The silver lining in a bankruptcy is that you get to begin again. The collection activity stops. The fees, penalty rates, and lawyers stop. In fact, in a Chapter 7 bankruptcy, virtually the entire debt may go away.

Without the ability to call a stop to the madness of credit gone awry, some people would never — and I mean *never* — be able to live a normal life again. Bankruptcy can allow that to happen.

You get credit education

Another plus of bankruptcy: The 2005 bankruptcy law says that anyone who files is required to get some credit education. This is an opportunity to look back at what happened, and to rechart your financial and credit course going forward.

If you take advantage of this opportunity, you'll walk away with a much better sense of how to manage your money — which means you'll be less likely to end up back where you started.

How to find a bankruptcy attorney

I always consider friends, family, or co-workers who have had a satisfied experience with an attorney as a good source of reference. I'm not suggesting that you put a note up on the company bulletin board, but someone who has already been through the bankruptcy process may be a good referral source.

The Internet also has some very good resources. Three that you may want to check out are

- American Bankruptcy Institute (www.abiworld.org)
- American Bar Association (www.abanet.org)
- Lawyers.com (www.lawyers.com)

If you have used a lawyer who handles other issues for you, ask her for a referral to someone who either specializes in bankruptcy or does a lot of it. Don't use your cousin, the real-estate lawyer. Get a pro.

The not-so-pretty consequences of filing bankruptcy

As you can probably guess, filing bankruptcy comes with some pretty heavy consequences. I outline them for you here.

You may still owe money

Bankruptcy may not wipe out *all* your debt. Some debts do not go away — even though you'd like them to — and they must be paid in full. The debts that don't disappear are

- Federal, state, and local taxes
- Child support
- Alimony
- Student loans from the government or a lender
- Money owed as a result of drunk driving

Your credit score plummets

Bankruptcy doesn't look good on your credit report. This event appears as a public record in your file and it stays there for ten years and sometimes more. Worse, it causes your credit score to plunge as many as 100 points. Declare bankruptcy and you're likely to see your score drop to 600 or worse. That is in the lowest 20 percent of all credit scores. Ouch!

Borrowing money becomes more difficult

When a lender sees a score in the lowest percentile, your interest rates and terms escalate. In some cases, a lender will decline to give you credit, because you no longer meet the underwriting guidelines.

Some lenders, however, specialize in giving loans to people with bad credit. They would be delighted to see you — the fact that you have just gone bankrupt is a big plus in their eyes. Why? Because under the law, you can't file a Chapter 7 bankruptcy again for eight long years. So while they get to charge you more interest as a risky borrower, you can't avoid repaying them by playing the bankruptcy card. If you fall behind, you can run, but you can't hide. Usually these lenders are very good at collecting overdue accounts. The bottom line: Avoid these guys at all costs. If you must borrow shortly after a bankruptcy only use a reputable lender.

Renting an apartment may become more complicated

Some landlords get credit reports on tenant applicants. They may refuse to rent to you, require a cosigner, or increase your required deposit if they see a bankruptcy.

Insurance becomes more costly

A bankruptcy will cost you more in insurance premiums, particularly for homeowner's and auto insurance. The insurance mavens and their actuarial henchmen love credit scores and credit reports. All those dispassionate numbers lend themselves to justifying rate increases much better than real claims do. So even if you have no losses, your premiums may go up. Credit reports are used mostly by homeowner and auto insurers, some states don't allow credit to be a factor in setting rates, but most do.

Employment becomes more dicey

Even under ideal circumstances, job hunting can be stressful. When you consider the fact that many employers run a credit check before making a job offer, your stress level can increase as your opportunities decrease.

The killer here is the unasked and, therefore, unanswered question: What happened to cause you to seek bankruptcy protection and will you do it again? The behavior, events, or judgments you made that resulted in the filing are all concerns for prospective employers who may suspect your bankruptcy means you'll be an unreliable employee. These are the silent killers, because although you can't legally be denied employment because you filed a bankruptcy, the prospective employer rarely asks the questions to find out the reasons. Going on to the next candidate is just easier and legally safer.

As a practical matter, some licenses cannot be given to people who have filed for bankruptcy, and security clearances can be denied.

Your self-image is likely to become tarnished

Having a major life event go against you never helps. You may think you're made of steel or maybe something softer, but either way, bankruptcy can take its toll. Like it or not, a great deal of how most people view themselves is wrapped up in their financial persona. Most people think of themselves as responsible adults. Many people have been taught that responsible adults pay their bills and keep their promises. Even though you know it's okay to file for bankruptcy and that you have no choice in the matter from a practical standpoint, you may find that you have an internal conflict to deal with that you didn't expect.

Considering a debt-management plan first

One of the stops you're required to make on the road to getting help from the bankruptcy courts is a credit-counseling agency. The court has recognized the value of the work done by these agencies by requiring that you run your situation by them (*before* filing). The courts have also named them as one of the providers of financial-management education (*after* filing).

The idea is that you'll get an unbiased assessment of your financial condition, and that you may, upon reflection, change your mind or find a less-damaging way to handle your debt. Additionally, if a creditor refuses to negotiate with a credit counselor, the court can order that their debt get a 20-percent haircut.

Understanding what a debt-management plan is

One of the mainstays of the credit-counseling industry is the debt-management plan. You begin with a an individually tailored spending plan that you create with the help of a credit counselor. A debt-management plan uses your available money to pay your creditors. It takes the equivalent of your disposable income after actual expenses and reallocates some or all of it to those creditors. The average debt-management plan may be set up for four to five years but in practice tends to be completed in about two years. (For more on debt-management plans, turn to Chapter 3.)

How a debt-management plan differs from Chapter 13 bankruptcy

Under a debt-management plan, the money left (if any) after you've paid your living expenses and paid your creditors may go into a savings plan for emergencies. Say your child gets sick and you have either a high deductible or no insurance. The money to pay for this emergency could come from your emergency savings account. If you file Chapter 13 bankruptcy, however, all your disposable income goes toward paying off your creditors. The amount you get to use for living expenses with minor adjustments comes from IRS guidelines.

Unlike the terms of a Chapter 7 or Chapter 13 bankruptcy, a debt-management plan is a voluntary arrangement with you and your creditors, using the credit-counseling agency as an intermediary. You can walk away from a debt-management plan at any time and still file for bankruptcy. Or, if you're on the receiving end of a windfall, you can pay off your creditors in one payment and be done with it.

Of course, your creditors don't have to accept the terms of the debt-management plan, whereas they *have* to accept it if you file bankruptcy. That said, most creditors do accept debt-management plans, because they know you'll be off to the courthouse to file bankruptcy if they say no.

Whereas a Chapter 7 bankruptcy liquidates many debts, a Chapter 13 bankruptcy forces creditors to accept a lower payment over a set period of time that may not cover what you originally owed. The difference between what was owed and what is paid under Chapter 13 is what the creditors lose. They also can't charge interest or fees under Chapter 13. A debt-management plan allows the creditors to collect finance charges, although many creditors reduce the rate to one that is more affordable and reflects your circumstances and your desire to repay the debt.

Perhaps one of the biggest differences between a Chapter 7 or 13 bankruptcy and a debt-management plan is the effect on your credit score. Bankruptcy has a large and not-too-positive impact on your score, which affects your ability to access credit at a good rate for years after the *end* of your bankruptcy.

A debt-management plan, on the other hand, doesn't have the same negative impact on your credit score. In fact, many creditors don't report to the bureaus that your account is being handled by a credit-counseling agency. Those that do report it to the bureaus report it as a description of the account (for example, credit card, real estate mortgage, credit counseling), not as a payment history item (for example, "pays as agreed" or "X days late"). Payment history items count toward your credit score. Further, your credit report will show the credit-counseling account description only until the time you pay off the account or decide to discontinue the plan, at which point the notation is removed. The description is not reported for the next seven years.

More good news: Even while you're in a debt-management plan, the FICO scoring system does not subtract any points. That's right — your credit score is not affected. A credit-counseling notation on your file is perceived as a neutral item — not a negative or public-record item — and your creditor reports the account as "pays as agreed."

If you decide to try the debt-management-plan route rather than a Chapter 13, and the debt-management plan doesn't work out for you, you can always file for bankruptcy without any waiting period.

So, if it can work for you, a debt-management plan may be less restrictive and damaging to your credit report and score than bankruptcy. I suggest that when you get your mandatory counseling on the road to bankruptcy, you explore making a debt-management plan work for you. Your credit score will be glad you did.

Qualifying and Filing for Bankruptcy

At this point, you may have determined that bankruptcy remains your best or only viable way out of your financial corner. But although bankruptcy may be right for you, *you* may not qualify for bankruptcy. Both Chapter 7 and Chapter 13 bankruptcies are limited by new requirements, which I cover in the following sections. For a quick look at the new rules, see Figure 9-1.

Checking your eligibility for Chapter 7

The most popular form of bankruptcy in recent years, Chapter 7 is now restricted by new rules under the Bankruptcy Abuse Prevention and Consumer Protection Act of 2005. Chapter 7 has been so popular because of its effectiveness and efficacy in getting rid of debts and collectors. Under a Chapter 7, you receive relief from virtually all your debts, with a few exceptions, and you get it fast — like the same day (unlike a Chapter 13, which may take years before you get a discharge). I cover the major changes to Chapter 7 in the following sections.

You have to pass the means test

The first hurdle in moving forward with Chapter 7 bankruptcy is meeting a means test. If you have too many means (that is, too much income), you can't declare Chapter 7. And, sorry, the courts won't take your word for it. You have to *prove* that your income really is as you said by handing in your most recent tax return. If your income is above the appropriate median for your state of residence, you can't file for Chapter 7.

Do you have family income above the median for your family size in your state of residence? To find out, go to the census Web site at www.census. gov/hhes/www/income/medincsizeandstate.xls.

If your income is above the average, don't give up just yet. Next, you want to determine whether you have *excess monthly income* of more than $166.66 to pay $10,000 of debt over five years. So what counts as excess income? You have to use the spending guidelines approved by the IRS. Allowable expenses are shown on the IRS Web site at www.irs.gov/businesses/small/article/ 0,,id=104627,00.html. The IRS guidelines may be very tight for you. (I know from personal experience: My dad was an IRS agent and his idea of a reasonable allowance was $5 a week — even through college!)

If you're beginning to get a little worried, you may have good reason. The monthly allowances are tight. If you live in Alaska or Hawaii, I can offer a little ray of hope. These states have a separate schedule to account for increased living expenses. But don't get too excited: In Hawaii, for example, the extra food allowance per month is $2 to $5, depending on your income level.

If you *can* squeak the $166.66 a month out of your budget, the best you can do is to file under Chapter 13.

NEW BANKRUPTCY CODE: **FILING PROCEDURES**			
Major Intent of Bankruptcy Reform	Cut down on abuse by requiring people who can pay all or some of their debt to do so.		
PROVISIONS			
In effect as of April 2005			
Homestead Exemption (Sections: 308, 322, 330)	(1) Exemption limited to $125,000 if property was acquired *within* the previous 1,215 days (40 months). (2) Cap is not applied to a property transferred from debtor's previous principal residence if acquired prior to the 40-month period.		
In effect as of October 17, 2005			
Means Test	Used to determine if you qualify for Chapter 7 or Chapter 13 bankruptcy.		
	Test #1 Are family earnings over the median income for your state? *(1997 U.S. averages)* Family of 1 = $18,762 Family of 2 = $39,343 Family of 3 = $47,115 Family of 4 = $53,165 • If "No," you can file Chapter 7. • If "Yes," proceed to Test # 2.	*Test #2* Do you have monthly income in excess of expenses equal to at least $166.66/month to pay $10,000 of debt over five years? • If "Yes," you can't file Chapter 7, but you can file Chapter 13. • If "No," proceed to Test # 3.	*Test #3* Do you have monthly income in excess of expenses greater than $100/month over the next 60 months to pay at least 25 percent of your unsecured debt? • If "No," you can file Chapter 7. • If "Yes," you can't file Chapter 7, but you can file Chapter 13.
Proof of Income	If filing Chapter 7 or Chapter 13 bankruptcy, you must provide the court a copy of your most recent tax return or transcript of a tax return at least seven days prior to the 341 meeting.		
Counseling	You must have had approved financial counseling within the last six months.		
Child Support and Alimony	These debts increase to a number-one priority and may not be discharged.		
Tithing	Up to 15 percent of your income can be given to charity. This may allow you to choose to pay either your creditor or your church in a Chapter 13, or get your income low enough to qualify for Chapter 7.		

Figure 9-1:
If you want to file bankruptcy, you'll need to qualify based on the newest bankruptcy code.

If you have less excess monthly income than the magic number of $166.66 a month left after IRS expense allowances, proceed to the next hurdle: Do you have an extra $100 a month over the next 60 months? And will that $6,000 account for at least 25 percent of your debt? If the answer to both questions is no, you can pass go and file for Chapter 7. If not, go directly to Chapter 13.

Tithing — giving money to your religious institution — is allowed in both Chapter 7 and Chapter 13 bankruptcies. You may donate up to 15 percent of your income and have it count as an expense that may lower your income. So much for rendering unto Caesar. Donating to your church, temple, or house of worship may just help you make the numbers work to become eligible for a Chapter 7 rather than a Chapter 13.

You have to go for counseling

At some point during the six months before you file for bankruptcy, you have to receive counseling from a court-approved credit counselor. The law leaves these requirements to the court (or bankruptcy trustee) to define. However, Congress did set certain minimum criteria. To be approved, a credit-counseling agency must

- **Be nonprofit.**

- **Have an independent board of directors, the majority of whom are neither employed by the agency nor directly or indirectly benefiting financially from the outcome of a credit-counseling session.**

- **Charge "reasonable" fees and provide services, even if you can't afford to pay the reasonable fee.**

- **Disclose its funding sources, counselor qualifications, possible impact on your credit history, any cost imposed on you, and how those costs will be paid.**

- **Offer adequate counseling encompassing an analysis of your current situation, what brought you to your current situation, and options to solve your problem without incurring *negative amortization* of your debts.** Negative amortization happens when you make payments on a debt, but the payments are too small to offset interest and fees on the account, so the debt grows instead of getting paid off.

- **Train its counselors adequately but not pay them based on the outcome of the counseling.**

The law also spells out minimum requirements for the personal financial-management course you must attend as part of the bankruptcy discharge process. The course may or may not be given by a credit-counseling agency, others are allowed to offer it if they qualify with the court, but all must:

- ✔ Provide experienced and trained personnel.

- ✔ Incorporate relevant teaching methodologies and learning materials.

- ✔ Be offered in an adequate facility or over the phone or Internet.

Just because the court has approved the counseling agency does not make it the right one for you, so exercise caution when selecting. (See Chapter 3 for guidance in choosing a credit counselor.)

Qualifying for Chapter 13

Because of the strict guidelines about who qualifies to file Chapter 7 bankruptcy, many more people will only qualify to file Chapter 13. The requirement for counseling and proof of income are the same for both types of bankruptcy, but although you must take the same means test, the outcome leads to different results.

Chapter 13 differs from Chapter 7 in that, after your income has been established and allowable expenses have been deducted, you must use all of your disposable income toward the repayment of debt. *Disposable* is defined by taking your income and subtracting the IRS allowable expenses. The means test establishes if your income is above the median for your state of residence. If your income is above the median average income level for your state, your disposable income gets disposed of (paid to your bankruptcy trustee who will forward it to your creditors) for the next five years, unless you can show that you can pay off 100 percent of the debt in less than 60 months.

The current bankruptcy law is intended to require those who can afford to make payments toward their debt to do so.

Just as with Chapter 7, those filing for Chapter 13 bankruptcy must establish that their family income is either below or above the median for their state. The law allows that if your income is below the median for the state in which you reside, your disposable income may be paid to your creditors over the next three years. (To find out what the median income is for your state, check out www.census.gov/hhes/www/income/medincsizeandstate.xls.) Because your income is under the state median for where you live, you get a break and may only have to complete a three-year repayment plan. The rest of the debt, the creditors eat. And there is no interest on any of the accounts involved.

If your income is above the median for your state, all the disposable income (income after allowable expenses) you have over goes to the creditors over the next five years.

Filing, then backing out

If you decide that bankruptcy is not for you *after* you've filed papers, you can ask the court to voluntarily dismiss your case before the discharge. Lets say you file a Chapter 7 and then find out that you have to give back that 3-carat diamond ring your sweetie gave you recently. Or in the case of a Chapter 13, you've been making payments and eating peanut butter for a month and can't go on. Or looking on the bright side, you get a windfall inheritance from a rich uncle and can pay off the Chapter 13 in one fell swoop.

No matter what the reason, you can call the whole thing off and get a dismissal. Keep in mind, however, that the credit-reporting bureaus will pick up the record of your filing and put the filing information out there even if you stop the process without getting out of any debts. The credit-reporting bureaus must also report that the filing was dismissed — but the record of your having filed a bankruptcy will stay on your credit report, and continue to lower your score, for the remainder of the reporting period (up to ten years). Both you and the creditor have the same rights and remedies as you had before your bankruptcy case was filed.

If you ask for a dismissal of your bankruptcy filing, you won't be the first to do so. In fact, the law has a specific section that deals with people who not only change their minds, but change them back again. Perhaps after backing out of the bankruptcy to save the diamond ring, your creditors turn up the collection heat to the point where you'd gladly give them the ring and your fathers watch if they'll just leave you alone.

Here's how the change works the second time around: In your first filing, after you file the paperwork with the courts, you get an automatic stay (or suspension) of collection activity on the part of your creditors. The length of time depends on the type of debt or action stayed and can vary in time allowed. But generally it's in place until you discharge your debts (that is, get rid of them). But if you refile after changing your mind, within one year of the original filing, the automatic stay (the stopping of all collection activity) is for only 30 days. So you have to get all your testing and counseling and paperwork done in the 30-day time period or the collectors and foreclosers return in force. If this is the third such filing in a year, you don't get *any* stay unless the court orders it.

So what this means is this: When you file for bankruptcy, do your best to make sure it's a decision you can live with for the long haul.

Managing Your Bankruptcy to Rebuild Your Credit

Declaring bankruptcy is more of a hassle than it used to be — and it's definitely harder to qualify for relief. But if you qualify and take the bankruptcy plunge, don't think you're out of the woods. You still have to live with the results of bankruptcy — on your credit report, your credit score, and the barriers that your new status creates. You're likely to discover that bankruptcy has an impact on your insurance rates as well as your ability to get hired or promoted.

Filing again for bankruptcy: A waiting game

Whether you file for bankruptcy via Chapter 7 or Chapter 13, be aware that you'll be restricted from doing so again within a significant period of time.

After you've completed your Chapter 7 filing and the court discharges you and your debts, the clock starts to tick. You cannot apply for protection of the court for another Chapter 7 — no matter what — for the next eight years. In the case of Chapter 13, after you've completed your filing, you can't file for a Chapter 13 again for the next two years or a Chapter 7 for the next four years.

Either way, it's important to be careful in your post-bankruptcy world because if an astronomical debt comes along, you may not be able to refile for a Chapter 7 or 13 right away.

Your bankruptcy is not something you want to let take care of itself. Your bankruptcy status will remain on your credit report as the mother of all credit negatives for up to ten years — and that's a long time.

So, just how do you get a handle on your financial future now that you've nuked the past? You get prepared with a good, short explanation; you rebuild your credit as quickly as possible; and you use credit carefully as you go forward — bankruptcy may not be available to you again for years (see the nearby sidebar, "Filing again for bankruptcy: A waiting game").

Preparing your statement

Now that your credit report shows a bankruptcy and will continue to for a long time, prepare for the consequences. To begin with, work on a short statement that describes your valid reasons for filing for bankruptcy. Businesspeople and potential lenders who have access to your credit report will want to know what happened so that they can judge whether to do business with you.

Note: This is not the 100-word statement you can attach to your credit report — this is an actual verbal statement that you'll make when you're doing anything that will require someone to see your credit report (apply for a loan, apply for a job). Be sure to tell them about this before they see your credit report — but only if you're sure they'll be looking at it. (Why raise the issue if they'll never know about it otherwise?)

A tight and targeted statement explaining your bankruptcy is similar to the spiel you give a prospective employer when she asks why you left your previous position. Whatever your parting circumstances were, your explanation is always a positive spin on the truth. It's short, sweet, and rehearsed. Having it at the ready allows you to convey yourself as confident, professional, and reliable — just the sort of person she'd love to hire. Same deal here. Come up with a succinct statement that briefly explains your decision to declare bankruptcy.

Although it's rare for one debt to push you over the edge, you're better off if you can attribute your situation to a single traumatic event. It may have been a divorce, a layoff, or an illness. Something beyond your control is a plus. Your efforts to pay the debts or deal with collectors are only of interest to you. All you need to say is that you tried everything you could think of to meet your obligations. End the short statement with some words of wisdom like: "I've learned a lot from this experience" or "I've become better at saving money as a result." Here's an example of a tight little speech that takes less than two minutes to share:

> When you look at my credit report, I want you know that you'll see a bankruptcy there. It's not something I'm proud of, but because of an illness, I ended up with bills for $100,000. I felt terrible about having to declare bankruptcy, but I had no choice. I've increased my insurance coverage and savings so that this will never happen again. I certainly learned a painful lesson, but that's all behind me now.

Keeping some debt: How it helps and hurts

As part of your bankruptcy rights, you can request to keep some of your debt if you can show the court that you can afford to pay it. What? After all that trouble to relieve yourself of the terrible burden? Isn't that sort of like going through a knock-down divorce and remarrying your spouse? Why would you do that to yourself?

Believe it or not, there are some benefits to keeping some debt (and its associated credit lines). This is often referred to as *reaffirmation*. For starters, having some ready credit available when you walk out of the courthouse may be a good idea. Also a chunk of your credit score is based on longevity of accounts. Keeping an old account may help with the score-rebuilding process.

Reaffirmations may not be the good deal they seem. A friend who declared bankruptcy was persuaded to reaffirm one debt so he could still have access to credit in his post-bankruptcy world. The card issuer reduced his credit line to the amount of the debt and raised his interest rate to the maximum. The result: He had no credit line left available to use and was stuck with a huge interest payment he couldn't afford. And after the first month, fees pushed him over his limit, so he began getting over-limit fees as well. And the creditor laughed all the way to the bank.

Beware of solicitations generated by your bankruptcy filing

After you declare bankruptcy, you'll face a flurry of solicitations and telemarketing calls from companies that received notices of your filing. Many businesses use these bankruptcy notices as mailing lists for the high-cost credit products they're selling.

Be very careful of solicitations you receive following a bankruptcy filing. Read all the fine print and be suspicious of a company anxious to give you a new start. You're very vulnerable, both from a personal and well as a financial perspective. This may be a good time to opt out of the credit bureau and direct-marketing mailing programs that a lot of solicitors use to send you those preapproved offers. It wouldn't hurt to make sure you're in the Federal Trade Commission's National Do Not Call Registry as well (to register, go to www.donotcall.gov).

If you want your name and address removed from mailing lists obtained from the main consumer credit-reporting agencies, go to www.optoutprescreen.com or call 888-567-8688.

The Direct Marketing Association can provide information about opting out of lists produced by companies that subscribe to their mail and telephone preference services. Contact them at the following addresses:

> Direct Marketing Association
> Mail Preference Service
> P.O. Box 643
> Carmel, NY 10512

> Direct Marketing Association
> Telephone Preference Service
> P.O. Box 1559
> Carmel, NY 10512

Include the following information with your request:

- Your first, middle, and last name (including Jr., Sr., III)
- Your current address
- Your home phone number (only for the telephone preference service)

If you decide to keep some of your debt, make sure that you really *can* afford to pay and that the terms of the card, including your original unused credit limit, don't change going forward because of the bankruptcy.

Working to repair your credit score

Your credit score is likely to suffer dramatically from a bankruptcy. The better your score originally, the more it will drop. If you had terrible credit before, a filing may not cause such a big drop. Either way, you'll likely have a very low score.

Now that your credit score has been decimated by bankruptcy, you want to take steps to repair it as best you can. In Chapter 5, I explain what factors influence your credit score. Here's how those factors are influenced by a bankruptcy:

✔ **Paying on time:** If you've gone bankrupt, this category may be heavily impacted. I say *may* be, because nearly half of all bankruptcies happen with no prior delinquencies. So you may have a long record of paying on time, with no delinquencies — just a bankruptcy. The more early problems you had, the lower your score will be.

✔ **Amount and proportion of credit used:** This category will also be affected. If you go bankrupt, you'll be closing most of your accounts — or your lenders will. Your credit available will drop to $0 in most cases.

✔ **The length of time you've been using credit:** Here again, your score will be damaged, because the history on your open accounts — if any remain open — will be shortened as a result of closing so many accounts.

✔ **The variety of accounts:** Chances are, you'll be left with only secured debt such as mortgages, student loans, or car loans. All your revolving and retail accounts may be gone, which means you won't have the variety of accounts that helps to boost your credit score.

✔ **The number and types of accounts you've opened recently:** After the bankruptcy, you may have more activity here than usual as you attempt to reestablish your credit. And your score will fall. (The more accounts you've opened recently, the lower your score.)

Keeping this in mind, a helpful tactic is to take steps to improve your credit in these five areas. And — don't forget — creditors don't necessarily report to all three of the credit bureaus. Now more than ever, you want to make sure that your "good" creditor experiences get on *all* the credit reports out there. Ask your lenders to report all your information to all three bureaus. If they don't, you can either try to get credit from someone who does, or you can ask the bureaus to use the information you send in to them (although there may be a fee involved).

Follow up on these tips, as well, in order to up that credit score as much as you can during the life of your bankruptcy:

✔ **Keep one or two of your older and lower-balance cards or lines open by reaffirming them.** See the preceding section for more information.

✔ **Apply for a secured credit card.** This type of account uses a deposit of yours to secure or guarantee that the payment will be made. They're reported to the credit bureaus as any other credit card would be.

✔ **Open a passbook installment loan, and then borrow against it to demonstrate that you can make those fixed payments on time every month.**

Establishing new credit

Yes, you can probably get new credit soon after you come out of bankruptcy. In fact, establishing some new lines of credit could be the first step in improving your credit score. You'll face some new challenges as you pursue new credit opportunities — you'll discover that the best loans at the most attractive terms and interest rates may not be available to you. Instead, you may discover you're being pursued by loan-shark types that would make Jaws look like a guppy.

I caution you to be extra-careful about committing to new lines of credit. Not only are you a target for unscrupulous lenders who specialize in post-bankruptcy loans, but — now more than ever — you're vulnerable to slipping back into an out-of-control borrowing situation. You don't want to get trapped in debt again. New credit is okay, as long as it's part of your plan to rebuild your rating and you're 100 percent confident you can pay it off.

Moving Forward from Bankruptcy

After you have a bankruptcy on your credit report, a number of things will be more complicated for you — I mention them earlier in this chapter under "Adding up the plusses and minuses." The good news though is that you'll have a chance to make a new start and a better life for you and your family. I strongly suggest that you begin your new life with a plan and some help. Without a plan, making the same mistakes is easier than you may think.

Coming up with a game plan

Moving forward with a plan is very different from moving forward *without* one. Although plans may not always work exactly as you want, they help you realize when you're drifting and give you a direction, motivation, and the tools to achieve your financial ends.

Begin by taking the post-bankruptcy education class you must attend as the springboard for your future. Then, if you didn't get one the first time you went to the credit-counseling agency (as you were required to do before filing for bankruptcy), work with your counselor to develop a detailed spending plan complete with goals.

A credit counselor will work with you to craft a spending plan that not only fits your current needs but allows you to set aside money for emergency savings and savings for those goals you want to achieve in the future. This will tell you how much money you can comfortably spend each month and help you to make sure that you're spending only on those things that you've consciously decided to spend your money on. No impulse buying for you. That money will be allocated to other choices you make — like a college fund, a vacation fund, or a retirement account.

Enlisting the help of a financial planner

Take your spending plan to a financial planner. Armed with this plan, you can work with a certified financial planner (CFP) or chartered financial consultant (ChFC) and lay out a savings and investment plan for you future. You'll start small, but with a plan in hand and goals to guide you, in no time you'll be moving forward to a brighter future for you and your family.

A good source for locating a planner are the friends, relatives and coworkers I mentioned before. If you're an orphan and have no friends, or even if you do, the attorney you used in the bankruptcy process may be a source of a good referral for you. Planners love referrals and are more apt to be patient with an existing customer referral while you acquire a nest egg.

Healing with time

No one can predict whether new laws or economic conditions will restrict future credit standards even more. Credit availability tends to swing like a pendulum from easy to difficult and then back again. Nevertheless, you can trust that by developing good credit habits, you can recover from the devastation that bankruptcy may have dealt. As time goes on and you continue to pay your bills promptly and establish new credit, the effect of your bankruptcy will diminish. Each month, it will move a little farther into the past and count for less on your credit report.

As with Monopoly, you're in this game for a long time. You *can* recover from landing on Boardwalk if you build up your savings and stay in the game.

Part IV
Building and Maintaining Good Credit

The 5th Wave
By Rich Tennant

"You have the first case of identity theft I've ever seen where the thieves actually returned the identity because the credit was so bad."

In this part . . .

Maybe your credit standing is now on the rebound after getting over some rough spots, or maybe your history has always been stellar. In any case, this part's for you! It's packed with chapters that address building — or rebuilding — an enviable credit portrait and keeping your good credit reputation untarnished. It includes a chapter on creating a workable spending plan (or budget), with tools to assist you through the process. You discover how a simple, useful, even fun financial tool allows you spend with confidence, while saving for the things you want. I walk you through the various life situations that can wreak havoc on your credit — including marriage, divorce, illness, unemployment, education, and death of a spouse — and reveal the secrets to getting through them with your credit intact. Finally, I give you the skinny on what you can and should be doing to avoid becoming a victim of America's fastest-growing crime: identify theft.

Chapter 10

Getting Back in Good Credit Standing

In This Chapter

▶ Developing a plan of action to clean up your credit

▶ Taking steps to improve your credit report and score

▶ Adding positive information to your credit report

*G*etting back into good standing with your creditors is a good thing. So is exercising. But for each of these activities, you're more motivated to do them and more likely to stick to them if you have specific, self-serving, and enjoyable goals. Credit — like exercise — is a means to an end, a tool and nothing more.

Like a fitness program that transforms your body into a healthier, more attractive *you,* building or improving your credit record is a tool that will help you achieve your life goals: buying your dream home, taking an around-the-world trip, sending your kids to college.

Identifying those goals is your first step. You don't have to lay out your whole future in financial terms, but taking a peek at least five years into the future is an excellent place to start — and it's easy and fun to boot!

This chapter is dedicated to helping you improve your credit and boost your credit score. Consider it your own fiscal fitness plan, designed to help you prevent those unwanted credit negatives from adding up. Allow me to serve as your personal trainer. So, lace up those sneakers and let's get to work!

Figuring Out Your Financial Goals

Some people think of credit as enabling them to spend more money for the stuff they want. Well, they're right *and* they're wrong. Credit doesn't put more money in your pocket. Having a credit card with a $5,000 limit does not mean that you have $5,000 more to spend. It *does* mean that today you can spend $5,000 you haven't earned yet (and, heaven forbid, may never earn). Credit is borrowing against the future or, as I'm fond of saying, "spending tomorrow's money today."

Problems often arise, however, when you spend *all* of tomorrow's money today — only to wake up tomorrow to find you have no money left. The government is the only entity I can think of that can get away with this, and even then I'm not sure it's a great idea. But in your case, spending *some* of tomorrow's money today can get actually help you lead a better life now — as long as you're spending those future dollars on things you've decided *you* want rather than things *someone else* wants to sell to you.

A good example: buying a house. If you had to wait until you saved up, say, $200,000 to purchase a house in cash, you might be ready for assisted living before you moved into your first home. Borrowing on future income to move in today makes sense and may well improve the quality of your life for years to come. On the other hand, buying a $200,000 Ferrari on borrowed money may be a mistake. Chances are you're buying the Ferrari because you were sold on the idea by some clever marketing campaign or plan.

This gets me to the concept of "the plan." Everyone I know who sells a product has a plan to get you to buy it. It is because of a *plan* that milk in a convenience store is always at the opposite end of the store from the door. It is because of a *plan* that candy at the checkout counter is placed low where kids will see it and ask parents to buy it for them.

What's your plan? If you don't have one, then like it or not, believe it or not, you'll end up following someone else's plan and you may end up sleeping in that Ferrari you bought instead of a house — until they tow it away for non-payment, that is.

Making a plan is easy. Set aside an evening or a weekend afternoon, sit down with your partner (if you're married) or alone without distraction (if you're single), and look into the future. No need to pull out the crystal ball or Ouija board. Simply sketch out what you want the future to look like. Consider the short term (generally from a few months up to a year) and long term (one year and later). Your goals may include such things as getting a car (maybe the Ferrari fits here), buying a home, having a family, saving for college or weddings, going on a fabulous vacation. In no time, you'll be having a ball as you imagine doing all those things you always wanted to do.

As you identify your goals, write them down. Documenting your dreams is important, because it makes them more real. Better yet, cut out pictures from magazines or newspapers that illustrate your goals. Maybe a picture of a big cruise ship or a tropical island surrounded by blue waters or, yes, that Ferrari.

Now you've taken the critical step toward creating a successful plan for yourself: You've established a reason to save some portion of your income. You have some shared goals to work toward. And you have the motivation to get your credit standing back on track. Believe it or not, achieving your goal is generally not the problem. Knowing were you want to go and — for couples — agreeing on a mutual goal is the trickiest part.

Take the list you made and keep it for reference when things get a little rocky. It'll be a big help in getting through difficult periods (for example, when something *not* on your list of goals is calling your name).

Selecting the Best Tools for Cleaning Up Your Credit

Now that you've established where you're going, the next step is to open up the big chest of credit tools and select which ones will best work for you to build your financial goals. Here are three credit tools you'll want to become very familiar with:

- ✔ A plan for spending and saving
- ✔ Copies of your credit report
- ✔ Your FICO score

Crafting your spending plan

Unless you're independently wealthy or you make a huge amount of money and just can't seem to spend it all, you need a spending plan. A spending plan, which will help you take care of today's responsibilities and tomorrow's goals, has three components:

- ✔ **Living expenses:** Your daily, weekly, and monthly financial commitments — from groceries and lunch money to rent or mortgage. Also consider those nonessential frivolities that crop up — your daily dose of designer coffee or the occasional boutique splurge.

✔ **Savings for financial goals:** This is where you account for the vacation, the college education, the dream house — or the Ferrari.

✔ **Emergency fund:** An emergency fund covers those unexpected (and usually unpleasant) wrenches, such as a medical expense or job loss. Saving for that unexpected emergency is as critical as saving for a desired goal. If you don't have an emergency fund — between three and six months of living expenses — when the emergency comes along, the money will come from one of two sources: the future (as in spending tomorrow's money today) or your savings (as in the money you were setting aside for that Ferrari).

Adding up your income

Here's how a spending plan works: You identify all your household income — that's the money coming into the house from salaries, tips, overtime, bonuses, royalties, all that stuff. Be sure to consider your payroll deductions (such as money you're putting into a retirement plan) as income.

Saving in your company retirement account makes sense, especially if your employer is contributing a match amount to the fund. Plus, saving for retirement probably ties into one of your goals (unless you plan to die at your desk).

Tallying your expenses

After you have the income part down on paper or in your computer, do the same with your expenses — making sure to include a savings category as an expense for each of the financial goals you listed earlier. The best way to manage this goal-based savings is to estimate how far in the future the goal is, what the goal will cost, and what you'll have to put aside each month to cover the expense in time.

For example, say you want to take a cruise on your wedding anniversary three years from now. The cost is $3,600 for the two of you. That's 36 months at $100 a month. If you can't afford the $100 a month, postpone the cruise for a year and save $75 a month — or take a cheaper cruise and still go in three years.

And the next time you find yourself standing before the flat-screen HDTV at the mall, your picture of the future will be in clear focus: the cruise or the TV — but not both.

Taking into account your existing debts

Don't forget to set aside money to pay your existing debts such as credit cards and car loans. You may need to tweak your plan a time or two so the numbers and timeframe for your goals reconcile. But you're now more firmly in control of your financial future. From here on, you make the decisions about what money goes to what categories — not those marketing guys.

On the CD included with this book are forms that help with setting up a spending plan. In Chapter 11, I get into more detail on budgeting for your future.

Paying attention to your credit report and credit score

Credit is an essential tool in achieving your future goals. If your credit isn't in decent shape, you'll be paying more for everything you plan to finance. And that difference could be tens or hundreds of thousands of dollars.

Order a copy of your credit report from each of the three credit-reporting bureaus. The FACT Act now requires the three major credit bureaus to provide you with a free copy of your credit report once each year. Get a copy of your report from *each* of the three bureaus — they often contain differing information. (See Chapter 4 for information on how to get your reports.)

When you get your credit reports, read them over and make sure that the information is accurate and complete and that there are no expired items that should be taken off. Chapter 6 provides information on how to scrutinize your credit report and fix any errors that you find.

Generally, negative items stay on your credit report for seven years. The most notable exceptions are:

- ✔ Student loan defaults, which remain until they're paid
- ✔ Overdue tax debts, which stay until resolved
- ✔ Child support defaults, which stay posted until cleared up
- ✔ Bankruptcy, which remains on your report for up to ten years

Positive account information will stay on your credit report for much longer. Some positive trade lines continue to be reported for 10, 20, or even 30 years.

Your credit score is a critical measure of your credit standing used by busy creditors who want a quick assessment of your risk potential as a borrower (see Chapter 2 for more info). The higher your score, the lower your risk of a default. Lenders look at your score and determine how you stand compared to all the other borrowers out there. Currently, the general population can be divided into five basic groups:

- ✔ Twenty percent have scores above 780.
- ✔ Twenty percent have scores in the range of 745 to 780.
- ✔ Twenty percent have scores in the range of 690 to 744.
- ✔ Twenty percent have scores in the range of 620 to 689.
- ✔ Twenty percent have scores below 620.

Steve Bucci's Theory of Good-Enough Credit

I often advocate the concept of *good-enough credit* as opposed to *perfect credit*. Your credit standing, which is represented by your credit score, is a reflection of your life in financial terms. Lose your job, get a divorce, suffer an illness — the fallout from all these life events shows up on your credit report and affects your credit score one way or another. Late payments and too much borrowing activity are some of the symptoms that may appear in your credit data. Although these events may lower your score to a degree, you shouldn't be driven to aspire to a perfect 850. Your life is not perfect, so don't expect your credit history to be. Again, credit is

a means to an end. As long as your credit score remains good enough to get what you need and want, you're in good stead to pursue your financial goals. No need to stay up nights worrying if your credit score has dropped from 745 to 744.

A bad credit score can cost a lot in extra payments. For example, say you bought a house for $150,000 — at a 30-year fixed rate with one point in fees and a down payment of 20 percent. If your credit score were 559 instead of 720, you would pay $184,695 more in interest over the life of your loan. That may even be enough for that red Ferrari!

Between the top two ranges, the difference in credit access and at what price and terms may be small. But the difference between the lowest group and the second-to-lowest is very large. Getting that extra point that moves you from 619 to 620 is much more critical that gaining an extra few points if you're in, say, the 690 to 745 range. To make more of those dreams come true, strive for at least the average, which is around the 690 to 700 mark.

The FICO credit score is the one that most lenders use. Although other credit scores exist, you want to see the one that your prospective creditors are judging you by. You can order your FICO credit score from only two places: the Fair Isaac Web site (www.myfico.com) or the Equifax Web site (www.equifax.com).

Using Small-Ticket Purchases to Build Credit

Because a lot of your score is based on using credit and making payments on time, I recommend using smaller purchases to get back in good standing more quickly. Why does making small purchases work so well? Because each item costs less (taking less of a bite out of your budget), and you'll have more purchases reported to the credit bureaus as well.

Creditors who don't report to the bureaus

Why doesn't every creditor report your history to all three of the credit bureaus? Because every time they send data on you to the bureau, they have to pay a fee. Some lenders don't think this is worth the expense. They may still order a credit report before approving your loan or credit card, but they want to save as much profit as they can. Typically, these non-reporters may include

✔ Credit unions

✔ Utilities

✔ Tradesmen

✔ Doctors

✔ Hospitals

✔ Local finance companies

✔ Landlords

✔ Insurance companies

Although these creditors don't report to the bureaus, you can still use your experience with them to help your score. You can send copies of statements and bills along with proof of payment to the credit bureaus and ask that they be added to your file. The bureaus don't *have* to do this, but for a fee, they might.

Major bank cards will certainly report your activity to the credit bureaus. Some store cards and credit-union cards only report to one bureau — or they may not report at all. To be sure your credit purchases are being reported and scored, call the customer-service number for your card and ask to which bureau(s) they report.

Pick up some extra points by following a simple plan when paying down balances. What you want to achieve for credit-score maximization is not having any cards that are above 50 percent of their credit limit. Some people suggest that you pay down balances based on interest rate to save more money on overall payments. Others say that paying off smaller accounts gives you a feeling of accomplishment and, therefore, you're more likely to achieve your overall goal. You get to make the choice about how you do this. My only advice is that *you* make the choice and don't let the first bill that shows up get the extra payment by chance.

Make a list of the smaller-balance accounts (under $200) and then a list of the larger-balance accounts (over $200). Next to each item, note the minimum payment and the credit limit. Starting with the smaller accounts, allocate available cash to the minimum payments first. Go through the entire list. Then with what money you still have available, go back to the smallest account and work on paying it down to 45 percent of the credit limit. This will get some great positive data in your credit report. As you pay down the smaller accounts, you'll work through each account toward the larger accounts. The big ones will take an extended amount of time to pay down to about 45 percent of their credit limit. This approach not only allows you to regain control of your accounts but helps you maximize your credit score, because accounts that exceed 50 percent of the limit count against you. When you're at the 45 percent limit on your cards, you may want to allocate more money to the highest-interest-rate cards.

If you don't have a major bank credit card, you may want to try a secured card. You can get one without a fee if you shop around. The secured card differs from the regular Visa or MasterCard in that you maintain a balance equal to your credit limit (some may allow more) to guarantee your payment. Secured-card activity is reported just as any other credit-card activity is reported, and it affects your credit score in the same way — so it can be a great option if you're trying to build credit.

Generally, if you make all your payments on time for a year, you should have enough of a positive payment history to get an unsecured card.

Turning Big-Ticket Purchases into Good Credit History

Big-ticket creditors — those lenders who specialize in expensive products or services — typically report to the credit bureaus. The reasoning is simple, they have a lot more to lose if they lend based on inaccurate information, so they want to see as complete and accurate a file as possible.

Making a major purchase may give your credit score a boost for two reasons:

✔ **When you make a major purchase, the lenders are more likely to extend credit in the form of a secured installment loan.** *Secured* means you have pledged collateral or the item you purchased as security for the loan. If you default on the loan, the lender repossesses the security you pledged — in other words, you don't get to keep it. Adding some secured credit to the variety of other types of credit you use, such as revolving credit, helps your credit score.

✔ **The payment will be the same each month.** When it comes to credit scoring, this equal monthly payment is an opportunity for the people who come up with your score to learn more about your creditworthiness. Your stability and ability to make a set payment at a set time every month can be measured. This scenario is different from paying on a credit card, where you can vary your payment up or down to a minimum, depending on how your month is going financially. Adhering to a regular payment schedule also indicates that you can handle what may be a higher limit than you may have on a store, gas, or credit-card account.

Examples of big-ticket items that might enhance your credit activity are

✔ Home mortgage

✔ Automobile

✔ Boat

- Student loan
- Furniture
- Appliances

Purchasing a vehicle

Because of the very large price tags on most cars, most people require some financing in order to afford one. Such financing typically comes in the form of a two- to five-year installment loan.

When lenders go on the hook for that much money, they want to be protected if you get in a cash squeeze at your end. Most car loans are secured by the car.

 Increasingly, homeowners are buying cars using the equity in their homes as collateral. Using a home-equity loan to buy a car may offer a tax advantage (with tax-deductible interest), but if you default on that home-equity loan, your car won't be repossessed — instead, your home may be foreclosed on.

Anyone lending you the amount of money it takes to buy a car receives and reports data to the credit bureaus.

Weighing the pluses and minuses of leases

Leasing is an increasingly popular way to get a car. Please note, I didn't say *buy* a car, because that doesn't happen in a lease arrangement. Consider a lease a long-term rental. Leases are popular because they generally require only a small down payment — or perhaps none at all. Plus, they're a tax write-off if you're a businessperson.

Signing the lease commits you to a stream of payments for an extended period of time. This activity is normally reported to the credit bureaus.

 Leases are very costly and difficult to terminate. Unlike with a car loan, you can't sell the car and pay off the loan. With a lease, you owe all the payments and you can't terminate without making all the payments first.

 If you're an active-duty serviceperson called away, you can get out of your car lease. Chapter 6 covers this in more detail. For the law itself, check out the Servicemembers Civil Relief Act (SCRA) on the CD.

Steering clear of upside-down loans

The term sounds as uncomfortable as it is. Basically, in an *upside-down loan,* you owe more than the item securing the loan is worth. Sounds good — you get the big bucks to buy the car and you only have to supply lesser-valued security to back it up. Well, the rub comes in when you want to get rid of the car and its payment. If you owe $10,000 on a car loan, and the value of the car is $7,000, you have to come up with the $3,000 difference or you can't sell the car. If you're in a car accident and the car is totaled, the insurance company will only pay what the car was worth — you get to pay the rest.

This situation becomes worse if you can't make the payments on the car and the creditor repossesses the car (whether they get you to agree to a voluntary repossession or do it the old-fashioned way — when you aren't looking). The car is worth $7,000 — but that was a retail value. At auction, let's say the creditor only gets $5,000. The fees on the repossession were $2,000 between the tow guy, the sales commission to the auctioneer, and the attorney's fees. So you get credited with $3,000 against the $10,000 you owe. Now you owe $7,000 in a lump sum to settle your account — and you have no car in the bargain.

Bottom line: Don't end up upside-down in a car loan — or any secured loan (upside-down house mortgages work similarly) if you can help it. Any repossession or default will show negatively on your credit report and your score will fall.

Leveraging your mortgage for good credit history

Owning a home and paying your mortgage can help build your credit in a few different ways. Credit grantors look at your credit report and credit score in order to rate your lendability, but they ultimately rely on you to be responsible for making the payments. Here is where those three Cs of credit really show up: Character, collateral, and capacity are really what credit scoring and lending are all about. A mortgage on your report tells the reader and the scorer that you have all three of the Cs and that some lender was so sure about you that she was willing to lend you a huge amount of money. The report indicates a large installment loan with fixed payments for a long period of time. All these items favorably impact your credit score.

A mortgage is secured by the house, so if you default, the lender forecloses and take the house back to pay off the loan. The average foreclosure ends up costing the lender an average of $25,000 when all is said and done. But don't feel too bad for the lender: *You'll* be chased down for any money still owed on the loan.

Home-equity lines of credit and home-equity loans are a popular subset of traditional mortgages. They're good ways to access money at a low interest rate. They also represent new and additional borrowing on your credit report. For example, you could have taken out a big mortgage and had only one lender report one loan to the bureaus. If you use a home equity loan or line of credit in addition to your mortgage, you're using the same collateral (your home), and you're borrowing the same amount as you would have with a bigger mortgage, but with more than one loan. Thus, more than one item gets reported to the credit bureau each month, building more positive information in the same time period.

There is a hitch, however: As you stack more debt on your home, you may reach the point where you and your castle are upside-down (that is, you owe more on your home than it's worth). This can also happen if the value of your home declines while your home-secured debt remains the same, and the two pass each other in the night, going in opposite directions. So, who cares? You have a 30-year mortgage and by then everything will be cool. But what if your boss offers you the general manager's job in a city too far to commute? Or what if the company lays you off and you either have to move to find work or downsize to reduce your mortgage commitment? You won't be able to sell the house to take advantage of a new opportunity, and you won't be able to sell it to lower your cost of living while you're trying to find work. When you're upside-down in a loan, your options are limited.

Lines versus loans

What's the difference between a home-equity loan and a home-equity line of credit? Here's the scoop: A *home-equity loan* is for a specified chunk of cash — say, $10,000. When you get the home-equity loan, you get the ten big ones to put down on that car (or whatever else you want to buy) and you have an installment payment due every month usually at a set interest rate for a set amount of time. In the old days, these were called *second mortgages* and they were a sure sign you were on the path to ruin. Today, they're called *equity products* and it seems everyone has at least one.

With a *home-equity line of credit,* you get a line of credit, maybe for $10,000, maybe for $20,000 depending on how much you want to have available just in case you need it. You don't have to take any money out of the line at all, unless you have a use for it. It just sits there like a wallflower at a dance, waiting for you to ask for a

tango. Generally, you have a set period of time (called a *draw period*) when you can access the line of credit and a set period before which you have to pay it back. So, until you use it all, the money is available and just sits there through the remainder of the draw period for free (or sometimes a small annual fee).

When you do draw money from the line, you generally have the option of paying it off anytime without a prepayment penalty. The loan terms often allow you to pay only the interest and not the principal (an interest-only loan); the principal is due at the end of a time set in the loan agreement. Or you can choose to pay both interest and principal until the debt is paid off. Some loans allow you to decide what you're going pay on a month-by-month basis. Pay principal and interest one month, but only interest the next. You decide.

Paying student loans to repair your credit

Because of the increasingly unaffordable price tag on higher education, more and more people have student loans. Student loans make a lot of sense to lenders: Although the person responsible for repayment may have no income at the time of the loan, the lender knows that good income is on the horizon, and the loan will soon be paid back. But what really makes these loans attractive to the lenders is that they can't lose. Almost all student loans are guaranteed by the U.S. government. The bank gets a fee for origination of the loan and for servicing it, but losses are Uncle Sam's problem.

If you have a student loan, chances are it appears on your credit report. It may also be reported more than once. Why? Each loan, be it on a semester or yearly basis, is reported as a separate loan for each enrollment period. So four years of loans add either four or eight loans to your credit report. If you make payments and/or file for benefits on time, your credit report will reflect a positive history and add to your credit score. This can be a lot of good news for your credit report.

Conversely, if you end up in default, you'll see a lot of negative marks on your credit report and credit score from all those individual loan entries. Any missed payments are reported to the bureaus, and you'll be subject to the full range of collection activity just like you would with any other loan.

If you've consolidated your loans after graduation, they'll show up on your report as one loan. (*Consolidating* is the process of refinancing all your individual loans into a single loan. The original loans are marked "paid in full," and the interest rate is often lower and the repayment term is typically longer for the consolidated loan than for the individual loans. The net result is the convenience of a single, lower monthly payment.) With consolidated loans, you typically have a number of different repayment options, including paying the same amount each month, paying less now and more later, and payment plans that change with your income.

Student loans are not secured with collateral in the normal sense of the word. When you're in default on a student loan, you can't defer payment of the loan. In fact, you may have to pay it all at once unless you come up with an acceptable repayment scheme. Additionally, you won't be eligible for further student aid, your school may withhold your transcripts, state and federal income tax refunds may be used to offset the loan amounts, and your wages (when you get that job) may be attached or garnished. Finally, student loans are not dischargeable in a bankruptcy (see Chapter 9 for more info).

Improving Your Standing by Using Cosigners

Getting a loan by having someone cosign for you is very much a double-edged sword. In fact, I consider it a triple-edged sword. A cosigned loan helps you get positive information on your credit report. As long as your lender reports to the bureaus, each time you make a payment on time and for the right amount, you'll accumulate more positive items. As time goes by, this will help offset earlier negative items on your report. Like snow falling on the ground, the good stuff will cover all the murk underneath.

I do have serious reservations about cosigning. Here's why I call it the triple-edged sword:

- ✔ **Edge #1: You may borrow when you shouldn't.** If a professional lender is reluctant to give you a loan, there may be good reason. So now the cosigner, who is not a professional and who likely has emotional ties clouding his judgment, decides to guarantee your loan.

- ✔ **Edge #2: The cosigner is at risk if you default.** The cosigner is fully responsible for the payment. If it takes 60 days for the cosigner to be informed that you haven't paid on time, the cosigner's credit gets dinged, as does yours.

- ✔ **Edge #3: A default could destroy a relationship.** If your ability to pay off the loan is compromised and you incur late fees or penalties, or you default on the loan, your cosigner is fully liable and his credit score may be damaged. Plus, he'll have to assume liability for the loan. This — no surprise — just may be the end of your relationship.

My advice: If you're going to ask a friend or relative to cosign a loan, make sure the life of the loan is for a short period of time. Also, put your agreement in writing to make it official.

Riding on Your Spouse's Credit Coattails

Just as with a cosigner, relying on your spouse's good credit history has its benefits to you and can allow you to offset your negative credit marks with your loved one's positive marks. Of course, your spouse can serve as a cosigner for your loan (see the preceding section), but another approach is to have your spouse add you to his or her credit card as an authorized user. Your spouse receives and pays the bills, but the account activity will be reported on *both* your credit reports. So good information flows to the damaged report like a blood transfusion to an ailing patient.

Community-property states: Till debt do us part?

Currently, nine states are community property states: Arizona, California, Idaho, Louisiana, Nevada, New Mexico, Texas, Washington, and Wisconsin. In these states, each spouse is liable for the debts of the other, even if they don't know about them. So particularly in these states, using your spouse as a cosigner or joint borrower can save you money at no additional risk to the spouse. Because both spouses are already on the hook for the loan if the loan is defaulted on, the spouse with the bad credit may as well get the benefit of the other spouse's *good* credit history to get a lower rate.

If you're not responsible with credit cards, you could run up purchases and exceed the limit or make payoff a challenge for your family budget. One way to avoid this is to remain as an authorized user on the card, but ask your spouse to keep the plastic away from you.

A word of caution to the *good*-credit partner: There is probably a good reason that a lender doesn't want to give your other half a loan. You need to understand that reason and then decide if you want to guarantee the debt. The worst of all possibilities: You end up on the loan, but not as a co-owner of the property. In my counseling days, I had a client who had cosigned on a car loan for his sweetie. After she got the wheels, she hit the road, and the collectors were all over him for payment. ***Remember:*** Love may be blind, but it doesn't have to be stupid.

Understanding Why Some Debt Is Good for Your Credit

No doubt about it: Getting into debt *can* get you into trouble. And if you're reading this book, chances are you've had some experience with that sort of trouble — or you're at least trying to avert a potential credit disaster. Although debt certainly has a downside, borrowing money can also do you a great deal of good. In the following sections, I tell you how.

Achieving goals with the help of credit

Debt allows you to take advantage of those opportunities and experiences that enhance your life and create joy and fulfillment: that dream home with

the white picket fence, the around-the-world cruise, the Ivy League school —
yes, even that Ferrari. When you can put your sights on your life goals and
develop a spending plan that allows you to get there in the timeframe you've
set, you've found the secret to the true value of credit.

Sending a message to potential lenders

If you had no debt — ever — then you'd never have used credit and wouldn't
have a credit report or credit score. Let's face it: In today's world, it's hard to
live without credit. Most people need credit to buy those big-ticket items —
vehicles, homes, higher education — not to mention rely on it in the case of
life's emergencies. By borrowing responsibly, you can create a positive credit
history — a credit reputation, of sorts — that says to prospective lenders
that you're a good credit risk. Showing that you can handle debt puts you in
a position to attract creditors who offer favorable rates and terms.

Not only is using credit wisely a good thing for your lifestyle, it gives prospective creditors the opportunity to know what a great customer you'll be based
on your past performance. Lenders prefer to loan money to individuals who've
borrowed before, who can show that they understand the commitment of
credit, and who have a history of prompt payment and reliable follow-through.
In fact, given the choice between lending to someone who's *never* borrowed
before and an individual with a history of debt — even a couple of blips on the
report — my guess is most creditors will go for the credit veteran over the
rookie.

Think of it this way: Let's say your two 20-year-old nephews ask to borrow
your car. One has no driving history, the other has a history, but with a parking ticket last year. Who would you pick?

Giving people a sense of how responsible you are

If you had no debt, and thereby no credit history, you might find yourself dis-
advantaged in other ways. If a prospective employer checks your record and
comes up empty, they'd probably see this as strange — and they wouldn't be
able to use your credit history as a positive factor when trying to decide
whether to hire you. Without that credit record, they'll miss one additional
tool in comparing your application to those of their other applicants.

The same holds true when it comes to renting an apartment, applying for
insurance, and so on. When you have no track record, you represent an
unknown risk.

Chapter 11

Budgeting for Your Future

. . . .

In This Chapter

▶ Recognizing what a budget can do for you

▶ Setting financial goals

▶ Maximizing your take-home income

▶ Keeping track of your household expenses

▶ Saving for the future

. . . .

Of all the topics in this book — or any other book that deals with the ins and outs of personal finance and its effect on credit — no subject is more basic and nothing is more important than budgeting. Based on the lack of attention that this topic gets from lenders, financial planners, and even schools, you might conclude that all Americans are born with a financial gene that innately allows them to sense when they're overspending or undersaving.

Unfortunately, nothing could be farther from the truth. The popular American misconception seems to be that credit can take the place of savings. I'm here to tell you the cold, hard truth: You may use credit in place of savings, but only for a limited period of time — and at a cost. When I say *cost,* I'm not just talking about the cost of interest or fees involved, but the cost of not being able to use the money that goes to repay the loan in more productive or enjoyable ways.

As I explain in Chapter 10, credit is only a tool. It does not give you more money to spend — it simply helps you leverage the money you anticipate having in the future. If you're borrowing to cover emergencies or big-ticket items, you're spending money today that you won't have earned until tomorrow.

So, what happens when you get to tomorrow and find that you spent all the money that was supposed to be there yesterday? Nothing pleasant, I can assure you. In my 15 years of helping individuals overcome financial challenges, I've rarely met a person who was applying the basics of budgeting to his daily life. Conversely, for the 11 years that I made my living as a management consultant to financial-services companies, every one of those companies had a keen interest in budgets and where they stood relative to their goals. What these companies knew that individuals didn't is that a budget is another critical tool — one that would lead them to success.

I know people who make upwards of $200,000 a year, spend it all, and have no idea how much they actually need to live on except that it must be their entire salary. Conversely, some moms I was speaking to at a Project Head Start spaghetti dinner told me that they couldn't afford to save anything either. How can both experiences at opposite ends of the spectrum say the same thing and yet still be wrong?! The truth? Most of your friends, neighbors, co-workers, and acquaintances do *not* have a personal budget or spending plan. Many use credit as though it were extra income and guess at whether they'll be able to pay all the bills when an unexpected expense comes along. Why? Primarily because no one ever told them that there is another way. One that will allow them to set and achieve important goals. One that will result in reducing debt — not adding to it. One that will allow them to provide for family or loved ones without an elevated level of stress arriving in the mail.

In this chapter, I show you how budgeting can be a valuable tool that allows you to

- Spend your income the way you want
- Save enough to be able to afford the goals that you set for yourself and your family
- Sleep peacefully at night

I walk you through the process of determining what you spend now and how you would like to spend your income in the future. You'll accomplish this task by allocating funds for particular areas of spending that you choose. I help you understand how budgeting and planning can help you get your credit back on track and keep it there.

So sharpen your pencil and get out those checkbook and credit-card records. You have some budgeting to do!

Defining Budget: A Tool for Crafting Your Financial Future

Simply put, a *budget* (also known as a *spending plan*) is a money-management tool that puts you in control of your spending and keeps you out of credit trouble. It is your personal plan for spending the income you have and using credit wisely. A budget can be as detailed or as general as you want. In order to create a budget, you need to know how much money you have to work with and what you plan to spend that money on, over a set period of time. Budgets can help you get by in the near term, as well as plan and save successfully for the future.

Many people incorrectly think that budgeting is like dieting, where you don't get to do what you want and have to suffer to achieve a goal. Actually, a budget used effectively has the opposite impact. You get to do *exactly* what you want to do. How can this be? Where does the money come from? It comes from not wasting money on things that aren't important to you or your family.

Look at this another way: If you couldn't see the speedometer on your car, what would the result be? You might go too slowly — but if you're like most people, you'd go way too fast. You wouldn't think you were speeding, of course, because you wouldn't have any reference points to tell you so. If all the other cars were whizzing by, just keeping up with the traffic would cause you to speed up, and you'd probably get in a destructive crash — or at least land yourself a speeding ticket.

Most people are spending out of control — but a budget serves as your own personal *spendometer,* putting you back in the driver's seat, controlling the direction of your financial future. It allows *you,* not the other out-of-control drivers, to determine the route to your personal goals.

Here's a short list of things that a budget can help you do:

- ✔ **Reach your financial goals:** Your budget is a compass that keeps you on course, helping you to put aside money to reach your goals. Whether your goals include an exotic vacation, an addition to your home, or a new car, a budget gets you there.

- ✔ **Control your money:** Allocating money for every aspect of your daily life allows you to decide how your money is used. Without a budget, your spending could easily get out of control and cause credit problems.

- ✔ **Live within your means:** You may notice when you begin the budgeting process that your expenses often equal or exceed your income, particularly if you have easy access to credit cards. Bringing spending in line with income is a great way to ensure you don't accumulate unmanageable debt and damage your credit.

- ✔ **Free up cash:** The best bonus of budgeting is that you get to decide how to spend. Instead of spending all your money on things you don't remember buying or didn't really want or need, a budget gives you the power to make better decisions on how your extra money is spent.

- ✔ **Focus on common goals:** An effective budgeting process involves the entire family. For example, your children are much more likely to go along with skipping pizza night for several months if they understand that doing so will allow them to go to Disney World! The same is true of your sweetie: If the two of you decide that an addition to your home is your top financial priority, you'll both be on the same page when it comes to making adjustments.

✔ **Prepare for the unexpected:** As part of your budget, you'll put aside money each month in an emergency savings account. This account will cover expenses such as major car repairs, large appliances that need replacing, or medical bills.

✔ **Reveal problem areas:** The process of budgeting helps expose the areas in which you overspend and gives you the freedom to decide to spend your money in areas that are more important to you and your family.

✔ **Get and stay out of debt:** Because budgeting helps you bring your expenses in line with your income, you'll stop adding to your debt. In fact, you'll *decrease* your balances with regular payments.

✔ **Attain peace of mind:** Gaining control of your finances provides relief from financial stress that could be causing sleepless nights, reduced productivity at work, and even physical symptoms (like headaches or ulcers).

Setting Goals: Turning Financial Fantasies into Reality

Focusing on your financial dreams is the fun part of building a budget, but many people overlook goal-setting as a key first step. Many people stumble through life with vaguely defined goals, letting the moment carry them where it will. Well, that's all about to stop for you. The first part of getting control of your finances is to decide what you want to do and when — both long-term and short-term.

Don't worry, this process doesn't involve a test, and there are no wrong answers. In fact, you can change your goals as often as you want.

Setting aside the time to plan

Set aside an hour or so — even an entire evening or afternoon — to explore your most treasured dreams. If you're sharing your life with a significant other, involving him or her in the discussion is critical. Heck, make it a date! Over a glass of wine or a steaming cappuccino, curl up on the couch and dare to dream. Or go to an inspiring place — a nearby park, the steps of a monument, a scenic overlook — and let your surroundings stimulate your aspirations.

Wherever you do your planning, use a stack of 3-x-5 cards, and write one goal on each card. Put a "due date" next to each item — this is the date by which you want to achieve this goal. If you're in the mood, you can have some fun with this: Get out the scissors and glue and cut out pictures from magazines, calendars, or other sources to illustrate your goals. These images can be powerful motivators in achieving your goals. Put the pictures up on your refrigerator or in a scrapbook that you can refer to as you make your plans.

At this point, don't limit yourself. Dream as big as you want. You've always wanted to retire and sail around the world in your own boat? Jot it down. Yearn to go back to school and launch a new career? Add it to the list. Fantasize contributing a substantial amount to your favorite charity? Good for you.

Buying a home, owning a sports car, taking a dream trip — this goal-setting stage is your opportunity to indulge yourself in *all* your financial fantasies. Getting them down on paper and discussing, assessing, and prioritizing them is an important part of the process of tailoring your budget to meet your own personal goals.

Be as specific as possible. For example, you may have written down, "Go to Disney World." But keep going: Will you stay in the park or outside? Go for a week — or two? Try to be as specific as possible. Not only will this level of detail give you a clearer target, it will keep your expectations in check.

Thinking long-term, short-term, and everything in between

Goals can be divided into four general categories:

- ✔ **Short-term goals** are generally things you want to do within one year. They may include taking a vacation to Disney World, beginning to invest in your retirement plan, donating to charity, saving money in your emergency fund, moving into a bigger apartment, buying jewelry or clothes, becoming a member of a local sports club, or reducing your debt.

- ✔ **Intermediate-term goals** are things that you'll need one to five years to accomplish. These might include saving enough money to buy a new car, beginning a family, or paying off your debts.

- ✔ **Long-term goals** are things you'll do at least five years down the road. These may include saving for your kids' education, starting your own business, buying a home or boat, or retiring.

- ✔ **Life goals** don't have a timeframe because you'll probably never *fully* achieve them. These are the goals that aren't necessarily money-driven, but capture the imagination. For example, America is the land of the free. Does everyone think he is as free as he ought to be? But freedom is a commonly held goal we all strive for. The same applies in your life. Have at least one goal you can reach for that may be unattainable through money. Who knows? You might find it if you look.

As you start thinking about your goals, try to think about which category each goal fits in. Make three stacks — one for long-term goals, one for intermediate-term goals, and one for short-term goals.

Pay attention to how big each pile is. Are all your goals focused on the short term? If so, spend some time thinking a little farther into the future.

Build in at least one or two goals that don't require money, if only to show the kids or your other half that you see the future in other-than-material terms. Camping can be almost free — and it's a great exercise in togetherness. Look for other opportunities to work "free" into your future.

Prioritizing your goals

After you've written down all your goals on 3-x-5 cards and put them into stacks based on when you want to accomplish them, you need to prioritize. You may not be able to achieve *all* your goals, so which ones matter most?

If your goals are too challenging, you may get frustrated. For more-difficult or long-term aspirations, break them down into stages so you can build on successes as you go along. If a goal calls for you to save a large amount of money, you may want to phase the amount in over time rather than try for too much too quickly. Be sure to recognize and celebrate each step as you attain it.

If your goal list is very long or requires winning the lottery to achieve, I suggest that you do some prioritization. You don't have to throw any dreams away. Just recognize that some are more important than others and concentrate on those that you have the means, motive, and opportunity to realistically achieve. Keep the others in the incubator and if the time and conditions are ever right for them to become real, bring them out into your life again.

Any plan requires minor or major tweaking as circumstances change. Building in some checkpoints will be helpful in allowing you to adjust. An unexpected bonus can move up a timeline; a layoff can set it back. Adjust your plan accordingly.

Building Your Spending Plan

After you've set your goals, your next task is to find the money to make them a reality. Here's where the budget comes in. *Remember:* You're not creating a budget to *restrict* your spending, but rather to *channel* it in the direction you want to go. You begin by listing your current income and expenses. You can't decide how much and where to spend until you know how much there is to go around.

Step 1: Figuring out exactly how much you're bringing in

Determining your income should be fairly easy. If you earn a salary or work a consistent number of hours every week, you're used to seeing the same figure on your paycheck payday after payday. But there are some tricky situations to consider. For example, if you work a service job — you're a waiter, for example — you may rely on tips, which may fluctuate dramatically depending on which shifts you're scheduled. Perhaps your work is seasonal (you're a landscaper or tax accountant, for example) and you bring in more income at certain times of the year. Maybe you have periodic bouts of overtime, which affect your income.

Whatever your situation, do your best to gather a good year's worth of income activity. Although you may find it helpful to come up with a monthly average, you still want to be aware of the natural ebbs and flows of your earnings rhythms and alter your budget accordingly.

In addition to your paycheck stubs, don't forget to gather details on other income such as child support, alimony, overtime pay, bonuses, investment income, royalties, or rental-property income. In addition, consider other money sources. Your garage band earns a few bucks paying for weddings and occasional gigs? Your monthly yard sales keep your closets cleared and add a bit of fun money to the household income? Your reputation as a first-rate résumé-writer has kept a steady stream of co-workers at your office door? Add it all to your money pot!

You can use Table 11-1 to list all the sources of income you expect each month. List your take-home, or *net,* pay rather than your *gross* pay (your salary before taxes). You may also want to list the expenses that are deducted from your paycheck. This can be useful if you think you might be able to reduce or eliminate some. Say you have $400 in federal taxes withheld each month, but you got a $2,400 refund last year. You may want to use half of the refund for current expenses by reducing your withholding by $100 a month. This will still leave you a cushion with the tax man, but add some extra cash to your budget. So list any expenses and savings that are deducted directly from your gross pay, that you want to consider reallocating. Add them back into your take-home pay, then enter the new amount of each deduction as an expense.

Table 11-1 Income Worksheet for _____			
Source of Income	Planned	Actual	Difference
Salary 1			
Salary 2			
Bonus			
Interest			
Dividends			
Child support/alimony			
Rental income			
Gifts			
Deduction changes/other			
Total income	$	$	$

After you've established all your income sources, come up with an average monthly income. Why monthly? Because most of your major expenses are paid out on a monthly basis — utilities, mortgage or rent, phone, even many charitable contributions are portioned out in monthly increments.

Be sure to use your *take-home* pay — not your *gross* pay — to come up with your monthly income. If you earn $60,000 per year, your gross income is $5,000 per month — but that's not what you're taking home after taxes. Instead, depressing as it may be, you're taking home $3,600 or so after Social Security, federal and state taxes, and other deductions are made.

Does that difference in gross and net jar your senses somewhat? Carefully consider your deductions. Some deductions, such as Social Security, are beyond your control (although if you earn enough to max out your contribution before the year is over — currently, around the $90,000-a-year mark — be sure to account for the extra income you'll be taking home after you go over that number). Other deductions, such as your withholdings for federal and state taxes, are worth review. My advice: Don't use withholdings as a forced savings plan — you lose out this way. After all, is the government paying you any interest for holding your cash for the year? You can do much better if you allow yourself a $600 annual cushion and adjust your withholding accordingly.

Look at last year's taxes: If your income and deductions are relatively stable, and you got back more than $600, increase your deductions. If you owed money, decrease your deductions to bring your refund into the $600 range. This strategy will improve your cash flow, while avoiding an unpleasant surprise in April.

Step 2: Identifying your expenses

Now that you know how much you have coming in, you need to look at what's going out — and where it's going. Using your checking- and savings-account statements, credit-card statements, or a financial planning program (such as Quicken), write down all the expenses you can identify to figure out what you spend each month.

Determining your monthly spending won't be difficult — though, as with gathering your income information, it may require some scrutiny. Many of your major expenses — mortgage, credit-card bill, utilities, car loans — hit monthly. If you have an expense that occurs other than monthly, prorate it to a monthly amount. For example, a $400 homeowner's insurance bill due once a year is $33.33 a month. For frequent yet varying expenses, such as groceries and entertainment, gather several months of history and then determine a monthly average.

Table 11-2 will help you get started. Start by collecting checkbook registers, receipts, credit-card bills, online statements, and any other financial records you may have. This will help you get the most accurate information. If you don't have complete financial records, use your best estimates to fill in the blanks.

Table 11-2   Expenses Worksheet for _____

Expense	Planned	Actual	Difference
Rent/mortgage			
Property tax			
Renter's/homeowner's insurance			
Home maintenance			
Water			
Sewer			
Garbage			
Gas/oil for heating			
Electric			
Telephone			
Car payment			
Car insurance			

(continued)

Table 11-2 *(continued)*

Expense	Planned	Actual	Difference
Gasoline			
Car repairs/maintenance			
Clothing			
Groceries/household supplies			
Doctor/dentist			
Prescriptions			
Health insurance			
Life/disability insurance			
Childcare			
Tuition/school expenses			
Child support/alimony			
Personal allowance			
Entertainment			
Eating out/vending			
Cigarettes/alcohol			
Newspapers/magazines			
Hobbies/clubs/sports			
Gifts			
Donations			
Work expenses			
Cable/satellite			
Internet connections			
Cell phone			
Student loan			
Other:			
Other:			
Other:			
Total Expenses	$	$	$

If you're like most people, you'll be able to identify where between 80 and 90 percent of your money goes. But you're likely to find that some fraction of your income inexplicably disappears on unknown items. I call these items "money gobblers" — these are the small cash expenses you make that never seem to register in your memory, let alone make it to the check register or any account ledger. I've assembled a list of some of these expenses (you may be able to add to this list, and not every item will apply to your life). These are all areas where your money may be flowing out — and each item is something you can save on if you're willing to get creative:

- **Allowances:** Your kids will hate me for this, but you don't have to give them allowances, especially if your own financial situation is tenuous.

- **Baby pictures:** You'll be surprised at what great pictures you can snap with your own camera. Dress your little one the same way you would if you were going to a fancy studio, drape a pastel-colored bed sheet behind her, and snap away. The shots you get will be even more special because of the time you spent together.

- **Babysitting:** See if you can work out a deal with one of your friends or neighbors and watch their kids one day in exchange for them watching yours the next. Or take shameless advantage of the grandparents — most will be only too happy to volunteer their services.

- **Beauty parlor:** Instead of going to a high-priced salon, look in the Yellow Pages for a beauty school in your area. You may be able to get your hair done for free (or for a very small charge), and the attention to detail you'll get will be phenomenal — the students are supervised by teachers and they're working to impress.

- **Beer and soda:** For some people, the thought of giving up brewskies or soft drinks may be akin to torture. But when you add up how much money you're spending, the motivation to get your calories elsewhere will be great. At the very least, try to reduce your intake of these nonessentials, and when you do drink them, do it at home instead of at high-priced bars and restaurants.

- **Fast food and vending machines:** The stuff is bad not only for your body, but also for your wallet. Shop at the grocery store instead; the savings will be amazing.

- **Books, magazines, newspapers, CDs, movies:** One of the greatest resources at your disposal is your public library. You can get all the books, magazines, and newspapers you want — free of charge. And most libraries will also lend out books on tape, as well as music CDs, free of charge. Some libraries charge a small fee for movies, but it's definitely less than you'll pay at your local video store.

- **Car washes:** Now, I'm not suggesting that you never wash your car. I'm just suggesting that, when you need to do it, you do it yourself, or toss a sponge, some soap, and the hose at your kids, and set them loose. They'll have fun, your car will be a little cleaner (if not flawless), and you'll save significant dough.

- ✔ **Cards, gambling, and lottery tickets:** A dollar in the bank (or put toward your credit-card bill) is much more valuable than a dollar spent gambling. End of story.

- ✔ **Charities:** I'm not suggesting you change your name to Scrooge, but if your own finances are stretched, you need to take care of yourself first. Then, when you're back on your feet, you can think about lending a hand to others. In the meantime, you can give to charities by donating your time. That's just as valuable as a check.

- ✔ **School fundraisers:** When your neighbor kids come a-knockin', just say no. This falls into the same category as the preceding bullet. If you want to be of help to your local school, you can volunteer at the library, coach a sports team, or lead a scouting troop.

- ✔ **Cosmetics:** Spending big bucks on makeup when you can't pay the bills doesn't make much sense. You can find inexpensive cosmetics if you look for it. If you have to, splurge on one higher-priced item, and make it last.

- ✔ **Dry cleaning and laundry:** Dry cleaning is a money-eater if ever there was one. Until you're in a better financial situation, stick to clothes you can wash at home. And launder your own shirts instead of sending them out. Your iron will wonder where you've been all these months.

- ✔ **Entertainment (concerts, movies, sporting events, and so on):** Look for ways to entertain yourself and your family free of charge. Instead of going to a Major League Baseball game, go out in the yard or to the park and toss a ball around with your kids or your friends. Instead of going to a movie, read a library book.

- ✔ **Film developing:** You can spend a lot of money getting film developed. Save the camera for special occasions, or if you have a digital camera, use that instead, and wait to get prints until you have money to spare.

- ✔ **Health foods:** Eating healthy is important, but health foods can be pricey. Shop the produce department of your grocery store, stick to whole grains and lean meats, and you'll be fine. Go granola when you've paid down your debts.

- ✔ **Hobbies:** Most hobbies cost money, and although they're fun, so is paying off your debts. Make *that* your new hobby.

- ✔ **Eating out:** Even if you're eating at fast-food restaurants, eating out costs a lot. You can save big money by preparing your food at home.

- ✔ **Pets:** If you're in financial trouble, getting a new pet isn't a good idea. (Let me tell you about my free cat!) Even healthy pets cost money, and if your pet gets sick, you're in for even more expense. If you already have pets, stick to the necessities (food, vaccinations) and avoid the store-bought toys. You can make a rope bone out of old T-shirts or throw a

> tennis ball around in the yard — all your pet cares about is that you're spending time together.
>
> ✔ **Tobacco:** You already know you shouldn't be smoking. Add up the financial costs, and you'll see the damage it's doing *beyond* the damage to your health.
>
> ✔ **Yard sales:** If your idea of a fun Saturday morning is going from one yard sale to the next looking for bargains, wash the car instead. Most people think they're getting bargains, but they usually end up buying things they don't really need.

You don't have to cut all the preceding items out of your life. Just be aware that you're spending discretionary money and cut the ones that aren't top priorities for you. For example, you may not be willing to scrimp when it comes to Fido's organic, super-premium dog food — if that's the case, just make sure to budget for it every month.

To get to the point where you're able to identify that last 10 to 20 percent of expenses, track your daily expenses. Record all those cash expenses that are such a part of your routine that you hardly notice them — items such as the morning coffee, newspaper, snack, kids' allowances. Again, I'm not saying you shouldn't *have* them — the goal is just to be aware of where your money is going so you can decide if that's the best use of your funds.

Was eating breakfast at the coffee shop every morning on your short-term goals list? I bet not. Did you know that if you took the $5 a day that breakfast costs and multiplied that times 260 business days in a year, you'd get $1,300 — which might translate to a five-night Caribbean cruise for two? You get to make the choices here.

The really good news about this tracking is that you only need to do it for two months to catch most everything. Now that's not so bad. After that you'll have a good handle on what's gobbling up your free cash — and you can either plug the hole or include it as an expense in your budget.

Step 3: Working your savings goals into your budget

Most people don't budget for savings, but I recommend that you do. The old saying "Pay yourself first" is a wise one, indeed. If you only save what drifts to the bottom line, you won't be getting the biggest deposit possible.

And now, a word from the Bureau of Labor Statistics: Are you an average spender?

You may be looking for some guidelines to tell you if your spending is in line with others. Look no farther. The nice people at the Bureau of Labor Statistics have been hard at work adding up grocery-store tapes and watching what you bought the last time you went to a liquor store. Their report is available for all to see at www.bls.gov/cex/home.htm. I'm only kidding about them watching you at the liquor store — but they do have their ways of getting the stats on what Americans are spending and for what. The latest data is a year or so old but probably still fine for your purposes. Here's the scoop:

✔ **Housing:** 32.9 percent

✔ **Transportation:** 19.1 percent (vehicles: 9.1 percent; gasoline and motor oil: 3.3 percent; other transportation: 6.7 percent)

✔ **Food:** 13.1 percent (at home: 7.7 percent; away from home: 5.4 percent)

✔ **Personal insurance and pensions:** 9.9 percent (life and other insurance: 1 percent; pensions and Social Security: 9 percent)

✔ **Healthcare:** 5.9 percent

✔ **Entertainment:** 5 percent

✔ **Apparel and services:** 4 percent

✔ **Cash contributions:** 3.4 percent

✔ **Education:** 1.9 percent

✔ **Personal-care products and services:** 1.3 percent

✔ **Alcoholic beverages:** 1 percent

✔ **Tobacco and smoking supplies:** 0.7 percent

✔ **Reading:** 0.3 percent

✔ **Miscellaneous:** 1.5 percent

The percentages were arrived at by taking an average expense as a percentage of an average income. So if you have $3,000 a month coming in and you spend $1,000 on housing, you're spending 33 percent. All the numbers work off take-home pay. (The government always allows for taxes!)

I'm not suggesting that you budget according to these percentages. Just use them to see if you're way out in left field on your estimates. For example, my family may choose to spend 40 percent of our income on housing and less on clothing and transportation, and yours may spend more on matching Corvettes or that infamous Ferrari and less on the old homestead. *Remember:* You get to decide.

Ideally, the money should go directly from your paycheck into a savings or checking account. When you get into the habit, you won't even notice the cut to your spending money — and you won't think to spend it if you can't see it. I do this myself and have found it to be painless.

Have your paycheck set up so that the amount of money you need to run your household goes into your checking account every pay period. Any raise, bonus, or leftover money goes directly into your savings. You never see it and never spend it — unless, of course, you want to. If you feel this is too

Saving strategies: The grown-up's version of the piggy bank

A technique that helps me make the most of my spare pennies is to roll change. No, I don't mean act like someone else, or switch from parker house rolls to crescent rolls. At the end of the day, I place my loose pocket change into those cute little tubes you can get (for free) at the bank. For guys, this is easy, as the coins usually fall out onto the floor when you hang up your trousers. For the ladies, not only will you be saving money, you'll save the strain on your shoulder from lugging around a pocketbook weighted down with coins. So stop giving exact change at the checkout register — and start collecting your pennies, nickels, dimes, and quarters for your change rolls. My experience is that this strategy will yield about $200 a year per person.

Use cash more. Not only will this retrain your fingers from reaching for the plastic every time you buy something, it may help establish a link between paying, earning, and the value you're getting. Buying a $100 item is easy with a swipe of your favorite, mileage-accruing credit card. If you have to peel off ten $10 bills, the experience is different. It's real money — and a lot of it! Plus, when the stash of cash is nearly gone, you really have to think about a purchase.

You can also save money by packing your lunch. Going out to lunch adds up to some real money: 260 business days in a year, $10 per lunch (including tax, tip, and gas, if you drive) equals $2,600 a year. If you pay 25 percent federal tax, 7 percent state tax, and 7 percent Social Security, your brown-bagging it will be the equivalent of a $3,614 raise. Think of the vacation you can go on with that money instead!

Finally, get a Sunday paper and cut coupons. Now that's real news. If you can put in a half-hour and come up with $20 in savings every week, you've made a great trade. How much? How about $1,445 a year!

extreme, you might at least consider directing half of all raises and bonuses into your savings account until you see how this strategy works for you.

Your savings plan is really two-pronged: You're saving to achieve the goals you've set for yourself, and you're saving so that you have money in case of an emergency. I cover both in the following sections.

Saving for a particular goal

At this point you've established your goals, calculated your income, and tracked your expenses. The next task is to revisit those goals that you're looking forward to attaining. Take an intermediate-term goal as an example: If you want to take a vacation, first you have to estimate the cost. Let's say the cost is $1,200. If your goal is to go in 18 months, you divide the $1,200 by the 18 months. The result — $66.67 — is what you must put aside each month in order to pay for the trip by the time you're zipping up your suitcase and canceling the newspaper delivery.

Avoiding backslides

For all your good intentions, there are five major causes of backsliding to be avoided in getting your plans in high gear. They are

✔ **Using credit cards outside of your budget:** If the expense is in your budget, how you pay for it is up to you. But if the expense isn't something you've budgeted for, putting it on a credit card is not a good idea.

✔ **Premature spending:** No, I'm not talking about a new medical problem. I'm talking about this situation: An item is in the budget to be purchased in the future, but you buy it early, before you have the cash for it. Instead, set dates and stick to them.

✔ **Lacking flexibility:** As situations change and opportunities appear, your budget will change. If it doesn't, it won't last. Remember who's in charge. Just don't charge like you're in charge.

✔ **Holidays:** They only last 24 hours, but the damage they can do to a budget is legendary. As gift-giving holidays approach, set a limit and use a list. Your family and friends will love you and won't notice you didn't overspend — but they will notice how relaxed you are and that your smile is genuine.

✔ **Summer vacation:** Immortalized in Chevy Chase's assault on Wally World, the summer vacation — any vacation, really — can become a frenzy. Vacations are supposed to be relaxing , rather than expensive — not just while you're on them, but after you return, too. You can't make up lost time with your family by spending more money. Learn this lesson and you've really learned how a budget can set you free.

But where will the money come from if your budget has little to nothing left after expenses? You need to either increase income or reduce expenses by the amount needed. Again, taking the vacation example, if you can get overtime at, say, $15 an hour, you'll need one hour a week, or 4.4 hours a month (15×4.4 hours $\times 18$ months) to swing it. On the expense side, you'll be looking to redirect $3.03 per workday ($3.03 \times 390$ days) or $2.19 per day ($2.19 \times 548$ days). Maybe your trip is as easy as passing up that latte and brewing your coffee at home.

Broken down into bite-size pieces, your goal becomes more easily attainable. If you can do that with *all* your goals, you'll be closer to a plan that works for you.

With some of your longer-term plans, it's fair to apply income that you're pretty sure will show up but hasn't yet. Say, you expect a 4 percent raise in six months. You may want to count that raise in your figuring.

Looking at your insurance options

Insurance is not the sexiest topic, and for that I'm glad. It is, however, an essential part of budgeting for your future. Catastrophic illness or loss to property can derail the most well-conceived plans. I don't advocate insurance for every little thing that comes up — which insurance you buy is a personal decision and to some degree depends on your resources and willingness to absorb the cost of some lower-level exposures in your lives, such as car-insurance deductibles.

But you should be concerned about the major life events and expenses that could dramatically affect your finances at all stages of your life — from the death of a spouse, to a major medical disability that prevents a wage-earner from working, to losing your home.

Here are a few critical coverage areas you want to consider as you pull together your budget for the future:

- **Life insurance:** If you have someone who will miss your income if you die, you need life-insurance coverage. You can get cheap *term life insurance.* Term life insurance covers you for specified term or timeframe but can usually be renewed. It has no cash or investment value — you get paid when you die, not before. But make sure you have enough coverage to bridge the gap your death will cause to the household budget. And, of course, you want to have appropriate coverage on your partner as well.

- **Long-term disability insurance:** If you're unable to work for an extended period of time, long-term disability insurance will help cover your expenses. Be good to yourself and your loved ones, and be sure that you get this.

- **Homeowner's insurance:** One of your biggest assets and one of your biggest liabilities is your home. As an asset, you'd have a tough time replacing it if an uninsured accident took part or all of your home. Keep up with building-code changes that will affect your replacement costs and add insurance that covers the unlikely stuff. If it happens you'll be glad you did. Some examples of the types of insurance you should have include: flood insurance, earthquake insurance, and umbrella coverage on top of your limits (to insure you for personal and medical liability if someone falls down your front stairs and you get to become the long-term disability insurer by default).

I favor high limits and as high a deductible as you can be comfortable with. The best use of insurance is not to reimburse you for everything that might go wrong — just the big things that you can't handle on your own. So, can you handle a $1,500 or even a $3,000 surprise, using your emergency fund? If so, set your deductible that high and you'll be saving enough in a few years to cover the deductible amount in lower premiums alone. After that, you get to keep it all.

- **Car insurance:** Insuring yourself against being sued for running someone over is actually more important than it is to have your car replaced. Many states require certain levels of insurance to drive. Your insurance rep will be able to help you choose a policy that meets your needs.

For much more information on insurance policies, check out *Insurance For Dummies* by Jack Hungelmann (Wiley).

Saving for emergencies

As an ultimate goal, you should have between 6 and 12 months of expenses in an emergency account for the unforeseen emergency. A number that big can seem impossible. But, realize this: You're aiming to cover *expenses,* not income. You don't have to replace that annual salary, but rather the expenses you'd have during say a lengthy period when you might not be working. You now know what your expenses are — thanks to your budget — so the number is at least a real one and not just some huge, unknown amount.

To start, shoot for just six months — or even *one* month. All you need to do is start building today. Even if you only have one week of expenses saved, that can be a world of difference from having none. Two weeks is divine. And a month — you're ahead of most people. So relax, get started, start small, and keep at it.

Do your emergency saving while you're saving for other things. But if you're saving for three things at once, won't it take three times as long? Not so! Because if you're saving for three things at once and at least two of them are things that have a personal payoff to you — like that vacation — you're more likely to stick with it. And that will get you there much faster. When you have that cash socked away for an emergency, turn those incoming dollars toward achieving one of your other planned goals.

I mention this strategy earlier but it bears repeating: Automate your savings plan. Arrange to automatically deposit part of your pay into different savings or checking or investment accounts. If you never see the money in your check, you won't miss it. As you get those raises and promotions or bonuses, put at least half into your savings account. Tax refunds get the same treatment. Make it easy and automatic, and your savings will grow before your eyes.

Step 4: Using credit and loans to your benefit

Yes, there's even a place in your budget for credit and loans. *Remember:* Credit is a tool to be used. As long as the tool fits the job, no problem. In fact, credit can make things easier. It can allow you to defer a payment to a more convenient time or to make a payment in such a way that it benefits you more than paying cash.

What I'm talking about here is consumer credit. There are a number of different incarnations of consumer credit, and you can use each type to your advantage:

✔ **Non-installment credit:** This is the type of credit I grew up with. My dad had a charge account at the local gas station. I gassed up the family car, and he stopped by the station and paid the bill at the end of the month. With non-installment credit, you pay in full each month and don't carry a balance. This type of credit is used in some retail stores, country clubs, and the like. It is credit in its simplest form, available as a convenience to you — and a benefit to the merchant: You're not deterred from spending simply because you don't have the cash at the moment. You get what you want, the merchant makes money, and everybody's happy — which is the essence of using credit properly.

You can use this type of credit in your budget to handle expenses for local services like trash removal, gardening or lawn care. The benefit here is that you get the service first and, if it's faulty, you're more likely to get it fixed — and get your money's worth — if you haven't handed over the dough already.

✔ **Installment, closed-end credit:** Frequently used by department or furniture stores, in this type of credit, an amount equal to the amount of a specific purchase is lent to you.

Here's an example of how you can use this type of credit: I bought a new bedroom set at a local furniture store, and they offered me installment credit allowing me 18 months to pay for the furniture in full. Normally, there is interest associated with this type of loan, but the Cardi boys were having a special sale — no payments for six months, and no interest for the next year. A sweet deal from my perspective, and a sweet sale from theirs.

✔ **Revolving, open-end credit:** This is how most credit cards work. With your card, you're granted an amount of credit — with a limit, say, of $5,000 — to be used as you want. You can choose how much of the limit you use at any point in time. As you use the card, you must make periodic payments, subject to a minimum payment required. As you repay the credit line, you in essence recharge the line. You can pay off the entire amount, which will restore the credit line to its original and full size or just make a smaller payment — or even make only a minimum payment. You get to decide.

You can use this type of credit in your budget to help offset the cost of airline tickets. One of my credit cards pays me cash back, which I put into my emergency fund.

Credit cards are the most misused form of consumer credit. Credit cards are tools designed to be used for convenience, short-term borrowing, and within their limits. When you do otherwise, they get very expensive very fast. *Remember:* You're supposed to benefit from the use of credit — you aren't supposed to get hosed. Choose credit cards as a tool when they fit with the

Building your future into your budget

Depending on your stage of life, your primary budget needs vary. The basic tools remain the same, but the emphasis shifts. Your priorities are different in each stage:

✔ **In your first job:** Chances are you have big ideas and little money. At this stage, you want to establish habits such as developing a spending plan and beginning a small savings program. Successfully dealing with any student loans to keep current on payments or getting deferrals is important, too.

✔ **As a newlywed:** Your focus may be paying off the wedding, learning to communicate about money, establishing joint and separate credit and savings, setting up a household account, dual income/dual budget planning, and preparing for a family.

✔ **With a growing family:** Adjusting to a stay-at-home spouse, paying for your kids'

sports programs and braces, expanding living expenses, and saving for education and weddings are just some of the issues a family faces.

✔ **Going solo:** Whether you never marry or you go through a divorce, you're likely to confront situations such as living and saving on one income, taking care of children solo, and perhaps paying off divorce expenses and dealing with alimony and child support.

✔ **In an empty nest:** As the kids fly the coop, you're left to re-budget for a new lifestyle — which may include saving for retirement, exploring estate planning, considering Social Security and Medicare issues, and having some fun with your savings.

job. For example, I could have used my credit card to finance the bedroom set, but I would have paid 18 percent interest and I would have had to make payments right away. Clearly, the installment, closed-end type fit the job better.

Credit should only be used to enable you to spend money you already have or know you'll have soon.

Step 5: Planning for taxes

Books have been written on the subject of tax-planning. Big books. Don't you worry, though, I'm not going to get into tedious detail about deductions or schemes that will save you money or how you can defer taxes until the cows come home. I want to look at the issue as an important component of budget planning. What do taxes have to do with budgeting? A lot if you owe tax money, if you're counting on your tax refund to bail out your budget, or if you're considering bankruptcy.

Typically, your employer deducts or withholds income taxes from your paycheck based on the number of your deductions. The deductions reflect an *estimate* of what you'll owe — but most people end up either paying something more to the IRS on April 15 or getting a tax refund.

You may have income *not* subject to withholding, such as dividends, interest, income from side businesses, tips, stock gains, gambling winnings, money paid to you as an independent contractor, small-business income, forgiven debts, hobby income, rents, and gifts above a certain dollar level. Because you haven't paid out taxes from these streams of income, be sure that you prepare yourself for that inevitability.

As you do your planning, you can choose one of three approaches to what I very generally call tax-planning:

- ✔ Overpay
- ✔ Underpay
- ✔ Strive to pay just the right amount

You can probably already guess which strategy is the right one, but just in case, I cover them all in the following sections.

Overpaying your withholdings

Many people tell me they deliberately overpay their taxes as a budgeting strategy: "I don't want to owe any money" or "I use my refund to pay down my cards after holiday shopping."

The problem with overpaying is that, at a minimum, you're giving the government an interest-free loan of your money — money that you could be using to pay down debt, build up savings, or achieve any of a zillion good purposes.

If you've overpaid all year and an emergency comes along in November, you can't ask the government for an advance of your refund to cover it. But you could use that money if you had it in a savings account, or even in a cookie jar.

If you're consistently getting a refund check every spring, talk to a qualified tax preparer and go over your situation. You'll likely be able to find a way to cover your taxes (and not owe something on April 15), without overpaying along the way.

Underpaying your withholdings

If you don't have a plan for your spending and savings, you may convince yourself that underwithholding your taxes provides the equivalent of an interest-free loan from the IRS. You tell yourself you'll figure out the tax issue when it comes up, which is a really long time from now. Besides, you have pressing needs for the money, and they have to be taken care of immediately. The backup plan: If you owe money April 15, you can always pay it with your credit card, right?

If you underpay your withholdings and owe a big tax bill in April, you'll find that your credit cards will be absorbing more unplanned items than just taxes, and they might well be full already. A further caution about taxes of all kinds, is that under current bankruptcy rules, local, state, and federal taxes cannot be discharged in a bankruptcy, nor can credit-card debt incurred from paying your taxes.

Paying the right amount of withholdings

Adjusting your withholdings so they jibe with what you'll owe at the end of the year is not as not as difficult as it may first seem. I suggest that you at least consult with a tax preparer to get a good forecast of your tax commitments for the year. You may get an early budget bonus if you find you're over-withholding and can increase your deductions — which may allow you to fund some of those short-term goals you've been saving for.

Conversely, if there is some shortfall in your future, you're much better knowing about it in advance so you can do something before it shows up on your doorstep like a big, wet, shaggy dog that just rolled in some very smelly stuff. Got the picture?

Considering help: Tax preparer or software program?

If you're using tax-preparation software for the first time, buy it well before you need it. You'll get some stress-free time to get used to the software, and you can anticipate what information you must save to complete the process. First-time users can also get a valuable lesson if they enter last year's return into the program (if the software allows). This way, you can see if you forgot anything, familiarize yourself with it, and anticipate your documentation needs for the coming tax season.

Until you get used to the software, having an experienced tax preparer talk things through with you is a worthwhile expense. The tax preparer may also have some comments on pluses and minuses of the various software packages you may want to use.

Remember: Whether you use tax-preparation software or a tax preparer, *you* are the only one ultimately responsible for the tax return you submit.

The right amount is not a precise number. Until all the figures are in, there is no way to say what your tax bill is going to be. However, I've found that allowing a range or spread will usually get you close enough so you have no big surprises. I like to shoot for a safeguard of $600 in excess of what you anticipate owing. This cushion will not make a big difference to your budget, and as long as your income is relatively stable and your deductions from last year haven't changed a lot, you should be in the ballpark.

Step 6: Planning for retirement

Retirement isn't what it used to be. If you expect me to wax eloquent about how good my father had it with three pensions, forget it. When I said it isn't what it used to be, I mean it is so much longer, better, healthier, and just plain different. No gold watch, no rocking chair — just the good stuff that you always wanted to do.

Retirement is a topic that warrants a book of its own. From the budgeting and credit perspective, I suggest that you find either a Certified Financial Planner (CFP), Chartered Financial Consultant (ChFC), or if you're in the heavy-duty-investment end of things a Chartered Financial Analyst (CFA) to help you set up a plan that will meet your retirement goals. Armed with a workable budget and goals, you'll be light-years ahead of most people who walk through a planner's door looking for assistance. If you tend to be more of a do-it-yourself person, you can find good resources at both Charles Schwab (www.schwab.com) and Fidelity (www.fidelity.com) on this topic.

Whichever approach you take, you'll need to make some calculations to help you determine how much you're going to have to start putting away to achieve your goals. Here are some simple tips for the budgeter looking down that long (or short) road:

- ✔ **Figure your life expectancy.** Chances are it's longer than that of your parents. Just don't guess too short. The Centers for Disease Control (CDC) estimate that 75 is the life expectancy for men and 80 for women. Those of you, like me, who weren't born yesterday and who are still in reasonably good health are looking at more than that. You can check out the good news at www.cdc.gov/nchs/fastats/lifexpec.htm.

- ✔ **Determine when you want to retire.** The difference between the age at which you want to retire and the age at which you think you might check out is what you have to budget for.

- ✔ **Consider inflation.** If you know you won't want to live on less than $40,000 a year in retirement, realize that you have to increase that number for the future because of inflation — the further out your retirement, the more you need to increase. A number of good Web sites or financial planning programs adjust for inflation and investment experience (how much your investments will earn). Check out "Using Cool Budgeting Tools," later in this chapter, for some suggestions.

✔ **Don't underestimate medical expenses.** The good news is that you're likely to live longer than earlier generations. The not-so-good news is that you'll likely require more medical assistance to live a quality life in your later years. Because medical costs have risen and show no signs of abating, getting your medical expenses and insurance coverages budgeted in your retirement planning is very important.

✔ **Remember that time may be money.** If you end up with too little money and too much retirement, there are three courses of action available: Save more, save longer, or cut the retirement budget. You can increase your current savings by earning more or spending less. You could just keep pushing out the retirement date until the surplus you've accumulated or an increased retirement benefit makes your numbers work. Or you could do with less later. The choice is up to you.

Using Cool Budgeting Tools

What with the advent of the computer, the world of home budgeting can be as slick an operation as a NASA command center. From high-tech pocket calculators to sophisticated software packages, tools to help you develop a spending plan — and stick to it — fill the shelves of most office-supply outlets.

The miracle of compound interest: Investing for the future

One of the key components of successfully budgeting for your future is to have your limited money in savings contribute as much as possible to your future needs, taking some of the pressure off you to earn everything, forever. We've all seen the charts that loudly proclaim that if you had only saved X-amount a year from the time you were 10 years old until you retired, you'd have a zillion dollars.

Well, behind all the hype and improbability of 10-year-olds investing their birthday money from Aunt Sophie in municipal bonds is a grain of truth. Investing is important. However, you have the right to feel comfortable with the process. So, if you haven't started, don't beat yourself up. Check out some of the resources in this chapter and start at your own speed, and with your own goals in mind.

Whether you do it on your own or with a paid professional doesn't matter. The compounding of interest and tax advantages available today from some types of investments make investing too great an opportunity to miss.

But not all budgeting tools have to be electronic to be cool or even useful. If you want a less technological approach to budgeting, here are some suggested tools to add to your budgeting kit:

- ✔ **Erasable board:** To write down your plan and maybe even chart how you money will be spent.

- ✔ **Pencil:** Lead, not ink, is the tool to use when developing a plan that you'll be changing throughput the process.

- ✔ **Sticky notes:** An easy way to supplement your planning ideas. They can be moved around to different places on a planning board or form as you make changes.

- ✔ **Envelopes:** They're handy for keeping dollars to be spent or receipts for what was spent, by category. You may consider one envelope for tax-deductible receipts, for example. Filing by expense categories or pay periods can be helpful, and envelopes can help you do that.

- ✔ **Accordion files:** They work similarly to envelopes, but they're more portable — and you'll be less likely to misplace them than you might an envelope.

Web-based financial calculators

Web-based financial calculators help you figure out where you stand and what it will take to get to where you want to be. They're a great tool to help manage your money, because they give you the information you need to make informed choices about what a course of action or purchase will actually cost you and for how long.

There are calculators to help you figure out your mortgage payments at different interest rates, calculators to tell you the true cost of a loan and its impact on your budget, even calculators that will tell how much you'll need to budget for how long to get those credit cards paid off.

Among the best in this class are the seemingly endless variety of calculators found at CCH, the tax and business information people who have published big books that accountants have used for years. You can find them at www.finance.cch.com. Their Financial Planning Tool Kit is at www.finance.cch.com/tools/calcs.asp.

For determining what effect differing credit scores will have on loan interest rates and total costs to you, go to the source: www.myfico.com.

General calculators for many financial functions are available at the home of the Debt Advisor, yours truly, at the financial megasite, Bankrate.com (www.bankrate.com).

Budgeting Web sites

You can find some easy-to-use, basic budgeting advice and tools at Consumer Credit Counseling Service of Southern New England's Web site at www.credit counseling.org/HelpfulResources/FinancialTools.asp.

The National Consumer Law Center site (www.consumerlaw.org) has a large amount of consumer-oriented material that you may find helpful in sifting through the competing claims of those who want to help you deal with financial issues.

A very good site for military personnel is found at the Military Network at www.emilitary.org. They have good tips and online budgeting tools that are tailored to service personnel — just look under the Pay and Budgeting tab.

Budget-counseling information sources

There is no shortage of places you can go to get support in putting together a budget that will work for you. In fact, one of the problems is sifting through those who are trying to sell you something or scam you. Here are two great places to start:

- ✔ **National Foundation for Credit Counseling (www.debtadvice.org):** They have good advice and referrals along with a good, high-level budgeting calculator that plots your spending based on income against national averages to let you know if you're in the ballpark of your peers. Their member-agency network offers budgeting assistance as well as debt-management solutions.

- ✔ **Association of Independent Consumer Credit Counseling Agencies (www.aiccca.org):** They have a listing of member agencies, many of which can help you with budgeting issues, but all of which have debt-management products.

Keeping records the fun way

Okay, you caught me. I lied. Here I was trying to show you some cool tools (incidentally, I have *never* been referred to as *cool* by anyone) and now I try to slip in record-keeping. Cool or not, record-keeping is important: You'll have a very difficult time knowing what to estimate for expenses or income if you don't keep some records. And keep them where you can find them. I have records — I just can't always find them.

You know you're not doing as good a job as you should in record-keeping if:

✔ You can't find your last three years of income-tax returns.

✔ You don't know where your original Social Security card is.

✔ You don't remember where or when you last saw your auto/homeowner's/umbrella insurance policy.

✔ You haven't made photocopies of all your credit cards, front and back, and the emergency numbers.

✔ You don't have a notebook or other single source of information to help your loved ones find all your bank accounts/insurance policies/investment accounts when you die.

✔ You couldn't tell your insurance agent, after you found the lost policy, what was in your house before it burned to the ground.

✔ You don't even remember who your insurance agent is.

Record-keeping may be one of duller ways to spend a rainy Saturday, but it really pays big dividends when you need quick access to important financial information. I'm pleased to be able to say that I can find the receipt for any purchase — no matter how small — for the last year and bigger ones for much longer. I may not be cool, but I *am* organized. Having a good system that works for you for keeping records such as policies, receipts, and such can save time, money, and frustration.

How can you accomplish this feat? I'll tell you: Any way you want. No, I'm not taking the easy way out. A number of perfectly good record-keeping methods and products are available, so pick one you like — or choose parts of various ones and put them together. I have a few guidelines to offer, of course:

✔ Keep all your stuff in the same place or general area, such as a desk, cabinet, or closet.

✔ Have some way of breaking down the information by subject: bank statements separate from investment statements, credit-card statements, and so on.

✔ If you have a spouse or partner, decide who is responsible for keeping records. It's okay if you each want to do your own. But someone has to assume responsibility — or it will be left to the budget elves, who aren't too reliable.

✔ Try to establish a routine to update things — once a week, once a month . . . it doesn't matter as long as you have a set schedule.

✔ Get a safe-deposit box for your irreplaceable papers. They don't cost a lot of money and the expense is tax-deductible if you itemize your deductions on your tax return. A fireproof safe may do just fine. Include documents such as car/motorcycle titles; marriage, divorce, and birth certificates; wills; savings bonds; and so on.

✔ Once a year or so, clear out old or outdated information like old policies or tax returns more than seven years old. Keep anything that relates to an item with an extended life (like a TV), including the receipt, warranty, and owner's manual.

Chapter 12

Applying Credit Strategies to Anything Life Throws Your Way

*Y*ou've heard it said, "Life is what happens while you're making plans." Well, here's my new twist on that old adage: Making plans will help your credit survive what happens to your life. Your credit report typically reflects what's going on in your life: If your personal life takes a dive due to divorce, you may see a drop in your credit score as well. If you lose your job, you may soon discover that your access to credit has been reduced.

Unemployment, marriage, divorce, illness, death of a loved one — you've heard time and again that all these significant life events can have a major impact on your emotions, stress levels, and health. Well, they affect your credit status, too.

The life situations themselves don't hurt or help your credit report directly — you don't lose points simply because you lose your job. No one's going to pull your credit report and stamp it "DIVORCED." You don't get placed in a lesser category if you become widowed. The events themselves have no impact on your report and score — but indirectly, they can pack a punch.

Here's how: All these situations, whether of your choosing (marriage) or something beyond your control (illness or death), have a financial impact on your life. For example, if you're unemployed for six months, you'll have a severely reduced income, which may cause you to miss or be late with some payments and max out your credit card. And these events *will* show up on your credit report.

In this chapter, I present some of life's variety and offer strategies to help you survive and thrive in these credit-challenging situations, making sure that you do your best to shelter your credit status from the financial curveballs that life throws your way.

For Better or for Worse: Building Good Credit as a Couple

Congratulations! As half of a married couple, you now have two sets of credit reports and credit scores to keep track of. Keeping your credit at its best can be tricky enough when you're only making financial decisions for yourself. Add another person to the mix, and the process becomes more challenging. On the other hand, marriage can also pose opportunities for at least one of the partners to improve his or her credit standing. In the following sections, I lay all the cards on the table.

Talking about credit compatibility

When my wife and I go out to dinner, she always looks at the dessert menu first. In the beginning of our courtship, this behavior baffled me. As a typical linear-thinking man, I approached my meal choices in the order I planned to consume them — starter, salad, entrée. In fact, I typically wouldn't even think about dessert until I was sopping up the last of the marinara sauce from my plate.

Finally, I got up the nerve to ask her about this display of, in my view, backward behavior. She explained that dessert, for her, was the most important part of the meal and she wanted to plan ahead to accommodate for her priority. If she saw tiramisu (her favorite) on the menu, she'd go for a light entrée or salad and skip the bread. If the dessert choices were fairly pedestrian, she'd order a heartier main course and perhaps settle for some tea.

I share this slice of our domestic life to illustrate two points:

- ✔ My wife's logic, as always, is unassailable and, what's more, her approach to dining out is a superb metaphor for household budgeting — one that has served our own relationship well. (I get to that later.)

- ✔ Understanding and communicating with each other is a critical component not just when it comes to ordering dinner, but in all aspects of married life — especially when it comes to financial issues.

Exploring all money issues

I advise all engaged couples to spend at least as much time discussing and exploring financial compatibilities, strategies, approaches, and goals as they do in choosing a honeymoon spot. Believe me, if you don't focus on a financial foundation, soon after the honeymoon is over, the honeymoon will *really* be over!

If you're soon to be married (or even if you're already married and haven't yet talked money), you need to openly discuss a range of money issues, including your current financial status. Yes, I know money can't buy love — but if you two are pooling your resources, you should know whether you're diving into a wading tub or an Olympic-size pool.

Here's a list of ten things you need to do with your betrothed before the wedding day:

- ✔ **Show each other your credit reports and credit scores.**

- ✔ **Discuss your current annual income or salary and your income hopes for the future.**

- ✔ **Find out whether you're a saver or a spender, and find out the same about your spouse.**

- ✔ **Talk about any of your debts and how you plan to handle them.** Will you each pay your own debts? Will you pool them together and split them 50-50? Or will the big earner pay more?

- ✔ **Tell each other about any bankruptcies or other major financial events in your past.** In some second marriages, a bankruptcy will be around longer than the kids, and you wouldn't forget to talk about *them*.

- ✔ **Discuss your spending and budgeting habits (whether you're frugal, indulgent, and so on).**

- ✔ **Talk about whether you've cosigned any loans.**

- ✔ **Discuss your personal budgeting approaches.** Will you count every penny, or go for estimates instead?

- ✔ **Discuss your financial goals for the next five years.**

- ✔ **Talk about your long-term financial goals and where you think the money may come from.** Will you retire at 50? Sail around the world? Give all your worldly possessions to charity?

I strongly advise that you each get copies of your credit report. These days, many newly dating couples request HIV blood tests and background checks. Credit is a critical relationship factor, too. You may have bared your heart and soul to your sweetie, but until you bare your credit, the job's not done.

If you've already gotten married, and you haven't yet discussed these issues, it's both never too late and later than you think.

Customizing a budget for two

I strongly recommend that you and your partner sit down and make out a budget for your new household. Budgeting is among the most important first steps you can take together to strengthen your marriage and reduce the risk of divorce because of financial stress and spending incompatibility.

Chapter 11 of this book includes suggestions on how to budget; you'll find a number of resources on the CD that will get you going, too.

As my wife would advise, when working your budget, always start with dessert — that would be the fun part: your future goals. What could be more fun than describing all the things you're going to do and the adventures you'll share together over the years? For example, my wife and I plan an extended road trip looking for the perfect piece of blueberry pie.

Explore together and agree on what you want to save for — a family, a house, early retirement. This discussion whets your appetite for all the spending steps you'll want to establish in order to get there. If you find that you just aren't able to get the numbers to add up, you can always refer back to Chapter 3 for a second helping of advice or consider a credit counselor. The good ones are not just for credit, debts, or problems — they can help you before disaster strikes.

Over the years, I've adjusted to my wife's ordering style in restaurants. I'm no longer a bemused bystander but often an active participant. If, for example, she's saving up for that decadent chocolate cheesecake but is tempted by the filling featured entrée, I'll offer to order the fat main course and give her a few bites, and she'll settle for a salad. But, of course, she has to share her dessert!

It's in this way — through a commitment to communication, establishing common goals, and working together for mutual benefit — that couples can achieve financial bliss. A perfect example of having your cake and eating it, too.

Considering the pros and cons of joint accounts

If your spouse has a less-than-glowing credit history, it will affect *you* as soon as you apply for credit together and open joint accounts, because both your credit histories will be reviewed. You each keep your own original histories but in addition, your new joint accounts will appear on both credit reports. So if you're concerned that your spouse may not be as diligent as you are in paying bills on time, paying the bills yourself is a good idea.

Many newlyweds decide to merge their financial accounts because consolidated accounts often make for easier record-keeping and enhance that feeling of "togetherness." But beware: Both of you are responsible for all debt incurred in any joint credit accounts. Regardless of which one of you takes the credit card out for a joy ride, if you miss a payment on a joint account, that missed payment will negatively affect both of your credit records. Also, if you miss a payment on an individual account, that missed payment may affect your ability to open joint accounts, because both credit histories will be considered.

In those states with community-property laws, you may be responsible for your spouse's debts even if you aren't on the account. Currently nine states fall into this category: Arizona, California, Idaho, Louisiana, Nevada, New Mexico, Texas, Washington, and Wisconsin.

Even if you decide to consolidate your accounts with your spouse, always keep at least one credit account in your own name as a safeguard in the event of an emergency. Keeping an individual account can also be a good thing in the event of divorce or untimely death of a spouse — having your own account can help you reestablish an individual credit history.

Keeping separate accounts

One alternative for those with a credit-challenged spouse, or for those cautious couples who want to take the credit-sharing slowly, is to keep separate accounts and allow one another to be authorized users on your accounts. Both of you can charge on the account, both of you get the credit history reported on your credit reports, but only one of you pays and is responsible for the bill.

Although this strategy may safeguard your credit score from a late payment, it will also expose you to the *potential* of at least one bigger-than-expected bill (if your spouse is a dangerous shop-a-holic, this setup won't protect you from his or her spending). But if you can trust your spouse not to go crazy with the credit card, this method allows your spouse to build additional credit history, while you keep responsibility and overall control for the account in your hands. (And, of course, if your spouse gets out of control with the credit card, you can always remove him or her from the account.)

Separate accounts (for those not in community-property states) make sense to some people. Especially those who come together later in life with substantial assets of their own. As long as you both agree, this sort of financial independence can keep you looking attractive to your sweetie long after your personal charms have become less charming. It can help each of you to feel that youthful independence and financial vigor that only money of your own can provide.

When money is the cause of conflict

The moose on the table. The elephant in the room. These are euphemisms I've heard to describe those huge, looming issues that couples or families pretend don't exist. But ignoring credit and money conflicts is done at great peril to a marriage. As in the case of the elephant, you can pretend it's not there — but it will still wreck your home.

Too often, couples convinced they're compatible on all fronts discover that they're polar opposites when it comes to spending, borrowing, and saving. Couples who thought they were in perfect — though unspoken or assumed — agreement on many fronts find out after the nuptials that they're opposites financially.

Of course, if you talk about your finances, you shouldn't run into credit conflicts — certainly not any that destroy your marriage. But money, as I point out earlier, seems to be a taboo topic, even among married couples. It's not until that bounced check, late-payment notice, or behemoth credit-card balance that money conflicts are discovered — and by then, the discussion may not be pretty.

Lack of careful and constant communication about money can lead to irreconcilable differences that result in divorce. When divorce is on the horizon, I think you can see how the fighting can escalate. Here are some of the pitfalls I hope you can avoid:

✔ **Not being open with each other about how you see and value savings, money, and credit:** *Remember:* Silence is your enemy.

✔ **Pooling all your funds, earnings, and credit:** Keeping some credit in your own name is important. The same goes for money.

✔ **Surprising your partner with a big expenditure (a car, boat, home theater, designer shoes, large donation to the cat-rescue fund):** Spending joint money without consulting your spouse is a big no-no. I recommend that any new expenses of more than 10 percent of your paycheck — or say $500 — be discussed in advance. You'll both be looking at any household purchases for a long time, so before you buy that great moose head for over the bed, talk about it.

✔ **Criticizing your partner's money style in front of others:** No one wants to be ridiculed — even in good humor — in front of others. If you're uncomfortable with your mate's spending behavior, talk about it when the two of you are alone.

✔ **Failing to set mutual goals:** Discuss them and agree on a plan for achieving them.

✔ **Letting kids set the rules:** If you have kids, they'll learn how to play one of you against the other to get what they want. This time-tested kid strategy can lead to discipline issues and fights between mom and dad. If you have a blended household (kids from different marriages), establishing the rules and standing together as a united front is especially important.

Protecting Your Finances in a Divorce

Marriage has its challenges, and, too often, financial issues are the trigger that can set off a divorce. If your financial and credit life was challenging as a married couple sharing a common future, in divorce it will become much more complicated. Plus, some of your expenses may be even greater as you separate into two households (you'll have two mortgage or rent payments every month, for example). Toss in one of the most emotionally stressful life experiences, and it's easy to anticipate what may be happen to your credit during a divorce.

The financial fallout from divorce may include difficulties in opening new accounts and obtaining new loans in your name. But you can take steps to protect and, if need be, restore your good credit.

Given that half of marriages end in a divorce, doing some "what-if" planning is a good idea, even if you're absolutely positive that you're living with your soul mate for all eternity.

Taking action if a split is a possibility

If you suspect that divorce may be a possibility in your future, I suggest the following:

- ✔ **Keep good credit in your own name.** One or two accounts chosen from a few different types — such as revolving (credit card), installment (car loan), and retail (department-store card) — should be sufficient. Be sure you handle the accounts wisely.

- ✔ **Build your own credit while you're married.** Remember that your credit score is made up of five main components: paying on time, the amount and type of your debt, the length of time you've held credit, the variety of accounts you have, and the number and type of new accounts you have.

- ✔ **Open your own bank account with checking and savings features.**

- ✔ **Get overdraft protection on your checking account.** This benefits you in two ways: by making sure checks don't bounce and by exhibiting responsible use of another type of credit.

- ✔ **Keep track of your joint credit by checking your credit report frequently or by enrolling in a credit monitoring service.** This may provide an early warning that your partner is having some issues. At a minimum, check one of your three credit reports every four months.

These strategies are good to follow even if you're sure you're married 'til death do you part.

Preparing for divorce

If the possibility of divorce becomes a reality, you'll want to ratchet up your credit-protection action. At this point, separating your financial selves to your best ability is important. Here's how:

- ✔ **After informing your other half that you're doing so, send a letter (jointly, if possible) to each joint creditor asking that the account be closed to any new activity.**

- ✔ **Attempt to come to an agreement about how accounts will be paid and who will be responsible for making the payments.** If you can't reach agreement, make the minimum payments yourself rather than let your credit deteriorate. You can always recoup the money in a reconciliation or divorce settlement — just keep track of what you're paying for.

> ✔ If possible, transfer the balances on closed joint accounts to individual accounts.
>
> ✔ Contact the three major reporting agencies and ask them to record your address and other contact information separately.

Even if your prospective ex is uncooperative, keep paying all bills on remaining joint accounts on time. Don't listen to uninformed but well-meaning friends and relatives who may tell you to ignore making payments or to run up debts to spite your ex. During the divorce process and as long as you still have joint accounts, be sure that at least the minimum payments are made, on time. Missed payments will stay on your credit profile for seven years, making it hard or more costly to obtain new credit in your own name.

If you change your name, be sure to write to all your creditors and the three bureaus to let them know. This will help keep your credit history from errors based on name mix-ups.

Establish credit independently as soon as possible. Start small and build up gradually if you have to. If your credit is damaged already, start with a credit card that has a small credit limit, perhaps from a local department store, gas station, or credit union. After paying your bills on time for six months or so, apply for another card and continue paying bills consistently. Remember that you can dilute negative credit information by adding positive experience to your history.

Lastly, check your credit more frequently than normal. You might consider subscribing to a credit monitoring service offered by the credit bureaus in order to be notified immediately of key changes in your credit report, such as late payments or new accounts being added.

Considering joint credit history: It may outlast your marriage

From the time you open your first joint account, you and your mate are linking your credit futures together. Your credit history and credit score will now be influenced by the behavior of your spouse. A blemish on your spouse's part is a blemish on yours, too.

How long will you have to suffer from your ex's joint-account misdeeds? Conventional wisdom says seven years. But what if I told you it could be longer? Maybe *much* longer. Just look at the numbers: Credit histories are reported for seven years in most cases. Your ex's credit may be part of your credit report for seven years from whichever event happened last:

- Seven years from when your honey first forgot to pay the credit card

- Seven years from when you got that notice saying your ex was 60 days late

- Seven years from the date your ex's loan charged off after going six months past due

- If, however, after the six months of charging off, the bill goes to court and, if, after another six months of insincere attention on your ex's part, the creditor goes for a wage garnishment, which precipitates a bankruptcy filing, the original account is reported for seven years, as is the public record of the court action and the bankruptcy overlaying that for up to ten.

It can get even worse in certain situations, but I think the point is made. 'Til debt do you part — but your debts may be with you for a long, long time after you go your separate ways.

Getting new credit in your own name

The first step in successfully getting credit in your own name is to find out where your credit stands. Begin by obtaining your credit report and your FICO score from myFICO.com.

The average credit score is somewhere in the 680 to 700 range. If you're at 680 or above, apply for the following in your own name:

- Checking account

- Savings account

- Small installment loan (use the savings account for collateral, if you must)

- Retail-store credit card

- Visa or MasterCard issued by a major bank

- Library card (because it'll save you money on books and videos)

This diversity of credit will help you respond to most financial situations that may arise and help build your credit score with on-time payments.

If your score is below 680, your journey toward establishing credit in your own name may be a bit slower. (If you have a sympathetic parent with decent credit, you may be able to move things along faster by having your parent cosign for you.) Reestablish credit on your own, if at all possible — you'll feel better and so will your parents. Begin with the following:

✔ Checking account

✔ Savings account

✔ Visa or MasterCard issued by a major bank (if you qualify)

✔ Secured credit card (if you don't qualify for a credit card). Secured cards give you a line of credit based on a savings deposit to secure the credit line. These show up on your credit report just like an unsecured card — no one but you and the issuing bank will know!

✔ Retail-store credit card (you're likely to qualify if you qualified for the bank credit card)

✔ Library card

If you apply for a credit card from your bank and you aren't sure whether you'll qualify, bring your credit report and have them look at it rather than have them pull one themselves. Why? If they decline you, a credit report inquiry will not show up on your credit report and lower your credit score unnecessarily (see Chapter 5 for more information).

Protecting your credit in a divorce decree

When the judge rules, be sure that all joint debts are clearly and specifically assigned and that both you and your ex understand that these debts must be paid on time. Close all remaining joint accounts by the date that divorce is granted. In the case of joint real estate that will eventually be disposed of, the party living in the property has the most interest in making sure that the payments are made and should ask the judge to rule that way, even if the money to make the payment has to come from the other party.

A divorce decree does not end either party's responsibility for joint debts incurred while married. This generally includes individual debts in community-property states. After all, you both promised the lender that you'd repay the loan. The fact that the judge says that only one of you has to make the payment from now on does not change your contract with your lender. Each person is fully responsible for the entire balance of joint accounts, from credit cards and car loans to home mortgages.

A default on a joint account by your ex will show up on your credit report. If your ex doesn't pay at all, you'll probably be subject to collection activity and have to pay, or you may end up in a different court. If this seems unfair to you, the rationale is that a creditor shouldn't be made to suffer (poor baby) because your marriage failed.

Overcoming your ex's defaults on your joint accounts

Given the stress associated with divorce, it is almost understandable that your ex may miss a payment or two. I said *almost*. Although you might be understanding of such a mishap, keeping your credit record as clean as possible is critical, in order to rebuild a positive credit history as a single person.

Because you want to address any missed payments as soon as possible, you need to stay up-to-the-minute on payment status. You may find out about a delinquency in a number of ways: a letter, a phone call, a credit-monitoring service, and so on. As soon as you know that a payment was not made, take action.

If your relationship allows, contact your ex to find out if the bill has been paid. If trust is a concern or if your relationship precludes such direct communication, let the lawyers handle it. Instruct your attorney to notify your ex's attorney that the court order has been violated, and ask for response. If the situation isn't resolved, you can always go back to court and have the ex reordered to pay as agreed or face the not-so-pleasant legal consequences.

Returning to court is a lengthy and expensive course of action, so you may consider making the payments yourself until the issue is resolved. Making the payments will cost you money, but perhaps less than bad credit (not to mention attorney fees) will cost you.

By now you've probably figure out two things: Life isn't fair, and paying a bill yourself may be a lot easier than having to deal with your ex.

Controlling the damages

Credit damage from divorce or its aftermath is not unusual, but you can take steps to lessen the negative impact to your credit record and score:

- ✔ **Pay your bills on time.** Paying on time will add positive credit history on top of any negative history. Over time, your score will count a large number of new and positive reports with more weight than older negatives. As your credit report ages, older items count for less, so make the most of new credit going forward.

- ✔ **Add a 100-word statement to your credit report.** You can explain mitigating circumstances that a prospective lender or employer might not know about in considering your application.

Be careful not to leave this statement on your report longer than you need to, because it may draw attention to a past problem that is no longer a factor in your credit score.

✔ **Review your credit report frequently.** Getting copies of your credit reports may be a good investment in controlling unexpected negatives, especially if your ex is still paying off joint or community-property debts. You can pay for monitoring services that alert you to any negative credit-reporting entries as soon as they occur, allowing you to take action to reduce your credit damage.

Keeping Credit under Control While Unemployed

On the predictability scale, finding yourself out of work, laid off, downsized, or just plain unemployed is more likely to happen than divorce. Although you don't expect to work for the same company for your entire career, you probably expect to make a job change of your own volition and for good reasons (your got a new job at higher pay, for example).

But considering the uncertain and volatile world we live in, the likelihood is that your *employer* will make the decision to say farewell at least once in your career. I can tell you from experience that the event will arrive at the least advantageous time possible. In the following sections, I help you through this almost inevitable fact of modern-day life.

Employment information is not regularly reported as part of your credit report. The bureaus are not keeping track of where you work or what you earn. As part of the loan process, a creditor may ask where you work, and that information may be reported on new loans, lines of credit, and credit cards. But unlike payment history, for example, your employment being included on your credit report happens infrequently. So unemployment won't show up on your record unless you fail to make your payments on time, go over your credit limits, or do something silly, like opening a lot of credit lines just in case you need them.

Preparing your credit for unemployment

Because your credit-report experience tends to follow your personal financial experience, you can do a few things in advance that will protect your credit in case of unemployment.

First and foremost, if you don't have an emergency savings account, start one. Fund it periodically so it grows to somewhere between six months to a year of living expenses (not income — your expenses are supposed to be less than your income). This is a good number to work toward, because six months to a year is how long you're likely to be unemployed if you're caught by surprise.

Having more than one or two credit cards or lines of credit is also useful. You don't want to draw undue credit-report attention to yourself if you're unemployed. So you want to make sure you continue to pay your bills on time, keep your credit-card balances to less than $1,000 if possible, and so on. (See Chapter 2 for more on what you can do to look "normal" and not draw attention to yourself.)

Using credit during unemployment

If you're already unemployed, don't beat yourself up. You're in good company. It happens to most of us, and it often happens more than once. Now that the unwanted event has arrived, if you've established savings, regardless of the amount, and you have some available credit lines, you have two tools that will be a big help to you to get through this time without damaging your credit. Using a combination of credit and cash you can put together a new plan that includes finding that new job and a budget/spending plan that works while you do so.

Prospective employers often pull a credit report as part of the employment process, so to maximize your chances of getting a job, you want the best credit you can realistically have.

Stay away from cash advances! The cost to spend money this way is much greater than using the credit card to pay for it. Even if it seems silly, using the card to buy a $10 item is better for you than using a $10 cash advance. Cash advances come with an extra fee, often have a higher interest rate, and often have a maximum lower than your credit limit.

Looking at credit differently

Now that you've shifted from spending to *conserving* your resources, your credit-use priorities have shifted. You need to recognize this up front by looking at credit differently. Originally, you used credit to spend your income in a different way from carrying around your paycheck in your pocket. You also used it for larger purchases that you needed some time to pay off.

When you're unemployed, possibly for a very long time, you don't have those earnings coming in (you may have a severance package or unemployment benefits, but they're only temporary — and they may not last as long as your unemployment does). Now you can use credit for basic living and job-hunting expenses only. This is just about the opposite of what most people will tell you, but you'll do this only for a limited period of time and for a specific, worthy purpose. If it helps, think of it as borrowing money to invest in a sure-fire investment: yourself and your future.

Preserve your cash for as long as possible by using credit first. This advice may be the opposite of what you've heard in the past. Conventional wisdom says to control expenses by paying cash for as much as possible. The opposite is now the case. Pay with credit for essentials as much as possible and save the cash. You'll keep your overall spending to essentials by closely following a budget (see the following section).

Refiguring the family budget

To keep your spending in line with your reduced resources, begin by sitting down with your family and discussing the situation and the need to temporarily reduce expenses. Don't be embarrassed in front of the kids. This situation is an important lesson in reality for them. And you can show them how adults face difficult issues and win.

On the CD, you'll find worksheets that are helpful when you're trying to put together a budget. Chapter 11 of this book is also devoted to the topic of budgets; if you've already created one, you'll need to revise it, trimming expenses wherever you can until you find a job. If you're starting from scratch with a budget, Chapter 11 is a good place to begin.

As you begin to figure your income into your spending plan, if your severance is being paid out over time or if you haven't yet received it, ask your employer or HR department to raise your deductions to the maximum allowed. The IRS wants a report of anyone with more than ten deductions. So, generally ask for ten (you don't want the IRS looking at you if you can avoid it). This strategy will result in more cash flowing through to you for the present, when you need it.

Yes, you may owe some taxes on this money in April (though your job-hunting expenses and reduced earnings for the year may offset that). You want to maximize today's income at the possible expense of tomorrow's demands.

Getting credit counseling

If you're overwhelmed and think you could benefit from some professional perspective or guidance, go to an accredited credit counselor. You can get more information on credit counselors and where to find them in Chapter 3.

Protecting your credit lines

The downside to using your lines of credit for your basic living expenses (a strategy I recommend) is that you *may* do some damage to your credit. Here are some tips for protecting your status while you leverage your available credit to help you get through this challenging time:

- **Keep balances at less than 50 percent of your available credit.** Spread your credit use over several accounts in order to keep your balance on each credit card at less than 50 percent. For example, rather than have a $2,000 balance on one card and a $0 balance on three cards, consider spreading the amount over four cards — with each balance at $500.

- **Make all payments on time.** Remember that 35 percent of your credit score has to do with whether you make payments on time.

Don't try to keep your same standard of fully-employed spending in place during this period of economic challenge. The more your balances grow, the more likely they'll attract the attention of someone looking at your credit report. You may need to use the credit, but not in such a way that you attract a crowd.

- **Pay your mortgage first.** Not all bills are created equal — and your mortgage is the most unequal of them all. If you can only afford to pay one bill, pay your mortgage. Partial payments don't work, and falling behind 90 days begins a very difficult-to-stop foreclosure process.

The 90-day period begins when the mortgage was originally due — it does not start from the end of the grace period. For example, if your payment was due on January 1, even though you had until January 15 to make the payment, count from January 1. You're considered 90 days late, then, on April 1 (not April 15). At the 90-day mark, you may well have to pay the entire three months of mortgage plus late fees in one shot. That can be thousands of dollars. Send in less, and they'll send it back. The bottom line: Always pay your mortgage in full and on time.

Do not contact your creditors unless you *know* you're going to default. If you just *think* you may miss a payment, it's none of their business — and they may whack your interest rate up to cover the additional risk you now represent in their eyes (even if you end up making the payment on time). If you're going to miss the current month's payment, telling them before it happens is important.

If you have any income, you'll want to ask for a *hardship program* (a special repayment arrangement that may be offered to a good customer in need of some extra help; they tend to last for no more than three to six months). Most companies have them, but the hardship has to be real and imminent and you have to ask for it.

If the hardship program is not sufficient to bridge the gap between what you can afford to pay and what they insist you pay, send a letter stating that you can't make any payments but intend to in the future as soon as you find employment. The letter might look like what you see in Figure 12-1. (You'll find this and other letters on the CD.)

Date

Creditor Name
Creditor Address
City, State ZIP

RE: Account #:
       Name on Account:

Dear Sir or Madam:

  I have been unemployed for *Insert Length of Time*. I
have exhausted my savings and unemployment benefits looking for work. For the present, I am
unable to pay the monthly amount required under
our agreement.

  Due to my desperate financial situation, I
cannot promise a date by when I will be able to
resume payments, although it is my intention to do
so. I can, however, promise to inform you immediately when my financial condition improves and I
am able to resume making normal payments.

  Thank you for your understanding and help.

Sincerely,

Your Name
Your Address
City, State ZIP
Your Phone

Figure 12-1:
Writing a
letter to a
creditor
when you're
unemployed
and can't
make
payments is
always a
good idea.

TIP

What to do when you run out of credit and options

If you aren't able to make any payments on maxed-out cards or credit lines and you still have no job on the way, something will have to give. There are only three sides to this triangle: income, expense, and credit. If credit is not an option, income and expenses are the only things you can alter.

Take out that budget you prepared when your unemployment started and consider some

extreme moves to cut expenses. Can you move to a smaller home? Can you move in with a friend? Can you sell things to raise some cash? On the income side, have you considered taking a job that will tide you over until something in your field opens up? The task here is to generate some income, not move a career forward.

Remember: Given time and perseverance, you *will* come out of this stronger than you went in.

Facing Student-Loan Default

These days, student loans are a lot like noses — everyone has one. Well, at least if you're in college or a recent grad, odds are you do. Studies show that about 50 percent of recent college graduates have student loans, with the average student carrying a loan debt of $10,000. The average cost of college is increasing at twice the rate of inflation, with public schools costing an average of $13,000 a year and private schools approximately $28,000 a year. Multiply times four — or, increasingly five — years, and the result is $65,000 to $140,000 of debt. Medical students routinely graduate with six-figure debt. If student loans are like noses, then these are the Cyrano de Bergeracs of student loans!

Student loans are critical to many people and their families as the preferred method for financing not only a college or technical-school education but a big part of the American dream.

Student loans are unlike most others in their generous terms, low eligibility standards, and flexibility. They also stand out as being among a select number of bulletproof debt obligations that are inviolate under the law. What this means is that neither bankruptcy nor the passage of time will release you from your obligations to pay off this debt.

Student loans are a powerful tool that has to be handled with care — often more care than the people who give them out use when they explain the ins and outs of these debt instruments to the borrower.

In this section, I help you deal with the aftermath of a student loan and its credit implications.

Preparing for payback: When student loans come due

Even though the price of a college education may seem high, the return on investment potential has always made it worthwhile. It is estimated that a college graduate will earn $1 million more than a high school graduate over the course of his career. And the figures go up for those with a graduate-school education.

If you're a typical student and you left school with $10,000 of debt, your payment will probably be between $75 and $100 a month, depending on interest and the length of the loan (which can run as long as 30 years). Medical students are looking at an average of between $500 and $1,000 a month.

You'll usually have a good idea of when you have to start paying back your student loans (generally shortly after leaving school) and at what rate well before you're out of school — the lenders are good about keeping you informed about this. So the first thing I advise is to come up with a plan for payback, even socking away some of that summer-job income to create a cushion in case your first real job doesn't bring in as much as you hope. Then adjust your living expenses to accommodate the loan payment.

Although student loans do offer generous terms, the danger here is that many young people just out of school don't have much experience budgeting and living on their own. When they find themselves in a real-live, "grown-up" job

---

Financial aid: The ultimate gamble?

Who would lend tens of thousands of dollars to a teenager with no income, no employment history, and no track record of handling money or credit? It happens every day in schools across the country. The idea is that these teens will mature into responsible, productive, self-supporting adults who will repay their debt and contribute to society with their new knowledge and skills.

The loan gamble really isn't as risky to the lender as it seems. Lenders expect that a parent will bail out an offspring if only to keep bad credit or the lack of transcripts from ruining a job hunt. And if that fails, Uncle Sam guarantees the loan for the lender.

That said, student loans are risky for the *borrower*. Instead of addressing the rising costs of education by making it more effective and efficient, our protectors in Washington have instituted a maze of loans that the government guarantees payment on, at very attractive rates that will allow kids to afford to be educated at increasingly inflated prices.

The result: Many kids graduate with huge debt loads and have to devote scarce first-job income to repaying their student loans. And those kids who don't graduate don't get their loans forgiven. They still have to pay perhaps 80 percent of the full amount a graduate does, but with significantly reduced income prospects.

with a salary, they may feel like millionaires — and they may start spending like millionaires, too. Without tools such as a spending plan, fledgling wage-earners may quickly lose control of credit and debt responsibility, finding themselves adding negative notes to their credit reports.

Create a spending plan (see Chapter 11). Don't start off on the wrong foot. The majority of student loans may be guaranteed by Uncle Sam, but they're all reported to the three credit bureaus. Missing a payment is not like cutting a class. Starting off a new life with debt is one thing, but starting off with bad credit is unnecessary.

Several repayment options are available for new grads:

- ✔ **Normal repayment:** You make principal and interest payments each month.

- ✔ **Graduated repayment:** You make lower payments at the beginning, and your payments increase at specified intervals throughout the life of your loan.

- ✔ **Income-based repayment:** Your monthly payments are set based on a percentage of your monthly gross income (for Stafford, Plus, and Smart Loan) and federal consolidation loans.

- ✔ **Extended repayment:** Your repayment term is lengthened.

- ✔ **Consolidation:** Your federal loans are refinanced into a single fixed loan with a long payback period.

- ✔ **Serialization:** You consolidate only the payments into a single payment but retain the original terms and interest rates on all your loans

Resolving overdue payment status

Because student loans are guaranteed against default and survive even a bank-ruptcy, the lenders and *servicers* (the people you send your payments into and talk to if you can't) have little to lose, so no one gets excited when loans are overdue (unlike the credit-card guys whose loans directly affect their bottom line and performance evaluations — and whose loans can disappear with a bankruptcy). But the fact that the lenders and servicers won't get all worked up about it if you're late shouldn't encourage you to put off repayment.

If you've already gone past due, contact your lender and explain the situa-tion. Ask what programs you may qualify for. All of this is much better done *before* you default — because more options are available to you. Student loans are one type of debt you cannot shake off. The full range of debt collection and legal options (including wage garnishment) are available to the lender — but bankruptcy relief is *not* available to *you* (if you declare bankruptcy, you still have to pay back your student loans).

Before you call or write the loan servicer (and I suggest you begin with a call and follow up in writing), organize your thoughts. Treat this as a very important job interview. Be able to explain coherently why you weren't able to pay: medical issues, job loss, pay reductions, armed-service call-up, family emergency. If you're calling to propose a payment alternative, have a number prepared and be able to justify it based on your budget.

The student-loan agencies and lenders generally accept regular monthly-payment alternatives that are both reasonable to the agency and affordable to you. Call your servicer or the U.S. Department of Education information line at 800-621-3115, but be sure to do it before you miss a payment.

Reporting your loan status to the credit bureaus

Student loans are reported unlike any other loan. They're similar in that a good payment history will help your credit and credit score, and a default will hurt it. If you're delinquent on your student loans, they may be referred to outside collection agencies that may also report your delinquency to the credit bureaus. But here's where student loans are different:

- **Each semester's or year's loan may be reported as a separate loan.** So you could have four to ten credit lines reported on what you think of as a single loan. That's four to ten negative items on your credit report, not just one.

- **Your tax refunds may be seized until the government gets its money back.**

- **You may be unable to get other government student aid.**

- **Your student loan will stay on your credit report until you pay it off.** How long will a student-loan default stay on your credit report? Well, if you haven't paid back your loan by the time you begin to collect Social Security, they take it out of your Social Security checks (along with fees and interest). No kidding.

Managing Medical Debt

If you have a lot of medical bills and you have health-insurance coverage, your approach to maintaining your credit will be different than if you don't have insurance, at least initially. Even if you're insured, dealing with health insurance and how it covers your medical bills can be a complicated and stressful issue. Problems can arise in terms of claims handling, and unless those problems are caught early, they can grow into major financial, credit-reporting, and legal dilemmas.

Understanding the Medical Information Bureau

Because the focus of this book is credit, I'd be remiss if I didn't mention the Medical Information Bureau (MIB). Yes, there is a bureau that specializes in your medical records. The information in your file can affect the price you pay for insurance (life, health, disability) — and the MIB can make mistakes. The MIB database, packed with health-related information on more than 15 million people, is used and shared by insurance companies.

Insurance companies use the MIB information to check your history before pricing or issuing you life or disability insurance and individual health-insurance products. Generally, when you apply for insurance, the insurance company asks you to provide information about your health or have medical tests. If something noteworthy turns up, the insurer reports that information to the MIB.

The MIB is a national specialty consumer-reporting agency (see Chapter 4), subject to the federal Fair Credit Reporting Act (FCRA). If you're denied insurance based on an MIB report, you're entitled to obtain a free report and to have erroneous information corrected. If you have an MIB file — and not everyone does — you want to be sure it's correct. You can obtain a copy for free once a year by calling 866-692-6901 (866-346-3642 TTY, for the hearing impaired), visiting the company's Web site at www.mib.com/html/request_your_record.html, or writing to Medical Information Bureau, P.O. Box 105, Essex Station, Boston, MA 02112.

Monitoring insurance claims for errors

You may be tempted to ignore the whole medical-payment process and assume that the insurance company and the doctors are handling everything satisfactorily. But you know better — what can go wrong often does. Claims payments or treatment-authorization communication between doctors and insurance companies is in codes, and one misplaced digit can make a big difference in the medical care paid for or allowed. Catching those small errors early is important — and you, as the claimant, have the most at stake.

Between the insurance companies — which have a better day when they don't pay a lot of claims than when they do — and the underpaid help in the medical office or hospital who must code all your procedures, errors are common, and legitimate claims are sometimes rejected. If your claim is rejected, always ask for the bills to be resubmitted and ask for an explanation of why they were rejected.

You don't have to be a claims whiz to keep track of your insurance process. Familiarizing yourself with your coverage limits is worth your time. Read through your insurance contracts (sorry, it's not the most scintillating reading). Get a copy of your coverage if you don't already have one. It may be a policy, a booklet, or something called a "summary plan description." (The insurance policy itself is the best and most complete source.) The health plan description is 20 to 30 pages or more. Points to pay attention to include

✔ **Schedule of benefits:** Explains what the insurance company pays and what you pay, deductibles, percentages, co-pays, and so on.

✔ **Covered benefits:** Often separate from the schedule of benefits, a laundry list of what is covered.

✔ **Exclusions and limitations:** What is not covered, as well as items covered but with limits.

✔ **Claims procedures:** Steps for filing claims and appealing denials. You may want to read that through, as there are usually some important time limits and details.

Reviewing these key components should give you a good idea of your coverage. If keeping track of medical expenses and reimbursements after or during an illness is just too taxing, consider a _daily money manager_ (DMM). Relatively new on the scene, the DMM is similar to a personal financial advisor, someone who can provide a wide range of services, depending on your needs. This individual can also keep track of medical bills and insurance forms. The best way to find a good DMM is through a referral. If you come up short here, contact the American Association of Daily Money Managers (AADMM) at www.aadmm.com or call 301-593-5462.

When your insurance doesn't cover it

If your insurance covers only a portion of a bill, you have a couple of alternatives:

✔ **You can ask for a discount.** The big insurance companies ask for discounts all the time and the hospitals grant them. Don't be afraid to ask.

✔ **You can ask the doctor to accept the insurance payment as payment in full.** Doctors do this all the time, too. If you're a doctor in a network and a network member comes in for something, whatever the insurer pays is all the doctor gets. The doctor agrees to this up front in order to be a member of the network and get referrals. You may be able to get the same deal if you ask.

Medical debts and your credit report

Most doctors and hospitals do not report payment histories to credit bureaus. They don't like to pay the fees — and some of them don't like to think they're in the credit business. However, if a debt moves from the medical provider to an outside collection agency, odds are it will hit your credit report. The message here is that you have more room to work with the medical provider — but to be sure, ask if they report your payment history to one of the credit-reporting agencies.

Keep in touch with the hospital and billing people. They'll assume that if the claim is denied by the insurance company, you'll pay the difference. Communicating that you don't consider the claim settled and need their help to resubmit or appeal a decision will make them a part of the process and keep their expectations in line with yours.

Lack of communication is not a good thing in these cases. Just as you take an active role in your health care and treatment as a patient, you also have to take an active role in the payment of your medical costs.

If you have a hard time getting your bills covered and you think the insurance company is wrong, complain. Most insurance carriers, believe it or not, do not like complaints. Here's a list of people to complain to, starting with the lowest one on the totem pole:

✔ Claims adjuster

✔ Supervisor

✔ Unit manager (over several supervisors by line of business)

✔ Assistant manager (over unit managers, but not in all offices)

✔ Claims manager or claims vice president (in charge of local office)

✔ Regional claims vice president (in charge of several offices in a region)

✔ Home office claims, senior vice president

When dealing with insurers, keep records of conversations (times, dates, and what was said), as well as copies of any paper you receive. If you write to an adjuster, copy his supervisor and request a written response in a set time-frame. Be polite and direct. Nasty complaints are easily dismissed or sent to a lawyer.

Lastly, if you reach an impasse, file a written complaint with your state insurance regulatory agency. Don't go into great detail — just give the very basic issues in dispute. To find your state regulator online, go to www.naic.org. Complaining to your state regulator is likely to motivate the insurer to pay better attention to resolving your claim.

Managing expenses to avoid credit repercussions

If, when it's all said and done, you're still left with medical expenses you're responsible for paying, you have some options:

✔ **Suggest a reduced repayment amount either in a lump sum (ask them to consider an ease-of-handling discount for cash) or a set payment every month.** Do this before you get billed. When a third-party biller gets hold of a debt, they're tenacious and the doctors, who consider themselves either artists, healers, or above it all, generally don't want to get in the middle. Deal with the doctor first, if you can.

✔ **Find out if your hospital is covered under the federal Hill-Burton Act, which prohibits** discrimination in providing services. In 1975, Congress amended the Hill-Burton Program, which established federal grants, loan guarantees, and interest subsidies for certain health facilities to require that they must provide uncompensated services forever. The U.S. Department of Health and Human Services at the Health Resources and Service Administration has information about where to find the 316 facilities covered under Hill-Burton. Check at `www.hrsa.gov/osp/dfcr/about/aboutdiv.htm`. There are no such facilities in Indiana, Nebraska, Nevada, Rhode Island, Utah, or Wyoming.

If you have no insurance, definitely let the doctor or hospital know this early on in the process and ask about discounts and payment plans. Be sure you can afford the payment plan before you agree to it. (You may want to follow the same process recommended in the "Keeping Credit under Control While Unemployed" section, earlier in this chapter, which involves resetting your spending priorities until you have the new bills under control.) Being willing to pay a reasonable bill over time is the best course of action to keep any collection activity off your credit record. *Remember:* Communicating with your doctor and hospital is the key.

Dealing with Debts of the Deceased

If you've lost a spouse, you're already going through one of the most emotionally draining experiences possible. Unfortunately, when a loved one dies, numerous financial matters surface, including credit and debt issues.

Stabilizing your credit in the event of a death can be difficult, especially if your spouse held all or most of the credit in his or her name. A creditor wants a death certificate and typically asks the estate to pay the bill. As a rule, the living spouse is not personally responsible for credit held in the deceased's name alone.

Keep in mind, however, that in community-property states — Arizona, California, Idaho, Louisiana, Nevada, New Mexico, Texas, Washington, and Wisconsin — credit accounts opened during marriage are automatically joint. That means you're responsible for any debt that your deceased spouse incurred during the marriage.

What happens to joint credit when there's only you

By law, a creditor cannot automatically close a joint account or change the terms because of the death of one spouse. Generally, the creditor asks the survivor to file a new credit application in his or her own name. If the creditor doesn't approach you with this option, close the joint account and open a new account in your name alone. The creditor will then decide to continue to extend credit or alter the credit limit.

Keep in mind that, when you're applying for new credit lines, you must use your name only. Including your deceased spouse's name will result in a joint account.

Credit bureaus automatically update records with periodic reports from the Social Security Administration. When the update is made, your spouse's credit history will be flagged and his or her name will be removed from any preapproved credit-offer mailing lists. This will reduce the mail you get in your spouse's name.

Understanding your liability

If you're a joint account holder on a credit card or if you live in a community-property state — Arizona, California, Idaho, Louisiana, Nevada, New Mexico, Texas, Washington, or Wisconsin — you may be liable for the debts of the deceased. In a community-property state, as long as the debt was incurred during the marriage, even if the other spouse received no benefit from it or didn't even know about it, he or she is still liable.

In the non-community-property states, credit-card and other debts that are only in the name of the deceased are not passed on to surviving spouses or children. When a loved one dies, however, notifying creditors is a good idea, even if you aren't liable. They'll ask for proof of death and generally request that a certified copy of the death certificate be forwarded to them. If there are assets in the estate, they may try to collect from the estate's executor. If there isn't enough cash and few assets that can be sold, that will generally end the issue.

Some loved ones feel that they should pay the debts, whether out of a sense of obligation or honor or just to set the record straight. Paying the debt of your deceased spouse is not necessary — unless you're required to by law. The creditors understand risk very well. When they charge a fee or an interest rate, this is just the type of risk they're collecting a premium for. So, in that regard, they've already been paid. If the creditor tries to pressure you to pay a debt that you aren't obligated to pay, I recommend telling them to go to *<insert your choice of venues>* and ask there.

Building your credit record — on your own

If the deceased was your spouse or life partner and you shared financial matters, you'll need to reestablish yourself as an individual once again. You may have done this once before when you were much younger. But the rules have probably changed, so I'll take you through the process from the beginning.

Notifying the credit bureaus

Begin by notifying the credit bureaus — Equifax, Experian, and TransUnion (see Chapter 4 for contact information). You want the preapproved and other junk mail in your spouse's name stopped. Also, although the Social Security Administration will notify the bureaus eventually, they aren't as fast as identity thieves. Some thieves make the most of the time between a person's death and when the death is reported to the credit bureaus. They use the deceased's Social Security number and identity to open fraudulent credit accounts. Generally, the family doesn't know anything about these accounts, because the criminal has the monthly statements sent to another address.

Prompt notification to the bureaus can help eliminate this crime. Some experts even suggest that you add a security alert on the deceased person's credit reports. Such a statement might say that the person is deceased, not to issue credit, and that any application for credit in this person's name is fraudulent.

Creating a new spending plan

Coming up with a budget or spending plan that covers your expenses as a single person is important. This budget will help you understand how your financial situation has changed — for better or worse. Chapter 11 offers suggestions on how to create a budget. Chapter 3 helps you figure out if you could benefit from the help of a credit counselor. I recommend a credit counselor — in stressful situations, a clear, professional perspective is an asset, especially one so reasonably priced.

After you have the income and the expense pieces in place, look at your monthly debt payments. The combination of these three categories — income minus expenses and debt — will give you a final number. If you're spending down your savings and investments as part of you retirement plan, consult your trusted financial planner or advisor to make sure you're still on track. If you aren't on track , you may want to use a professional counselor to help you find ways to make ends meet.

Budgets can be as simple or a complex as you make them. When I helped my mother with this process, I used a planning program and my mother just looked at the amount of money she had to move from checking to savings each quarter to gauge where she was. You get to pick what works for you.

Like so many things after you've suffered such a major loss, fine-tuning your budget may take several months. Be patient with yourself.

Familiarizing yourself with your credit report

When you know where you stand financially, you can begin deciding how you want to use credit. Because your credit score determines what you pay for credit and under what terms it may be available, I suggest you get your FICO score from myFICO.com, along with your credit report. The better your score, the less you'll have to pay to borrow or use credit.

To get headed in the right direction, I suggest the following strategies:

- Open a checking account and a savings account in your name.
- Open a retail-store credit card.
- Open a line of credit such as an overdraft-protection line on your checking account.
- Open one or two Visas or MasterCards issued by major banks.
- Get a library card. You'll save money and meet new people, too.

If you already have some of these, all the better.

Don't close old accounts unless you have to. The length of time an account is open counts in your favor for credit-scoring purposes. A variety of accounts also help your score. If you have a mortgage or a car payment and you can afford to pay them off, you may want to consider keeping them open for a short while (instead of paying them off), just to keep new positive information flowing into your credit file.

In no time, you'll have established your credit on your own.

Chapter 13

Steering Clear of Identity Theft

*W*hen someone steals your identity, he pretends to be you. No, he may not dress up like you, change his hair color, and immerse himself in the role, as Meryl Streep would for a role in a new film. Identity thieves don't have to be able to master dozens of accents — they have critical information that proves they're you more effectively than a pair of color-corrected contact lenses and a photo ID.

They have your credit-card numbers, your address, your birth date, and your Social Security number. They have your user IDs, your passwords, maybe even your mother's maiden name. Whether they steal your mail, hack into your computer, break into your home, or sift receipts and personal information from your trash can, identity thieves gain access to valuable data that allows them to tap into your existing lines of credit or to open new accounts.

With your data in hand, they can take vacations, buy cars, rent apartments, order designer furniture, pay for a week at the Ritz, get a job, run all the credit cards they have to the max, and profit financially because the businesses they're dealing with believe they're *you*. This activity, of course, hits your credit report. But if the thief is lucky — and you aren't — you might not discover that your evil twin is living it up and wrecking your credit rating for months. You may apply for a line of credit and discover you're rejected. Or you may get a flurry of aggressive calls from collections agencies who are sure you did it.

Of course, you get to defend yourself and prove otherwise, but the process can be expensive and may take a long, long time to resolve. And while you're doing it, you may be passed by for that new job you've applied for, be turned down for a credit card or car loan, or miss out on all kinds of other opportunities, because your credit report didn't look right. In this chapter, I let you know how you can protect yourself, your identity, and your credit from these crooks. And I help you deal with the situation if you've already been hit.

Protecting Yourself from Identity Thieves

For the past five years, the Federal Trade Commission (FTC) has ranked identity-theft issues as its number-one consumer complaint. The most recent rankings indicate identity theft makes up nearly 40 percent of all complaints — and those complaints represent a reported loss value of $547 million. In response to growing concern, Congress amended the Fair Credit Reporting Act (FCRA) with the Fair and Accurate Credit Transactions Act (FACTA or FACT Act) to help reduce the threat of identity theft and help victims with new rights.

Find out more about the FACT Act in Chapter 6 and at the FTC Web site, `www. ftc.gov/bcp/conline/pubs/credit/idtheft.htm`. (You can also find a copy of the FACT Act on the CD.)

Most identity thefts are perpetrated by people we willingly let into our lives — more often than not, friends, relatives, or co-workers are the culprits. These people have access to the places where you keep information about yourself. So you can greatly reduce your chances of falling victim to identity theft by making yourself more secure in your home: Don't leave financial documents and confidential information where they can be easily seen.

As a teenager, I vividly recall my father using the dining room table as a sort of open-shelf filing system. In the middle was a great heap of letters, bills, statements, and the like. To greater or lesser degrees, the rest of his family adopted the same system. But no more. Leaving bank statements or checks on the table today is like putting them out in the middle of the street. Anything you wouldn't want in the middle of the street is something you should take care to hide. Try to envision my analogy of putting an item in the middle of your street as you read on. This simple image will help you keep focused. Do you want your bank statement in the middle of the street? No? Then put it away.

In the following sections, I walk you through some simple steps you can take to reduce the chances of your identity being stolen.

Taking advantage of online transactions

Whenever possible, handle bill-paying, information transfers, and financial transactions electronically. Having bills and statements delivered to your password-protected computer is much better than having them delivered to your mailbox outside your home. Or as I like to say, dropped off in the middle of your street. The more information you send and receive electronically, the lower the chances of identity theft.

Using a computer has other benefits as well: When you get your information online, as in the case of your bank statement, you can look at it anytime you want. No need to wait for the end of the month. In fact, I recommend that you do a quick once-over every week — that way, you can spot a problem early.

Take precautions when conducting business via the Internet. You still may be at risk for identity theft. But assuming you're careful, you're much better protected than you are with snail mail.

Avoiding phishing scams

Phishing is when a stranger pretending to be someone you trust (for example, a representative of your bank or credit-card company) e-mails you and asks you to confirm critical information about your account (for example, by replying with your password, Social Security number, or other personal information). It can also be a spyware program that you download to your computer (without realizing you've done so) by clicking on a link or opening a file; the program then records any personal information you've stored on your computer and sends that information to others.

Over a recent six-month period, the number of phishing Web sites nearly doubled from 1,707 to 3,326. And that's just the ones that have been identified. Not only is the number of scams increasing, but they're also becoming more sophisticated. Bottom line: You need to be extremely careful when giving out your personal information over the Internet.

Here are some suggestions that will help keep you and your personal information safe:

- ✔ **Be suspicious of any e-mail with urgent, exciting, or upsetting requests for personal financial information.** The sender is using your emotions to stimulate an immediate, illogical response to the request.

- ✔ **Don't give out personal or financial information unless you're certain of the source and you confirm that the link is secure.** You can tell you're on a secure Web site if you see a little padlock or key icon in the lower-right corner of your Web browser. Also the address of the site will begin `https://` rather than `http://`. *Note:* Your e-mails are almost *never* secure, which means you should never e-mail your credit-card number, Social Security number, or other personal information to anyone — even if you're sure it's someone you can trust.

The exception to this rule is if you're communicating with a co-worker using an internal network at work or if you and the person you're e-mailing both have special security software in your e-mail programs. These exceptions are pretty uncommon, so to be safe, I recommend never giving private information out via e-mail, no matter what kind of network you're on.

✔ **Never respond to e-mails that are not personalized.** If the message has your name wrong or doesn't have your name at all, don't reply.

✔ **Never click on links in e-mail messages to find out what the great offer is.** If you click on the link, you may end up downloading spyware onto your computer, and your security may be compromised.

✔ **If you suspect that you're being phished, forward the e-mail to the Federal Trade Commission at spam@uce.gov, and file a complaint at the Internet Fraud Complaint Center (IFCC) by going to www.ifccfbi. gov.** The IFCC is a partnership between the FBI and the National White Collar Crime Center (NW3C). The IFCC Web site not only lets you report suspected Internet fraud but provides disturbing statistics about this growing crime. If you fill out a report, you won't be alone. In 2004, more than 200,000 others did, which is up 66 percent from the year before.

Keeping computer data safe

I recommend that you safeguard your computer so it doesn't end up in the middle of the street, metaphorically speaking. Here are some computer-safety rules to consider:

✔ **Don't leave your laptop out where it can be picked up.** Whether at home, in a hotel, or at work, when you're not in the same room as your laptop, put it away and out of sight. Would you leave a $100 bill laying out there? The same consideration applies here.

✔ **Don't walk away from your computer and leave files with personal information open — particularly if you're online.** My wife does this all the time and it drives me crazy.

✔ **Come up with a user name and personal identification number (PIN) or password that isn't obvious, and set your computer so that this information is required in order to turn your computer on.** You can also use a screensaver that has a password, so that if you walk away from your desk for a certain period of time, and the screensaver comes on, you need to enter a password to get back to your desktop.

Including at least one number or character in your password is good (for example, Steve@1). Don't use birth dates or Social Security numbers — they're too obvious for hackers to guess.

✔ **Don't keep a list of your passwords near the computer.** That's the computer equivalent of leaving your house key in your front-door lock.

✔ **Install a firewall.** If you use a wireless network, make sure the firewall is encrypted. (You can get firewalls for your home computer at most office-supply stores like OfficeMax or Staples.)

✔ **Use antivirus and spyware protection to keep** *key loggers* **off your computer.** Key loggers are programs that send out any information that you type to the crook, including your credit-card numbers, user names, passwords, Social Security number, and so on.

✔ **Make sure to thoroughly delete all personal information on your computer if you decide to get rid of it and really put it in the middle of the street.** Your best bet is to completely reformat your hard drive, which wipes it out and gets rid of everything. (Check with your computer manufacturer to find out how to rewrite your hard drive.)

Loose lips: Keeping passwords private

It is a testament to the trusting nature of Americans that if you want to know something personal or secret about them, all you have to do is ask. I can't count the number of times I've been at the office working on my computer and, when I've needed people to do something technical for me, they've said, "Steve, give me your password." That the tech-support people continue asking for this information leads me to believe that they must be getting it from other people, and not getting their hands slapped for asking. Me, I slap 'em. "No thanks," I say. "Just tell me what to do and I'll do it."

Seriously, this problem is so widespread that it has a name: It's called *social engineering*. It's using social situations to get information about otherwise secure data out of the unwitting.

To make sure you're not being socially engineered, follow these suggestions:

✔ **Don't give** *anyone* **your password.** If the guy in the next cube over wants to be helpful, you can enter your password for him.

✔ **If you have to give out your password, be sure you trust the source — and then change your password immediately.**

✔ **Don't share your clever password with co-workers or friends.**

✔ **Don't use your kid's or pet's name or birthday for your password.**

Most of the time if your identity is stolen, it will be stolen by someone you know. Avoid giving out confidential information to friends, acquaintances — even your kids. They may not be identity thieves, but they sure are great, naive sources of information.

Identifying vulnerable spots for theft

Although people seem to be spending more time than ever on their computers, most of us still spend more time in the *real* world as opposed to cyberspace. Not surprisingly, so do the identify thieves. Most identity theft occurs in the most mundane of situations. In 2004, in fact, the most frequently reported source of information used to commit identity fraud was a lost or stolen wallet or checkbook. Although you won't hear it on the evening news, computer-related identity fraud represented less than 12 percent of the known cases.

Recent research indicates that identity theft may have peaked. This news offers hope that as people become more aware of the crime and, consequently, take steps to prevent it, identity theft will continue to decrease. You probably won't hear that on the evening news either.

The top five sources of identity theft are

✔ Lost or stolen wallet or checkbook

✔ Friends, relatives, and acquaintances

✔ Corrupt employees

✔ Offline transactions

✔ Stolen snail mail

Half of all identity theft is committed by someone known to the victim. Your mother always told you to be careful who you hang around with — some advice never gets old.

Safeguarding your mail

Although tampering with the U.S. mail is a federal crime, your mailbox is one of the most common targets of identity thieves. The culprit removes some statements from your mailbox and, before you miss them, begins the process of changing addresses and opening new accounts. He can also easily convert that check you sent off for the heating bill into ready cash. Acid-washing the original recipient off the check and replacing the name isn't difficult for enterprising thieves.

I suggest the following tips to help you reduce your exposure to mail fraud:

✔ **Convert as much of your financial business to online transactions as possible.** This will help you avoid delivering information to the waiting hands of the criminal scouting your unattended mailbox. Many retailers, mortgage companies, and utilities services now provide online payment features, and make your account information available online at a secured site.

✔ **Explore alternatives to your unlocked, end-of-the-driveway mailbox.** Consider using a post office box or a locked mailbox that will accept mail (not unlike the old slot in the door).

✔ **Don't mail checks or financial information from your home mailbox.** Use your local post office mailbox or bring your mail to work with you. (Don't forget the stamps, or the boss may cancel your work identity.)

✔ **Ask your bank to hold new check orders and pick them up at the bank.**

✔ **If you're away for a day or more, have someone pick up your mail or, better, have the post office hold it until you return.** Don't let it sit in your mailbox overnight.

TIP

Protecting active-duty military

The last thing the United States wants its active-duty servicepersons to worry about when they're safeguarding you and me is who's safeguarding *them* from identity thieves. As a credit counselor, I worked closely with many clients enlisted in the Navy. I can tell you from experience that they are as fine and trusting and *naive* a group of young idealists as I have ever met. They're often targeted for scams when they step outside of their military environments. Fortunately, amendments to the Fair Credit Reporting Act (FCRA) have taken this into account with the *active-duty alert*. The active-duty alert requires creditors to verify a serviceperson's identity before granting credit in his or her name.

If you're in the military and away from your usual base or deployed, you can place an active-duty alert on your credit report. This alert helps minimize the risk of identity theft by requiring that a business take "reasonable" care to verify your identity before issuing you credit. However, if you're in some distant land trying to keep the peace, that may not be feasible. So to keep the creeps away from your credit, you can appoint a personal representative to place or remove an alert.

Before you leave your base or home for active duty, be sure to appoint a personal representative and provide contact information to the credit bureau. If you don't, a creditor only has to

"utilize reasonable policies and procedures to form a reasonable belief" before granting credit to someone who claims to be you. This is way too *reasonable* for my comfort level. Be sure to appoint someone you trust!

An active-duty alert on a credit report requires a creditor to take extra steps to verify your identity not only before granting new credit, but also when issuing an additional credit card on an existing account or raising your limits. When you put an active-duty alert on your credit report, you receive a copy of your credit report and, as a bonus, your name is removed from preapproved-offer lists for credit cards, insurance, and loans. You can place additional alerts if your deployment lasts longer than a year.

To place or remove an active-duty alert, call any one of the three major credit-reporting bureaus. Whichever one you call will require you to provide appropriate proof of identity, which may include your Social Security number, name, address, and other personal information.

You only have to contact one of the three companies to place an alert — the companies are required to contact the other two. (If you call all three, they'll be calling each other and getting confused — and they're easily confused.)

Remember: If your contact information changes before your alert expires, update it or have your representative do so.

Keeping and maintaining financial data in your home

When you gain control of the mail flow in and out of your home, you can feel more comfortable that you've closed off some key avenues for potential identity theft. Yet, inside your sanctuary, that pile of documents must be protected and secured. Your information is still accessible to house thieves, not to mention others who may gain access to your inner sanctum through other means.

Storing your confidential documents and information

Sometimes it's the simple things that save the day. Making and securely storing a photocopy of the contents of your wallet and account numbers is one of them. If you haven't already done so, empty the contents of your wallet or purse and photocopy everything, front and back. Write the contact phone numbers next to each item and file the paper in a locked cabinet. Voila! You're now better prepared to deal with an identity crisis.

Keep all financial, confidential, and legal documents and information in a secure place — a strong box or a metal filing cabinet. Not only will your valuable data be safe from prying eyes and sticky fingers, you'll benefit from having all critical information in one place in case you need to access it quickly.

Shredding the evidence

Your mailbox is not the only source of private information for identity thefts. Your garbage can is also ripe with potential (not to mention banana peels and dog-food cans). A determined thief won't mind sifting through your detritus if it means snagging a credit-card number from those coffee-ground-covered receipts. A fishing expedition in the backyards and trash cans of suburbia promises a good catch.

Purchase a good home crosscut shredder, and shred all financial mail that contains account numbers. This includes savings, checking, and credit-card statements. Don't overlook all those preapproved offers for credit you receive.

I recently purchased a shredder, and I recommend that you get a model that has a large capacity, because the shredded paper takes up a lot of space and they fill up fast. Also be sure the shredder is easy to empty — the shredded, confetti-like material will try to fly all over the place. This pleases my cat but not my wife.

Freezing your credit information

Frozen daiquiris, frozen snickers, frozen credit? The topic of freezing your credit to keep it from identity thieves has been cropping up on more legislative calendars recently.

The concept is simple: You can freeze or lock up your credit information so that anyone who is looking to extend credit will have to ask you to *thaw out* (unlock) your file. Freezing your credit information would seriously hamper an identity thief from opening credit in your name without your knowledge, because few lenders will do so without a credit report in hand.

But the strategy is not foolproof. Existing accounts could still be pirated, used, and abused by such tactics as simply swiping your mail, changing your address from Peoria to Las Vegas, and getting replacement cards issued. So a freeze might help protect your *information,* but it might not protect your *money.* Given the low personal level of liability on credit cards, however, your monetary losses would not be significant.

If your information is stolen, and the thief opens new lines of credit in your name, you can get all sorts of grief from collectors who are trained not to listen to excuses. "But I *swear,* I was never *in* Las Vegas and I never autho-rized that purchase of a $5,000 lap dance." They've heard it all before. So the bottom line of freezes is as follows:

- ✔ **Only a few states — California, Colorado, Louisiana, Maine, Texas, Vermont, and Washington — have adopted credit-freeze laws.** As of this writing, bills are pending in 22 more states.

- ✔ **Freezing doesn't prevent abuse of existing accounts.**

- ✔ **Some freeze laws require that you be victimized before you can implement them.** California law allows anyone to freeze his information, but you have to pay a fee to the credit bureau to freeze and another fee to thaw each credit report.

- ✔ **Thawing an account takes a few days and might keep impulse or sale purchases from happening — which can be a good thing or a bad thing, depending on how you look at it.**

A fraud alert is similar to a freeze, but it only requires verification of identity and when you place a fraud alert on your file, it's on your credit report for a specific amount of time after a theft has occurred.

The main consideration surrounding to-freeze-or-not-to-freeze, when you get past whether you can do it in your state, is whether you value access to instant credit more than you fear your personal information being compro-mised. Only you know the answer to that question.

Spotting Identify Theft When It Happens

If your identity is stolen, there may be no obvious indication that you've been victimized — there's no broken window or missing masterpiece to serve as a clue. The evidence, unfortunately, may not make itself known until your credit has been sorely compromised and you're fighting on multiple fronts to restore your good name.

That said, by being vigilant, you can spot signs of identity theft. This crime is one that you'll probably be the first to notice, and vigilance on your part can make all the difference between a minor or a major identity crime. In the following sections, I give you some key signs to watch out for.

Receiving a collections call

The call, likely an unpleasant and adversarial one, will be one demanding a payment on an overdue account, one the collector is certain you made. What should you do? The FACT Act, designed to address identity-theft issues, states that you need to tell the collector very clearly that you did not make the purchase and you believe that your identity may have been stolen.

When you tell the collector you think your identity may have been stolen, the collection agency is required by law to inform the creditor. You're also entitled to get a copy of all the information the collection agency or creditor has about this debt, including applications, statements, and the like, as though this really were your account or bill.

The best part is that, under the FACT Act, as soon as you notify the creditor or collector that the debt is the work of an identity thief, the debt cannot be sold or placed for collection.

Discovering unrecognized credit-card charges

In order to find charges on your statement that you didn't make, you have to actually read your statement in detail. Many people just look at the amount due and write a check. Instead, take a minute and review your charges — you just may be surprised.

Don't rely on your memory as you review your statement. My memory isn't the greatest in the world (or so my wife says, although I can't remember why). So I make sure to keep all my credit-card receipts in a file — and I pull them out when reviewing my monthly statement. Keep all credit-card receipts in a convenient place — at least until you receive, verify, and pay your statement.

If you see any unauthorized charges on your statement, call the customer-service number and get the details. You may have to dispute the charge, but that's no big deal. Also, the representative may see some indication of an identity theft. That happened to me once — I saw a stray charge, called the credit-card company, and the customer-service rep recognized it as a fraud right away. Make the call.

Getting denied credit or account access

Rejection is always a painful thing — but it's especially painful when you're rejected because of something you're not responsible for. If your credit application is rejected and you don't know why, this is a sign for concern. Someone may be wreaking havoc on your credit history, which has affected your standing. If you get rejections for credit, you may want to ask why — but your best bet is to order a copy of your credit report and look for evidence of credit theft (accounts you never opened, activity you don't recognize).

Another sign of identity theft is receiving a notice that you've been rejected for credit you never asked for. Take this seriously. Someone may be applying for credit in your name.

You may try to access an ATM and get a denial message. If this happens to you, contact your bank immediately to determine whether it's the result of identity theft.

Missing account statements

Your monthly statement is really late. Hmm . . . now that you think of it, you didn't receive a statement last month either. Yes, I know this was one of your birthday wishes, but the real reason you're not hearing from your creditors may be more sinister.

If your statements or bills fail to arrive when you expect them, it could mean an identity thief has changed your address in order to use your bank accounts, hoping you won't notice for a few months. It may also mean that a neighborhood troller nabbed your mail recently and now has access to your account numbers.

Create a system in which you remind yourself when statements are due and bills must be paid. This way, you're more likely to stay on top of your payment schedule and be alerted when something is amiss. Then you can contact the creditor, who may alert you to a serious problem or may report that the company is simply having a problem with this month's mailing and the statement will be out shortly. As you may imagine, if you pay bills and get statements via computer instead of snail mail, you make it harder on the thieves (and easier on yourself).

When Identity Theft Happens to You

If you discover that you're a victim of identity theft, you need to act quickly and comprehensively. Don't rely on others to resolve this mess. You have the biggest interest in getting this situation stopped, fixed, and behind you. And you need to assume all responsibility for making sure it does.

If your identity has been stolen or if you believe it has (you don't need a smoking gun, video tapes, or a confession to act), do everything I recommend in the following sections right away. *Remember:* Most of these places are open for business 24 hours a day, so a late-night call won't wake anyone.

Who you gonna call? Contacting the bureaus, creditors, police, and more

You may read different advice on whom to call *first* if you discover you're a victim of identity theft. Some sources recommend calling the police, others suggest you call your creditors or the credit bureaus. My advice is to begin in one of two places, depending on your circumstances:

- ✔ If your existing accounts have been compromised, call your creditors first.
- ✔ If you're hearing about accounts you've never had, call the credit bureaus first.

Either way, don't wait long between the two calls.

Before you pick up the phone, you must do one more thing: Get a notebook and a pen and start writing down everything that happens from now on. You want names, badge numbers, phone numbers, names of supervisors, and so on. Documentation is critical because this situation may go on for a long time and require a lot of calling and writing to resolve. Don't trust your memory or count on anyone calling you back when he says he will. It happens all the time. Be responsible and get the facts.

On the CD, I've included a handy worksheet, courtesy of the Federal Trade Commission, that may be useful or that may give you some ideas for one of your own. It's called "Chart Your Course of Action."

Canceling your credit cards

If your credit or debit cards have been compromised, call the card companies, ask for the fraud department, and cancel the cards immediately. You can find the phone number on your monthly statements or in your terms-and-conditions brochure. Your card may also have a customer-service number you can call.

A small comfort: Your liability on stolen credit-card accounts is relatively low — just $50 maximum. Even so, you need to contact all your creditors as quickly as possible so that the thief doesn't continue to wrack up charges in your name, creating a bigger loss for the credit-card company.

For ATM and debit cards, your maximum liability is $50 if you report the loss within 48 hours of noticing it, but $500 or even *unlimited* liability (including any overdraft protection) if you delay too long.

Contacting the credit bureaus

Calling one of the bureaus results in a fraud alert being placed on all three of your credit files within 24 hours.

If you live in one of the credit-freeze states (see "Freezing your credit informa-tion," earlier in this chapter), put a freeze on your accounts until you know how severe the damage is. You can always thaw your accounts later, and a freeze will shut off access to your information much more completely than a fraud alert will.

You can also add a *victim's statement* to your credit report. A victim's state-ment may be particularly useful if you live in a state that doesn't yet allow freezes. The victim's statement informs anyone getting your report that there is a problem with your file and it may not be relied upon to be completely accurate. Most creditors take strong notice of this fact and don't issue new credit in your name.

Adding a victim's statement to your report may motivate creditors to close existing accounts that weren't affected until they can determine you're safe again — which may keep you from using your accounts for a while.

After you've notified the credit bureau of your situation, you'll receive a credit report from each of the bureaus. Be sure to keep a copy of all reports (store them with those copious notes you're taking).

Calling the police

Call the local sheriff? Will he flip on his blue and red lights and tear around the town to find the thief? Not exactly. But the FACT Act requires that you be official on your end, just as the government is required to be on its end. You have a crime on your hands, so you need to call the police and report it.

The police report is also a way that others in the process can get a straight, consistent story from a third party about what happened and when. You'll have less difficulty convincing that collector you aren't kidding about the Las

Vegas lap-dance bill if you can refer him to your local police or send an offi-cial police report to bolster your story. Be sure to get a copy of the report as soon as it's available — or at least get the police-report number for reference.

Some police departments may not recognize identity theft as a crime they're responsible for handling. They may question their jurisdiction and not want to take the time to take a report. Furnish as much documentation as you can to prove your case — debt-collection letters, credit reports, your notarized Identity Theft Affidavit (see the following section), and so on.

Be persistent if the police seem reluctant to take your statement, but be polite. They may just not have done this before. Remind them that, without a police report, credit bureaus may not block fraudulent items on your report, and they may be inadvertently helping a crook.

The FTC advises that if the police are reticent to take your report, you ask to file a miscellaneous-incidents report or try another jurisdiction (such as your state police).

Contacting the Federal Trade Commission

The Federal Trade Commission (FTC) supports an entire department that handles identity-theft issues. The folks in the identity-theft clearinghouse don't follow up on specific instances, but they play an important role in look-ing for patterns and accumulating statistics that help everyone concerned with stopping identity thefts.

Call the FTC's ID Theft Hotline at 877-438-4338. From a purely self-serving perspective, contacting the FTC will bolster your claims regarding unautho-rized credit-card charges or accounts opened by thieves in your name. Go to `https://rn.ftc.gov/pls/dod/widtpubl$.startup?Z_ORG_CODE=PU03` to fill out the Identity Theft Affidavit form. You can use a copy of this form when disputing accounts or charges with creditors, as well as when filing a police report.

Notifying the post office

Many identity-theft cases are the result of unauthorized and illegal access to your information via the U.S. mail. Messing with the mail is a federal crime. The post office recommends that if you're a victim of identity theft and think your mail played a role, you contact the nearest U.S. Postal Service Inspection Office and report your concerns. If you know for sure it was the mail, call to report a crime. Find the office closest to you by contacting your local post office or go online to `http://usps.com/postalinspectors/ifvictim.htm`.

Taking advantage of the FACT Act

The new FACT Act (also known as FACTA) has numerous provisions for businesses, credit reporters, and you. An entire book could easily be written on the topic, but in essence FACTA was designed to address issues surrounding incomplete or inaccurate credit reporting, not to mention identity theft.

In the following list, I highlight the consumer-oriented provisions of the act that I think you'll find most informative or useful:

- ✔ **You can receive at least one free credit report each year from each of the three bureaus.** Under certain circumstances, you can get more than one. Specialty reporting agencies, such as insurance and landlord reporting services, must also give you a free report if you ask. (See Chapter 4 for more information on specialty bureaus.)

- ✔ **You have the right to dispute the information in your file directly with the party furnishing the data, instead of having to go through a third party.** The credit-reporting agencies have up to 45 days to respond.

- ✔ **You can sue creditors and the bureaus for violations of FACTA for two years after discovery or five years after the violation took place.** Your case is especially strong if they continue to sell, transfer, or place your account for collection after you've communicated that it is because of identity theft and placed a block on the trade line.

- ✔ **Creditors and collectors cannot continue to report information based on an account that you've reported as fraudulent or that you've shown to be inaccurate or incomplete.**

- ✔ **You must be notified about any adverse credit actions, such as being offered less-than-favorable credit terms or a creditor sending a negative item to your credit report.**

- ✔ **Businesses must cooperate with you to help clear your name in the case of identity theft.** They must provide copies of records about goods or service they provided to the thief. The business may require a police report and may take up to 30 days to comply.

- ✔ **You can opt out of information-sharing between affiliates.** So, if you don't want Citibank to tell Smith Barney (their brokerage affiliate) that you're a big spender (and should be called to invest some of that money), they won't.

- ✔ **You may place a 90-day fraud alert, a 7-year extended fraud alert, and a 1-year military active-duty alert on your file.**

✔ **You may have fraudulent trade lines on your credit report blocked if you've reported the crime to a police department or law-enforcement agency.**

✔ **You may request that your Social Security number be** *truncated* **(shortened) on your credit report and communications in case it falls into the wrong hands.** And credit-report users can't just throw your used reports in a Dumpster. They have to dispose of the report in an approved manner.

✔ **Businesses must truncate your credit-card number on credit-card receipts.** In other words, your restaurant receipt shouldn't show your entire credit-card number — just the last four digits. Merchants that still make out manual receipts have until 2007 to switch over to the new format.

Sending out the fraud alert

As I mention earlier in this chapter, contacting the credit bureaus is one of your first steps when you discover an identity theft. When you contact them, you have the opportunity to place a fraud alert and a victim's statement in your file. These two items indicate to anyone looking at your report that the request for credit they've received recently may not actually be from you. Generally, the creditor contacts you before approving the credit request.

If your ex-brother-in-law is pretending to be you and he's at a car dealership waiting to drive away with a new Rolls Royce, the fraud alert and victim's statement work well. The dealership would have to verify who he was. The fraud alert does create a bit of an extra step or delay if you're simply trying to legitimately open a new credit card to take advantage of a 10 percent discount on items you're purchasing today at the local department store — but this may be a delay you're willing to live with because of the protection it provides.

A fraud alert is placed on your account for 90 days. Any new activity, including your own, is researched and reported to you. So if you open new credit lines during this time, you may notice a slower-than-normal process. Although inconvenient, this safeguard is in place to protect you.

If you aren't sure whether your identity has been stolen, but the information necessary to do so has been compromised, consider an *extended alert* on your credit report. An extended alert will last seven years. Why use an extended alert? Let's say you lose your wallet. A thief may not use your information right away — he may save your information for future use. The extended alert covers a long enough time period so that if the information is used to open an account next year, the alert will stop it. Sort of like that weed killer you use to keep the little creepers from sprouting in the first place. Though a nuisance, an extended alert will serve to warn you of any suspicious activity — even after you've forgotten about the original event that triggered you to establish the alert in the first place.

A small silver lining: After you put the alert on your file, you're entitled to *two* free copies of your credit report at any time during the next 12 months from all three agencies, not just the annual report now available to all consumers.

Block that line

"Block that line" may sound like a football cheer, but it can be a powerful tool. Be sure to request that the bureaus block any lines of credit that you believe are fraudulent. This will prevent those items from being sold, transferred, or placed for collection.

In addition, ask the credit bureaus to remove any inquiries on your record as a result of those fraudulent lines.

Finally, ask the credit bureaus to notify anyone who may have received reports over the last six months with the erroneous information and inquiries on them. This will help alert creditors and other interested parties to the situation — and save your reputation.

Accessing Credit after Identity Theft

If you're a victim of identity theft, you're likely to experience those emotions typical to any victim: You'll feel traumatized, battered, fearful, and angry. You're likely to avoid any experience with credit and borrowing in the future.

But I encourage you to strive to overcome these feelings. After all, credit — though it certainly can be abused and exploited — also brings great benefits to responsible individuals, allowing them to achieve personal and financial goals they otherwise wouldn't realize. I strongly suggest that you adopt a strong offense and move forward with your personal goals. Whether you're planning on buying a house or you're simply buying back-to-school supplies at their lowest prices, don't be afraid to use credit to your advantage. Here are some steps you can take to get your credit going again, without putting yourself at renewed risk to identity thieves.

Closing and reopening all accounts

Whether your personal accounts were broken into, stolen, or just sniffed at, change all your PINs, passwords, user IDs, and account numbers. You'll probably have to close accounts and reopen them. A hassle, perhaps — but if you've been a victim of identity theft, you already know the real meaning of *hassle*.

Here's a list of which accounts to close and reopen:

- **Bank accounts:** When your information is compromised, you never know if or when trouble will pop up. Changing the account numbers will result in a dead end for a thief.

- **Credit-card accounts:** When you contact the card companies, you'll be asked for proper identification. (This is good — you *want* them to be suspicious!) They're used to closing accounts and reopening new ones quickly and painlessly. I suggest that you only reopen those you use. As a rule, if I haven't used a card in two years, I begin to wonder why it's taking up space in my wallet.

    But be careful about closing your older accounts. These accounts tend to help your credit score.

- **Other accounts:** Contact your Internet service provider and utilities companies to alert them to your circumstances. Get new account numbers in every situation. If your long-distance calling card has been stolen or you discover fraudulent charges on your phone bill, close your old account and open a new one.

Changing your PINs and passwords

When you change those accounts at the bank, change your personal identification numbers (PINs), too. And be sure, when you access money at ATMs or in public places, that no one can see you enter the number. Getting close to the machine may block the sight of a camera with a telephoto lens or someone using binoculars across the street. (Yes, thieves really *do* go that far.)

Switch to a *pass-phrase* instead of a password. A pass-phrase uses a short series of words like "ElvisIs#1" instead of a single password. Pass-phrases tend to be longer and harder to crack. Include some numbers and characters in them if you can.

Beware of bogus ATMs

I'd like to share a story from my early counseling days about an ATM fraud. A crook made a realistic-looking ATM complete with a TV screen. He set up the ATM on a busy sidewalk on a weekend and got inside. As passersby came by and inserted their cards, the display told them the machine was out of order and to check with their bank on Monday. This was, of course, after they had entered their PINs, which he wrote down for use later. Late at night, he and the bogus machine disappeared.

The moral of this story is that crooks will continue to come up with new ways to get information out of you. When a door is closed, they'll try to open a window. So be vigilant and be safe.

Changing your Social Security number and driver's license

If you can't seem to shake the damage done by the identity theft (either because new theft occurrences keep popping up or collectors keep landing on you like blue-bottle flies), you may need to take more-serious action. Contact the Social Security Administration to inquire about getting a new Social Security number.

Getting a new Social Security number is a huge pain to everyone, including you. Imagine all the places you've used your old number. Prepare to change all your records yourself — no one does this for you.

If you go this route, you won't be the first. Besides the storied federal witness-protection program, Social Security numbers are also changed for domestic-violence victims when warranted. But with all the emphasis on national security, changing your number won't be easy.

Be sure to document everything. This dog can have a very long tail. You may need to dig up some documentation a year or two after you thought all the dust has settled. Good records, with everything in writing and names and dates, will be a godsend.

For more information, visit the Social Security Web site at `www.social security.gov` or call 800-772-1213 (800-325-0778, TTY for the hearing impaired).

While you're at it, grab a good paperback book, go down to the Department of Motor Vehicles, and get your driver's license number changed — especially, if someone is using yours as an ID.

Keeping positive about the war on identity theft

Yes, it is bad out there, but information and vigilance are the tools that will safeguard you and your identity. The government is doing its share of work to get this under control. The FACT Act is a big step in the right direction.

And here's some promising news: A recent study released in January 2005 by the Better Business Bureau and others updated the Federal Trade Commission's 2003 Identity Theft Survey Report. It showed that, despite the hype and hysteria about identity theft, these crimes are more frequently committed offline than online, regardless of how many databases have been compromised. Internet-related fraud problems are actually less severe, less costly, and not as widespread as previously thought.

Need more reasons to turn to the Internet to conduct your financial business? This study shows that those whose accounts are online detect crimes earlier than those who rely only upon mailed monthly paper statements. Further, and I think remarkably, people who detected identity theft by monitoring accounts online experienced less than 12 percent of the losses of those who detected the crime via paper statements ($551 average losses when detected online, versus $4,543 average losses when detected on paper statements). The study concludes, "Our numbers show that fears about online identity fraud may be out of proportion to the relative risk, causing consumers to ignore the most glaring issues. Indeed, most instances of identity fraud occur through traditional channels and are paper-based, not Internet-based."

Finally, the FTC and other federal agencies have been directed by Congress to conduct several studies of the credit-reporting industry. The results of these studies may help to further improve reporting accuracy and consumer awareness.

Part V
The Part of Tens

In this part . . .

Good things come in tens — at least, *these* good things do. In the Part of Tens, you get short, concise chunks of valuable information to help you tame, improve, repair, and protect your credit. I summarize all the salient bits in quick-reference lists of ten. Look for ten tips to protect your identity, and ten steps to take if you didn't read the *other* list. You can also tick off on your fingers ten warning signs your credit is in trouble, ten ways to deal with financial emergencies, ten quick fixes for your credit standing, and ten great ways to make your credit look good. Got ten minutes — or even ten seconds? This Part of Tens is bound to benefit your credit.

Chapter 14

Ten Ways to Make Your Credit Look Good

In This Chapter

▶ Applying for the kind of credit that boosts your credit image

▶ Keeping your financial records and credit information safe

▶ Getting the good stuff on your credit report

"*A*lways look your best." That's what my mother told me as she wiped a smudge from my face and straightened my collar before we visited the new neighbors. Good advice. And it applies to your credit, too. When lenders and others view your credit report, they're sizing you up based on the way your credit looks — similar to the way my family's new neighbors sized us up.

In this chapter, I tell you ten things you can do — some as easy as straightening your collar — to improve your credit appearance. Keep in mind that truly beautiful credit can take time. Believe me, there's no such thing as plastic surgery when it comes to credit repair (other than cutting up the plastic if you've exceeded your credit limits). But you can work with what you have to set it off in the most flattering light. These ten tips for good-looking credit are sure to help.

Paying Down Debt

One of the fastest ways to improve the appearance of your credit is to decrease your *credit-availability-to-credit-used ratio.* Simply put, this means paying down the balances on your revolving credit accounts.

For example, if you have a credit card with a credit limit of $5,000 and your balance is $3,000, your credit-availability-to-credit-used ratio is 60 percent — you're using 60 percent of the credit you have at your disposal. Lenders like to see that ratio lower than 25 percent — 25 percent of $5,000 is $1,250, which means you'll be more attractive if your balance is $1,250 or less.

The nice people at Fair Isaac (www.myfico.com) will ding your credit score if your ratio is above the 50 percent mark. So if you want to up your credit pizzazz, start by paying down your balances to below 50 percent, and then shoot for a ratio of less than 25 percent to look even more desirable.

Making an Entrance with Secured Cards

A *secured credit card* is issued by banks and credit unions and looks just like any other credit card, but it has one small difference: You, the cardholder, must deposit money into an account at the issuing institution to partially or fully cover the credit limit for the card. The deposit is used to secure the line of credit for the purchases you'll be making with the card. The account is reported to the credit bureaus as a revolving account. You make payments, just as you would with any credit card. But the creditor is guaranteed payment for your charges by your deposit, which they'll pull from if you default on the payments. That's where the "secured" part comes into play.

How does a secured credit card improve your credit appearance? If you're establishing credit for the first time, or reestablishing credit after clearing up past mistakes, you can immediately add some positive information to your report. A new account with on-time payments for a period of months goes a long way to improving how you look on paper.

Here's how to get started:

1. **Contact your bank or credit union to find out if it offers secured credit cards.**

   Watch out for annual processing or maintenance fees. You can get secured credit cards free — you just have to look around for banks or credit unions that offer them. If the bank you use doesn't offer one, or only offers one with fees, try other banks or credit unions in your area, or search online for secured credit cards.

2. **Deposit the funds to be used as security for the card.**

3. **Use the card for purchases, making sure that you have the funds available to pay the balance.**

   You don't need to use the card a lot. Just make a few purchases each month.

4. **Make on-time payments every month.**

Some people may encourage you to use a cash advance on your secured card to open another secured card — and so on. Sure, this approach may allow you to open several lines of credit and chalk up more positive entries on your credit report. But it also exposes you to the risk of multiple negatives if you can't make payments — *and* it can cost you plenty in interest payments. My advice: Only get secured cards when you have the cash on hand to put down as security.

Applying for Passbook Loans

A personal loan using your savings as collateral is an excellent way to add positive information to your credit report, thus improving your credit's appearance. You'll need to have some money in savings to begin with. Your goal is to prove that you can borrow money and repay a set amount each month as agreed. A passbook loan is reported to the credit bureaus as an installment loan because you pay off the loan with a regular monthly payment in the same amount for a specified period of time.

These loans are generally low-interest-rate loans — and they should be because there is almost no risk to the lender. The combination of secured credit card (see the preceding section) and passbook loan can springboard your credit image, with its mix of credit types (one revolving and one installment). The two accounts in good standing will make you look as if you're dressed to the nines and ten years younger!

Check with your bank or credit union to make sure that the loan is reported to at least one but preferably all three of the major credit-reporting bureaus. If the loan is not reported to at least one of the major bureaus, request that the bank report it. If the bank is unwilling to do so, take your business elsewhere.

Using Retail Store Cards

Just as a secured credit card can help you look good, retail cards are relatively easy to get and can boost your credit appeal. These cards generally have lower credit limits, so they'll have little effect on your available-credit-to-credit-used ratio, which you want as low as possible. Use the cards for purchases and pay the balances on time and in full each month. The goal here is to establish accounts that will reflect that you pay as agreed — a positive mark in the credit good-looks department.

Make only planned purchases that you have the cash to cover. Then use that money to pay the balance when the bill arrives. You don't want to add the extra weight of unnecessary debt while you're working to enhance your credit.

Keep Those Old Accounts Open

Like throwing out your favorite old shirt or that famous little black dress, you'll regret canceling an old account. The credit mavens will lower your score if you close out a longstanding account. They like stability and they spell it *o-l-d*. So keep those accounts, especially if you open a new one. The combination of closing an oldie-but-goodie and adding a new account will hurt your score twice.

Taking Advantage of the 100-Word Statement

You have the right under the Fair Credit Reporting Act to add a 100-word statement to your credit-bureau file. You can use this statement for many different reasons, including to improve your credit image.

Keep in mind that a good deal of loan underwriting is done by computers, so a consumer statement may or may not be helpful in this situation. But in the case of a prospective employer or a landlord looking at your report, the 100-word statement will be of more value.

Start by assessing which aspects of your report are the most negative. You may have charged-off accounts, a medical collection account, a paid judgment, several 120-day-late accounts, or all of the above. Whatever your situation, use the statement to place the most offensive listing in the most positive (or least offensive) light — much like telling folks you got that black eye by bumping into a door (as opposed to in a barroom brawl).

For accounts that are reported 120 days late, your statement may look something like this:

I was injured on the job in January 2003 and was unable to work for three months. During that time, I did not receive any compensation and was unable to pay my bills. Please note that, when I returned to work, I caught up my accounts in a short period of time (120 days) and they are now all paid on time. The problem is now resolved and my finances are no longer affected.

For a medical or other collection account, your statement may look like this:

> I incurred medical expenses for a procedure in March 2004. I disputed some of the charges included in the bill, and my account was sent to collection before the dispute was resolved. I paid the revised bill in full as soon as the dispute was resolved in November 2004. The problem is now resolved and my finances are no longer affected.

The credit bureau will help you write the 100-word statement if you ask for help. TransUnion offers help on its Web site. The other credit bureaus require you to write the statement first, and then they'll help edit it after it appears on your credit report. *Note:* If you live in Maine, your consumer statement may be up to 200 words.

After you place the statement on your report, don't forget it's out there. A 30-day delinquency may only cost you a few points for a year, while a charge-off (usually over 180 days late) from your ex-spouse's account could hurt more and for longer. How long depends on how much positive information is on your file and the volume of new information being reported. So as your credit recovers over time, you may want to pull the statement or you'll be drawing attention to an old negative unnecessarily.

Performing Periodic Checkups

Having a mirror to check your appearance before you head out the door is helpful. And so is getting a reading on how others view your credit report.

Review your report from each of the three major credit bureaus at least once a year. Read the reports carefully to make certain no inaccurate or outdated information is included, and that none of the positive information is missing. Dispute inaccurate entries with the credit bureau and request that positive data be added to your file (see Chapter 6 for more information).

If you're checking credit reports because you think someone (for example, a lender or a prospective employer) may be looking at your report soon, check all three at once. You may not know which one will be pulled. If you're checking your report just to monitor progress, I recommend that you order a different one every four months — that way, you're able to check your credit report more often, by rotating among the three. See Chapter 4 for help on getting copies of your credit report.

Protecting Yourself from Identity Thieves

Now that you're working hard to correct past credit mistakes and make your credit look as good as possible, the last thing you want is for an identity thief to mess up what you've struggled to achieve. To help protect yourself from this growing epidemic, follow these tips:

- ✔ **Guard your account numbers.** Be careful with credit-card statements, bank statements, and other financial documents that contain account numbers and personal information. Shred any of these documents that you don't file in a safe place.

- ✔ **Be wary of phone transactions.** Never supply credit-card or Social Security numbers over the phone, unless you initiated the call and you know whom you're dealing with.

- ✔ **Protect your Social Security number.** Do not keep your card in your wallet or purse, where a thief could find it.

- ✔ **Check credit reports for evidence of identity theft.** Review one of your credit reports every four months or all three at least annually. You can order a copy of each report for free once a year. And even if you have to pay (because you've ordered more than once per year), consider the expense valuable insurance.

- ✔ **Don't put bills in an unlocked mailbox.** Do not send bill payments by mail from your unsecured home mailbox; anybody driving by can reach in and get your account numbers. And keep track of your statements to be sure that you receive all of them in the mail. Mailboxes are often the targets of identity thieves.

Maintaining Good Records

A surefire way to make your credit look good is to pay your accounts — every last one of them — in full and on time. In order to accomplish that goal, keep track of your bill due dates, your checking- and savings-account balances, and pretty much all other financial information. Some tips to keep in mind:

- ✔ **Attend to your checkbook.** Keep track of all debits and deposits to your checking account, including debit-card transactions. Balance your checkbook every month to make sure you know how much money you have.

- ✔ **Devise a bill-paying system.** Come up with a system that makes sense to you and one that you'll use to make sure you don't miss payments or pay late.

- ✔ **Pay on time.** Allow enough time for your payment to get to your lender. I suggest at least seven days for mail and four days for electronic bill payment.

Getting Professional Help

If all else fails — or if you just like to bounce things off someone else to make sure you've covered all the bases — consider these two sources of help:

- ✔ Your attorney
- ✔ A legitimate credit counselor

As a bonus, the credit counselor will help you create a spending plan that satisfies all your needs as well as the needs of your creditors. I only recommend credit-counseling agencies that are certified by the Council on Accreditation (see Chapter 3 for more information).

Chapter 15

Ten Signs That You Need Professional Help with Your Credit Problems

In This Chapter

▶ Recognizing financial red flags that cry "help"

▶ Identifying the right professional to assist you

▶ Knowing that it's okay to get help

*I*f you feel sick, you may stay home from work and load up on chicken soup — but if your condition doesn't improve, you'll call the doctor. If you're selling your home, you may try to sell it yourself — but if it's a tough real-estate market, you'll enlist the help of a real-estate agent. And come tax time, you may be comfortable doing your own taxes — but if you have complex situations such as business write-offs, investment properties, and complicated deductions, you'll hire an accountant to prepare your returns for you.

Just as with health, real estate, and taxes, your financial state may be so challenging that you're much better off turning to a professional to help you resolve your situation. Depending on your circumstances, that professional may be a credit counselor, an attorney, or even a marriage counselor.

In this chapter, I identify ten key warning signs that signal it's time to seek help. For more detail about how a credit counselor can help you stay or get back on financial track, read Chapter 3.

You're Spending Too Much on Debt

If more than 20 percent of your monthly take-home income goes toward paying off debt, not including your mortgage or rent, you may be ready for some professional help. If you're typical of most American consumers, after you allocate your earnings to normal living expenses such as food, shelter, kids, pets, entertainment, and so on, you should have enough left over for that emergency fund or short- and long-term goals such as vacations and retirement. My experience tells me that when you begin to factor a large recurring debt payment (such as a credit-card payment) into your budget, you end up compromising your savings goals.

If you're spending 20 percent or more of your income to pay off debt beyond your housing, see a credit counselor to find out how you can restore balance to your finances, meet your current obligations, and save for a secure financial future.

You've Missed More Than One Mortgage Payment

A popular bumper sticker says it best: @#$% HAPPENS. That may explain why you may have missed one mortgage payment. If you've missed *more* than one mortgage payment, however, you're most likely confronting serious financial difficulties — and you're closer to major calamity than you may realize.

Many people who pay their mortgage late may be lulled into false security by that 15-day grace period normally offered in mortgage arrangements. But after you've been 30 days late once, the grace period no longer applies. And if you reach 90 days past due, all three months of payments and fees must be paid at once, or you enter the realm of the foreclosure process — and the penalty for a misstep here could be your home.

In the case of payment problems with your mortgage, the best type of professional guidance may come from a HUD-certified housing-counseling agency. (HUD is the government's Department of Housing and Urban Development.) HUD is not limited to low-income housing — it's good for all income levels. Not all credit- or housing-counseling agencies are HUD-certified, so be sure to ask. Beyond the agency certification, you want to ask for a certified housing counselor. A number of independent bodies (such as Neighborhood Reinvestment Corporation and the National Foundation for Credit Counseling) certify individuals. One last and pleasantly surprising reason to insist on a HUD-certified agency is that the counseling should be free. In fact, in order for an agency to become HUD-certified, it has to agree not to charge homeowners a fee.

You Can't Make Your Minimum Payments

Having trouble making even minimum payments on your credit cards? This could be a sign that professional debt exorcism is required. Like a bad dream that keeps you up at night, struggling to pay the minimum saps your strength and lowers your resistance to more financial challenges. If you can barely afford to make minimum payments, chances are you can't afford to save — and that will put you at risk for ending up deeper in debt from unexpected illness, car problems, or temporary unemployment.

Your Utilities Have Been Shut Off

Generally among the friendlier creditors, utility companies do not see themselves as lenders. Because they're guaranteed a profit by most state regulators, they can afford to be a bit more tolerant of late payments — which means that, if you're receiving shut-off notices, this is a clear sign that you're in trouble.

Seeking help from the utility company may not be enough — financial problems seldom exist in a vacuum (that is, if you're in trouble with the electric company, odds are you're having financial trouble in other ways). So, in addition to seeking help from your utility, get help in managing your finances.

If you get a shut-off warning — or expect one — call your utility provider and ask about payment programs for which you may qualify. Also ask for referrals to local credit counselors: Many utilities companies can connect you with reputable agencies.

You're Arguing with Your Partner about Finances

Unless your names are Ward and June, Ozzie and Harriet, or Lone Ranger and Tonto (and they had a silver mine), fighting about money is going to happen at one time or another in just about every committed relationship. When the arguing is ongoing and unresolved, however, you may benefit from the guidance of a professional. Money-related disputes are the number-one cause of divorce in this country. My experience says that even when financial conflicts end in divorce, the financial problem doesn't go away — it leads to a more serious meltdown instead.

Instead of letting such issues destroy your relationship or your credit history, get some professional help. If the issues are more about financial problems (such as paying bills late), a credit counselor may help. If the root of the problem is a destructive behavior (such as gambling or out-of-control shopping), getting a therapist for the person with the problem may be in order. If the conflict is more about a difference in financial philosophies, turning to a marriage counselor may help. In any case, look to friends or trusted professionals for referrals.

You've Been Refused Credit

After the embarrassment of credit denial wears off, you'll no doubt recognize this critical warning sign — something must be seriously wrong if a creditor is not willing to extend credit, even at an extremely high interest rate. Some categories of lenders do profit by offering high-cost loans to folks with low credit scores. And you may be able to shop around for a high-risk, high-interest lender.

Or you could take another course: If you're turned down by your usual credit source (your bank, credit union, or finance company), you could recognize this as a sign that you need help in repairing your credit. If your banker says no to a loan request, ask for a recommendation of a good credit-counseling agency to help get you in better credit shape, so you can come back and give them your business.

You've Written Bad Checks

If you've recently written a bad check, consider this a serious wake-up call! Knowingly writing bad checks is a crime — one that may be punishable with jail time and fines. But you don't get off the hook just because you didn't do it on purpose. Writing bad checks by mistake means you've lost control of your checking account, and you need to take immediate steps to remedy the situation. Be aware that a number of specialty credit-reporting agencies report your history of writing bad checks (see Chapters 4 and 6 for more information).

If you regularly receive nonsufficient funds (NSF) letters from your bank, you can be sure you're losing money to bad-check fees and penalties. The two best places to turn to for help are your bank and a credit-counseling agency. A bank representative may sit down with you to analyze the cause of your overdrafts. The problem could be as simple as not balancing the account every month — or it could be more serious.

Multiple Creditors Are Calling

If you fall behind on one bill, chances are you can handle it yourself. As the number of creditors calling you for late payments grows, the problem becomes exponentially more complex. Why? Because collectors want all the money due, and they want it *now*. Often the only way to get rid of a collector is to promise the payment requested. But you can't do that with them all. If you could, you wouldn't be receiving these calls in the first place.

Dealing with multiple conflicting requests for more money than you have can quickly escalate. My experience is that juggling the demands of three or four collectors is nearly impossible. A professional who knows the creditor policies and is empathetic but not personally involved can advocate on your behalf very effectively. Turn to Chapter 8 for help.

The Courts Are Involved

Getting mail from a debt-collection attorney about a past-due debt is a bad sign. Getting a summons to court is worse. Creditors are within their right to sue you in civil court if you don't make your payments on time or as agreed. If you receive a summons to appear in court concerning a debt, by all means go to court. If you don't show up, the judge will automatically enter a judgment against you. This will be reported to the credit bureaus, which will lead to a lower credit score. Depending on your state laws, your wages may be garnished and you may have a lien put on your property.

When you're required to appear in court, the advice of an attorney may be critical to you. If you can't afford an attorney to represent you in court, go on your own. You'll fare much better if you present a plan to pay the debt than if you don't do anything. A short visit to an attorney to understand your rights, followed by a longer and less-expensive visit to a certified credit counselor to work out a repayment and spending plan, will help you get a result that won't come back to haunt you.

If you don't have an attorney and don't know where to begin to find one, visit the American Bar Association at www.abanet.org and click on your state for a referral service.

Your Vehicle Has Been Repossessed

People who are struggling to make their car payments are sometimes mistakenly relieved when the tow trucks appear outside their residences to repossess their vehicles. But your financial headaches won't end with the repossession of your car, and any relief from eliminating the monthly payments is short-lived.

Most lenders sell the repossessed vehicle at an auction. But *you* are responsible for the difference in the price for which the car sells and the balance due on the loan (known as a *deficiency balance*) plus some hefty fees for towing, storage, legal services, disposal, and, of course, ongoing interest, often at a higher rate.

If your vehicle is repossessed, you may be confronted with a much larger debt than you originally had. The services of a credit counselor — and possibly an attorney — may be required.

Chapter 16

Ten Tips for Avoiding Identity Theft

In This Chapter

▶ Using technology to help keep you safe

▶ Monitoring your mailbox for signs of identity theft

▶ Safeguarding your Social Security number

*H*ardly a week goes by without a new report of a compromised database or a hacker gaining access to personal financial data. The Federal Trade Commission reports that identity theft is the number-one consumer complaint. In 2004, 9.3 million Americans were victims of identity theft. In addition to the hundreds of hours spent by each consumer trying to correct problems caused by the thefts, identity theft accounted for $52.6 billion in losses to businesses in 2004.

In this chapter, I help you avoid adding *your* identity to those numbers. I discuss ten fairly simple but effective ways to prevent identity theft. The reality behind the statistics is that most identity theft occurs from *paper* rather than electronic sources — paper that you can do something about. In this chapter, I tell you how.

Going Online with Bills and Statements

Paying bills online is more than just a convenience that saves the cost of a stamp: It can save the cost of late fees from checks that arrived past due — and the damage to your credit score that would result. Going online can also prevent the information on your monthly bills and statements from ending up in the wrong hands.

To pay your bills and get your statements electronically, simply call your creditors or visit their Web sites and make the request. Most creditors' Web sites make it pretty easy for you to switch to electronic statements and pay your bills online.

Currently, the majority of identity theft occurs *offline*. You still want to be sure, however, that information is not accessed online without your knowledge. Protect your financial information stored on or accessed from your computer by installing firewall and antivirus software. Also, make sure you're on a secure Internet connection before submitting personal information. Typically, a locked padlock icon shows up on the bottom of your screen to indicate you're secure.

Scrutinizing Your Statements

Whether you get your statements online or through the mail, take the time to look them over carefully. If a thief has obtained your credit-card information and is making purchases in your name, those charges will appear on your statement and may be your first indication of a theft. Promptly review your paper statements each month to verify all the charges listed are yours. If you're banking electronically, I suggest you check your activity more often — perhaps weekly.

If you find an item you don't recognize and believe is fraudulent, contact your creditor immediately. The phone number to call is likely listed on the back of your credit card. You may be required to sign a statement attesting that you did not make the charge(s).

Using Passwords Responsibly

Passwords are essential to help protect your financial information online. Here are a few of the basics rules that will help keep you safe from prying eyes:

- ✔ **Never store your passwords near your computer or in your wallet.**

- ✔ **Choose passwords that are at least eight characters in length and combine both upper- and lowercase letters, as well as numbers or symbols.**

- ✔ **Use words you know, but with a twist — like the use of letters you see on license plates in place of words.** For example, if you like going to the beach, you may use "cshore." Using a word that is in the dictionary is a bad idea, because it's too easy to crack.

✔ **Substitute numbers for letters, for example using 1 in place of I or 0 in place of O.** For example, if you're a waiter, you might use the password "w8ter."

✔ **Change your passwords periodically.** Experts recommend every six months.

✔ **Never give out your passwords.** If you or your kids do give them out, get new ones immediately (the passwords, not the kids).

Nothing can be more frustrating than forgetting a password! If you forget your password, look for hints or password reminders on the Web site. Most companies will have you answer a few security questions and then they'll e-mail you a new password, which you'll have to reset. If that doesn't work, contact customer support.

Shielding Your Social Security Number

All children over the age of 1 year must have a Social Security number in order to be claimed as a deduction on their parents' federal income-tax returns. Schools that receive federal funding use the Social Security number as the student identification number, beginning with elementary school and continuing all the way through college. Most kids today know that number as well as their telephone number. Some states still use the Social Security number for driver's license numbers. Even libraries may use it for their cards. In addition, insurance policies and medical records are often tied to the Social Security number.

Needless to say, your Social Security number is requested, required, and referred to numerous times in the course of your daily life. And if you're like most people, you freely give it out without question. But your Social Security number — unlike your name — is unique to only one person in the world: you. It's like a numeric thumbprint that can open the doors to personal and confidential information. And to an identity thief, getting hold of your Social Security number is like striking gold.

The following tips may help you protect your Social Security number:

✔ **Do not carry your Social Security card in your wallet.** You should keep it with other important documents — such as birth certificates and insurance policies — in a secure place. A bank's safe-deposit box is ideal.

✔ **Be sure any requests for your Social Security number are legitimate.** You're within your rights to refuse to give it out. Simply ask why it is needed and state your concern — most legitimate businesspeople will respect your reticence.

- ✔ **Don't give out your Social Security number over the telephone or Internet when you've been solicited for the information.**

- ✔ **If your state is still using the Social Security number as an identification number, you're within your rights to ask them to use an alternative number.**

- ✔ **The same applies for insurance cards, library cards, employee badges, and most other forms of identification that use your Social Security number.** Ask them if another number can be used. If they have to use your Social Security number, ask that the number not be visible on the card (an employee badge or student ID, for example).

- ✔ **If your Social Security number is stolen, contact the FTC at 877-438-4338 or at www.ftc.gov.** This may be the prelude to the opening of accounts that aren't yours and a credit-report nightmare that can last for months or years. Carefully check your annual earnings record through the Social Security Administration on a regular basis. Unexpected earnings may be your first indication that your identity has been stolen and is being used by another person.

Getting a new Social Security number is extremely difficult. Guard your number jealously, and teach your family members to do the same. However, under certain circumstances, the Social Security Administration may assign you a new number if all efforts to resolve your identity-theft problems have failed to help. For information on getting a new Social Security number, call 800-772-1213 or visit your local Social Security office.

Reading All Your Mail

Don't throw away that junk mail so quickly. It may not be junk mail after all. A thief may have opened a new credit account in your name using your personal information, including your address, and the statement may be mailed to you. Open all your mail, even if it's from a bank you don't recognize.

In addition, you should always open mail from an attorney's office or collection agency. Sometimes a thief will use one of your credit accounts and have the statement sent to another address. In this case, the bill would go unpaid and be turned over for collection. The collector might try the previous address on the account and send you a letter requesting payment, which may be the first time you become aware that your account has been compromised.

Keeping Credit-Card Offers at Bay

Those unsolicited credit-card offers that come in the mail are a goldmine for an identity thief. Taking the offer out of your mailbox, filling out the information with a change of address, and having a new credit card in your name mailed to them is quite easy for a thief to do.

Call 888-567-8688 or visit www.optoutprescreen.com to stop these offers. You'll need to provide your name, address, previous address (if it changed less than two years ago), and, of course, your Social Security number.

Also, contact Direct Marketing Association to remove your name from mailing lists. Visit www.dmaconsumers.org or write to:

DMA Consumer Affairs
1111 19th St., NW
Washington, DC 20036

Until you can get these offers to stop, be sure you're shredding the solicitations before throwing them out. (See "Shredding the Evidence," later in this chapter.)

Locking Up to Protect Your Mail

You wouldn't leave your wallet out on the curb in front of your house, would you? And yet your mailbox is full of as much valuable information for an identity thief. Just think of the personal detail that's sitting in your mailbox between the time the mail carrier drops it off and the time you get home from work:

- Credit-card statements that identify your account number, name, and credit limit
- Checking-account statements that reveal your account information
- Cancelled checks that can be chemically treated to remove the ink, leaving an essentially blank check
- Credit-card and other loan offers

To keep your personal information safe, keep your home mailbox locked or use a post office box. Also, do not put bill payments and checks in an unlocked mailbox. Instead, take them to the post office to mail.

Knowing Where Your Mail Is

An overflowing mailbox may be too much of a temptation for an identity thief. When you're away from home, have your mail picked up by a trusted friend or relative — or place a hold on your mail at your local post office. To be safe, start the hold the day before you leave and have it resume the day after you return. Visit the post office to pick up the mail.

Sherlock Holmes solved a mystery by noticing that a dog did not bark when it should have. You can stop an identity thief by looking for mail that hasn't come. The bill that did not arrive in the mail may not be a blessing. It could very well be that an identity thief has obtained your account information and requested that the statement be mailed to a different address so that you aren't aware of the fraudulent charges accumulating on your account.

Always make sure that you receive monthly statements from each of your credit-card issuers and that you receive your monthly checking-, savings-, and investment-account statements — and that you get them on time.

Defending Your Credit-Card Number from Strangers

Most people know to be leery of phone solicitors that request their credit-card number or other personal financial information. However, you may naturally trust the innocent-looking college student who comes to your door soliciting donations to save a whale or a tree. Even if the person looks trustworthy, don't give out a check or a credit-card number — the tree-hugging, whale-saving college student is still a stranger. If the charity is legitimate and you want to contribute, do so with cash, or, if you don't have cash on hand, donate later by check or credit card when you've had time to check out the charity and the requestor. Better safe than sorry.

Shredding the Evidence

No matter what the documents are, the message is clear: If a piece of paper has an account number, Social Security number, or subscription number, or if it will allow you to open a new account, it needs to be shredded before you throw it out. You probably wouldn't think twice about having a burglar alarm installed at your home to protect your stuff against intruders. To protect your stuff against mail intruders who would steal your identity as quickly as a burglar would steal your silver, buy a good shredder.

I suggest that you get a shredder that has a cross-cut feature — this makes the confetti harder to read. I also suggest that you buy one that is easy to use — otherwise, you won't use it. Find one that will take multiple pieces of paper at once. I like at least six pages at a bite.

Make sure that the container catching the shredded material is both large and easy to empty. The shredded paper takes up more volume than the unshredded stuff and it's very dusty. If you have a hard time emptying the container, you'll either get dust and shreds of paper all over the floor or you won't use the machine.

Keep your shredder in a convenient place where you handle your mail, so you can use it on a regular basis and for everything.

Chapter 17

Ten Signs Your Credit May Be in Jeopardy

In This Chapter

▶ Recognizing the signals that foretell credit crisis

▶ Reading the signs in your credit report, credit score, and other credit information

▶ Recognizing your own credit-risky behaviors

▶ Taking action to preempt credit problems

"WATCH FOR FALLING ROCKS!" "CONTENTS MAY BE HOT!" "DANGEROUS CURVE AHEAD!" Everywhere you turn, signs and labels warn you about situations that could cause you harm — from drinking scalding coffee to ironing your pants while wearing them.

With credit issues, however, few signs are so clear. Maybe all credit cards and loan agreements should include a big disclaimer: "WARNING: BORROWING MAY BE HAZARDOUS TO YOUR WEALTH." Then perhaps, eventually, the pitfalls of credit carelessness would be as apparent as "PLACING YOUR HEAD IN THIS PLASTIC BAG MAY CAUSE DIFFICULTY IN BREATHING."

In this chapter, I shine a light on ten warning signs that predict impending credit calamity. Some require that you have recent copies of your credit reports from the three major credit bureaus. (If you haven't ordered them already, what are you waiting for? Turn to Chapter 4 to find out how.)

So, turn off the TV and turn up the lights. The signpost up ahead says "WARNING: YOU MAY BE ENTERING THE CREDIT TWILIGHT ZONE."

A Low FICO Score

A low credit score is one of the prime indicators of a credit crisis ahead. Obviously, it can also mean you're *already* in trouble. But sometimes you can pay all your bills on time and keep your credit below the limits on all your cards — and *still* have a low score. Late payments and high credit usage are only two of the factors that make up your score. FICO scores are calculated based on more than 20 variables and their interrelationship with each other. For more on FICO scores and how to raise yours, check out Chapters 5 and 6.

Fees on Your Credit-Card Statement

Being charged fees on your credit-card statement is not normal. Well, it may be normal for some people, but not if you're striving for a healthy credit report. Fees are a sign that you're doing something the issuer does not think is safe. Fees are a sign that you've raised your risk level — hence, the creditor's need to charge you more to offset that risk. If your perceived risk level has risen in the eyes of your creditor, then believe me, it has not escaped the elves that work in the FICO workshop.

Over-limit fees mean you're using up too much of your credit line — that'll drop your credit score. You should strive to keep your credit-card balance under 50 percent of your limit. Late fees warn you that your on-time payment record is suffering — and your credit-score points are dropping like rocks on a mountain road.

If you see fees on your card statement, beware of credit problems ahead!

Having Your Credit Card Denied When Trying to Buy Something

Besides causing embarrassment and frustration, having your credit card rejected when you're trying to make a purchase is a sign that your credit is in trouble. This signal is akin to the check-engine light coming on in your car. You don't have a clue what it means — but you need to check it out.

Cards can be refused for any number of reasons, ranging from being over the credit limit to possible identity theft. No matter what the reason, the system has picked up data that your credit may be on a crash course. Your job is to follow up and look under the hood.

A Jump in Your Insurance Premium

An increase in your insurance premium — whether homeowner's, life, or auto insurance — is a warning sign. I don't mean a couple of bucks' increase — I mean something with a little *wow* factor to it (maybe a 20 to 50 percent increase). Insurance companies not only rate your loss history, but they also consider your probability of having a loss. If you live in a high-accident area, chances are greater you'll be in an accident. If you have too low a credit score, your financial life may appear to be slipping out of control. The insurance company deduces that maybe your car or house or health will be next.

The actuaries at insurance companies love to play with numbers. They even play with numbers that aren't there yet! Those numbers are called *incurred-but-not-reported* losses (or IBNR losses, for short). This factor is loaded into rates that account for losses that have already happened, but that they don't know about yet. Bizarre, yes, but true. People with bad credit statistically will have more losses than those with good credit. An unexpectedly high increase in your insurance rates is a sign that your credit may be in jeopardy.

Getting the This-Is-a-Great-Rate-for-Your-Score Story

Risk-based lending allows lenders to make loans today that they would have turned down a few years ago. It enables more people to get the financing they need, although at a higher price. If you're told that something on your credit report has pushed up your rate, you need to know what that something is.

About 25 percent of all credit reports have some errors on them. If you knew that one person out of four gets short-changed at your favorite breakfast place, wouldn't you at least count your change? You may be getting charged more for an error — or an error on top of what you already know is a ding or two in your record. Be sure to check it out and verify that your record is accurate. There is a second benefit to this: You'll be making sure that you aren't being overcharged through an error on your lender's part — or an intentional and unwarranted hiking of your rate to increase the lender's profits at your expense.

Using Credit to Cover Living Expenses

When you rely on your credit cards for day-to-day needs, you could be on the road to credit chaos. I'm not talking about using your credit cards to purchase groceries or fill your gas tank. I'm talking about putting the groceries or other regular living expenses on your credit card and carrying the balance over to the next month or two (or more). Not only are you paying a premium interest charge, but this is a clear sign of a problem.

If you're running out of money before the month ends, it's only a matter of time before your credit report shows high balances. And it's only a matter of time until an unexpected emergency comes along, pushing your cards to the max or above. Using credit cards to cover living expenses, and carrying the balance into the future, is a sign that you need to cut your expenses or increase your income. Eventually, your credit will suffer — if it hasn't already.

Tying the Knot

I'm not saying that getting married gives you bad credit — I'm married and I have very nice credit, thank you — but it does mean sharing much of your life with another person. Part of that sharing includes credit history and spending habits. Few people explore financial behavior and issues before they commit to happily-ever-after. Talking about money and credit is one of the last taboos in the United States. You may know if your significant other snores, but do you know his score? If she pay bills on time? Or even if good credit is important to your betrothed?

If you live in one of the community-property states listed in Chapter 7, you'll also be sharing any debts incurred by your spouse. The sad fact is that about half of marriages end in divorce — and *more* than half of those divorces credit financial issues as one of the main causes.

Getting married? You show me yours and I'll show you mine — *credit*, of course! Discussing credit and financial habits before you walk down the aisle is a great wedding-planning idea.

A Lack of Emergency Savings

How can the lack of an emergency fund be a credit warning sign? Emergencies happen. They aren't a matter of *if*, but a matter of *when*. Without an emergency savings cushion, you're sailing without a lifeboat. None of us would take a cruise on a liner with no lifeboats. But some people think nothing of set-ting sail into life without a lifeboat of three to six months of living expenses.

Savings are important to head off a stormy credit future. No one can predict when you may face a job loss, serious illness, divorce, or other financially devastating event. However, you'll probably have at least *one* of these events in your future. As long as you have a savings cushion to cover expenses when your income is interrupted or takes a dramatic plunge, you'll be way ahead of the game in protecting your credit. If you can't afford a three- to six-month cushion, set aside what you can and work to save more.

Approaching or Exceeding Your Credit Limits

As long as you don't go over your limit, things are fine, right? After all that's what a limit is for, isn't it? Unfortunately, no. If you're approaching or are at the credit limits of your credit cards or credit lines, you can bet your credit score will reflect this. Keeping your borrowing under 50 percent of your total credit limit is in your best interest. Creeping close to your credit limit will put you on a slippery slope — one where you could easily misstep, slide over the edge, and further harm your credit.

To address this warning sign:

- ✔ Stop charging right away.

- ✔ Pick the card with the balance closest to its credit limit and begin paying it down as aggressively as possible.

- ✔ When the highest-balance card is paid down to within 50 percent of its limit, move on to the next card and keep going until you pay off all cards. Even *one* card with a high balance can have a big impact on your score.

- ✔ Keep the card accounts open, because closing them could negatively affect your score.

Receiving Collection Calls and Letters

If you're getting calls and/or letters from collection departments or agencies, take this as a clear signal that things are not right in your financial world. Don't blame the caller or ignore the warning and think it will go away!

If the debt in question is yours, the appropriate action plan is to reassess. In Chapter 3, I provide a worksheet that can help you get things organized and back on track.

Collectors must follow the rules of the Fair Debt Collection Practices Act and may not call in regard to your debt before 8 a.m. or after 9 p.m., or call you at your place of employment if you inform them that your employer prohibits those types of calls. (See Chapter 8 for more tips on dealing with debt collectors.)

If you don't recognize the debt, you may be the victim of identity theft. If this is the case, you can place a fraud alert on your credit report and start the process of rebuilding your credit by disputing the bill and notifying the credit bureaus. (Check out Chapter 13 for more on handling identity theft.)

Chapter 18

Ten Ways to Reduce the Damage of Identity Theft

*T*he best way to dodge damage from identity theft is to avoid being a victim in the first place. (In Chapters 13 and 16, I address a number of ways to do this.) But the sad fact is this: Identity theft is reaching epidemic proportions in the United States and, despite your best efforts, you may become one of its victims. From sophisticated Internet *phishing* (in which thieves posing as banks or other companies with which you do business e-mail you asking for your account number or Social Security number) to low-tech dumpster-diving, criminals bent on stealing your identity bombard you from every direction. If you have gas, water, or electric service at your home; own a computer or telephone; put out the trash; or pick up your mail from a typical mailbox outside your home, you're vulnerable. When you're victimized, it's up to you to fix the problems caused by the theft.

But what if you're not certain you've been victimized? Say, you lose your wallet or leave your credit card behind at a store. My advice is this: Act anyway and act fast. By the time you have evidence of identity theft, it'll be too late. Don't wait more than two days before taking action. Why wait even one day? Because you may have only misplaced, forgotten about, or left whatever it is you're concerned about in your car, at a friend's, or at a trustworthy merchant's. Why not three days? Because after two days, your liability may increase.

What to do, when to do it, and who can help you get on with your life is what this chapter is all about. So read on — in the pages ahead, I tell you the information you need to get through the trauma of being an unfortunate victim of identity theft with as little damage as possible.

Canceling Your Credit Cards

If you have reason to believe any credit or debit cards have been compromised, call and cancel them immediately. The numbers to call are included on your monthly statements, on the back of your card, and/or on the Web site of the issuing bank.

For credit cards, you're only responsible for the first $50 of any unauthorized charges that occur before you report the cards as lost or stolen. You have no liability for any losses after you report that the card has been lost or stolen; you also aren't liable for any losses resulting from someone getting a hold of your number but not using the actual card itself (say from a receipt or writing down the card number and using it later).

ATM and debit cards are a little different: Here, time is of the essence. A loss reported within two days of your noticing it carries the same maximum $50 liability as a credit card. If you report the loss more than 2 days and up to 60 days from the date your statement is mailed, your liability can be a whopping $500 maximum per card. And if you delay your report beyond 60 days, you may have unlimited responsibility for charges, including any overdraft line that may be associated with the card. Ouch!

You may be able to recover some of your loss through your homeowner's insurance. Check with your policy. Most insurers offer reimbursement of the $50 fee(s), up to a limit, as part of basic forgery and fraud coverage. You can usually buy additional coverage if you have many cards and possible $50 fees to cover.

Contacting the Credit-Reporting Bureaus

Good news: You only have to contact *one* of the big-three credit bureaus, and your theft will be communicated to all three. Each agency is bound by law to contact the other two agencies.

A fraud alert will be placed on your account for 90 days. Any new activity will be researched and reported to you, including your own. So if you open new credit lines during this time, you may notice a slower-than-normal process. Although inconvenient, this safeguard is in place to protect you.

If you aren't sure whether your identity has been stolen, consider an extended alert on your credit report. If, for instance, you lose your wallet, a thief may file away your information for future use. The extended alert, which stays in effect for seven years, is a bit of a nuisance, but it will serve to warn you of any suspicious activity after you've forgotten about the original event that triggered you to establish the alert.

A small silver lining: While the alert is on your credit file, you're entitled to additional free copies of your credit report from all three agencies, not just the annual report now available to all consumers.

Calling the Police

Identity theft is a crime and must be reported, even if you don't have a stolen wallet or actual documents missing. The police may be able to do little to keep your identity from being stolen and misused — but filing a police report is a very good idea. It will be useful in challenging unauthorized charges on any credit or debit cards. In addition, if new, unauthorized accounts are opened in your name, the police report helps to document your experience.

If the police are reluctant to take your report, the Federal Trade Commission advises that you ask to file a "miscellaneous incidents report," or try your state police. You also can check with your state attorney general's office to find out if your state law requires the police to take identity-theft reports. Look in the Blue Pages of your telephone directory for the phone number or go to www.naag.org for a list of state attorneys general.

After you file your report with the police, be sure you have the file number and the name of the officer who took your report. If you can get a copy of the report, all the better. This information will serve as evidence if you have problems with creditors because of unauthorized debt, and it'll back up any challenges you make.

Notifying the Post Office

Yes, even the Postmaster General wants to help. Not that Lance Armstrong will ride around like Paul Revere and give out the warning to every "middle-sex, village, and farm." But tampering with the U.S. mail is a crime. If someone has gained access to your credit card and bank information by way of stealing or tampering with your mail, the U.S. Postal Service wants to meet them. If you're a victim of identity theft and you believe that the U.S. mail was used in the theft, they recommend you contact the nearest U.S. Postal Service Inspection Office and report the crime. You can find the office closest to you by contacting your local post office or going to `http://usps.com/postal inspectors/ifvictim.htm`.

Contacting the Federal Trade Commission

The folks at the Federal Trade Commission (FTC) have a department dedicated to identity theft. Call the FTC's ID Theft Hotline at 877-438-4338. You'll be asked to fill out an identity theft affidavit; you'll then be added to their database of victims.

How does being added to the FTC's database help you? Well, the FTC uses the database to search for patterns in tracking down identity thieves, and even though yours is only one crime, it may assist in future cases. In addition, just like the police report, the affidavit will support any claims you may need to make regarding unauthorized credit-card charges or accounts opened in your name that do not belong to you.

Protecting All Your Accounts with Passwords

Not since Groucho Marx offered $100 for guessing the secret word have passwords been so important. You may not have had passwords for all your accounts in the past, but now that you've suffered the misery of identity theft, you'll be eager to protect all your accounts — online and otherwise — with a guess-proof password. See Chapters 13 and 16 for more password help.

Notifying the Social Security Administration

If you're a victim of identity theft, you want to make sure this most essential of numbers has not been compromised. Report the theft to the Office of the Inspector General at the Social Security Administration. You can find them at:

Social Security Administration Fraud Hotline
P.O. Box 17768
Baltimore, MD 21235
Phone: 800-269-0271
Fax: 410-597-0118
Web: www.socialsecurity.gov/oig

They'll take your information and follow up on any fraud or illegal use of your Social Security number.

Beyond identity theft, they're concerned about possible terrorist theft of Social Security numbers to establish false identities having nothing to do with credit.

Having done your patriotic duty, you'll also want to carefully check your annual earnings record through the normal channels at the Social Security Administration and keep doing so on a regular basis to see if there are entries that don't look correct to you or that you can't account for. You can check your information by contacting the Social Security guys at www.social security.gov or calling 800-772-1213.

If you've done all you can to fix the problem and you continue to find evidence that your number is being misused, the Social Security office may assign you a new number. However, you cannot get a new Social Security number if:

✔ You've filed for bankruptcy.

✔ You intend to avoid the law or your legal responsibility.

✔ Your Social Security card is lost or stolen, but there is no evidence that someone is using your number.

Checking Your Checking Accounts

If your checks or checking-account numbers have been stolen or misused, close the account(s) and ask your bank to notify the appropriate check-verification service. Unlike credit or debit cards, no federal law limits your losses if someone steals your checks and forges your signature. However, state laws *may* protect you.

Most states hold the bank responsible for losses from a forged check, but they also require that you take reasonable care of your account. For example, you may be held responsible for the forgery if you fail to notify the bank that your checkbook has been stolen or is missing. Your local bank manager may be able to help put you in touch with the right department in your state. If not, contact your state banking or consumer-protection agency for more information.

Notify all check-verification companies — or *registries,* as I call them — if you believe your checking information has been stolen. (Turn to Chapter 2 for more information.)

ChexSystems (www.chexsystems.com) is the most comprehensive of the check-fraud sites. You may place either a 90-day or a 5-year security alert. For the 90-day alert, call and get a password to allow you to file a report online. To extend the five-year alert, you'll need to download the form, have it notarized, and send it to them.

Check, Check, and Check Again

After you've canceled your cards and protected every account you can with a password, you can relax, right? Sorry, but the answer is no. If your personal information has been compromised, chances are a thief will use this knowledge — somewhere, sometime — for his personal gain and your loss. Review your credit report frequently. Place an extended, seven-year alert on your credit report. You may want to resort to a monitoring service as well.

If your home were broken into, you wouldn't think twice about buying an alarm system. Consider these precautions your own personal alarm system to notify you and your "security service," the credit bureaus, that there's been an identity break-in.

Even if your thief is caught and prosecuted to the fullest extent of the law, continue to check your credit reports often — at least two or three times a year for the first two years. Be diligent in reporting any errors and make sure inaccuracies are corrected and errors are removed from your reports. Do the same with your annual earnings statement from the Social Security Administration. Protect your information and teach your family members to do the same.

Keeping Good Records

Good record-keeping on your part is important in repairing identity theft damage. Keep contact information and follow up by snail mail or e-mail with everyone you've contacted. For snail mail, use certified mail and request a return receipt.

Set aside a file drawer or area for originals and copies of all correspondence or forms you send. Don't send originals of police reports or statements. Write down the name of anyone you talk to, what he or she told you, and the date the conversation occurred. A good example of such a form for record-keeping is "Chart Your Course of Action," available on the CD. You can also find the form at www.ftc.gov/bcp/conline/pubs/credit/idtheft.htm#Identity.

While you're gathering and securing documentation of theft activity, take inventory of your other valuable documents — containing information that may have led to your current identity-theft woes and how you handle or store them. I have some suggestions:

- ✔ **Buy a shredder, and use it regularly.** Never throw away any papers with any type of identifying information without shredding them first. This includes all those preapproved credit-card offers that flood your mailbox, in addition to actual account statements that you no longer need.

- ✔ **Keep your information safely locked away.** Although I don't suggest you turn your home into Fort Knox, keeping your personal papers out in the open is not the way to keep them safe. A locking file cabinet or drawer will deter at least a casual thief from stealing your valuables. They may get the silver, but they won't get your account numbers!

- ✔ **Get a safe-deposit box at your local bank.** A safe-deposit box is the best bet for valuable papers, Social Security cards, birth certificates, citizenship papers, automobile titles, and the like. If you don't want to get a box, at least purchase a fireproof safe for these papers.

- ✔ **Password-protect your computer and its programs.** Most computers allow you to set up a password at startup and, similarly, most software will allow passwords to restrict access to certain documents. If you keep banking or financial planning/investment information in files on your computer, use a password.

Chapter 19

Ten Ways to Handle Financial Emergencies

In This Chapter

▶ Implementing a plan *before* an emergency strikes

▶ Drawing on resources you may not have considered

▶ Weighing the pluses and minuses of bankruptcy

*F*or many people, an unexpected emergency is what launches them into credit trouble. Individuals who responsibly pay their bills on time, credit-card users who pay off their charges monthly, homeowners who keep up with their mortgage payments — all can easily be thrown into financial crisis when certain surprises strike. A serious illness or accident can rack up astronomical medical expenses in no time. A job layoff can eat up that last paycheck before the rent is paid. And suddenly, responsible people are facing down a financial firestorm that ravages their good credit standing.

A financial emergency is not much different from any other type of emergency. You can prepare and respond in ways that will reduce the casualties and improve your recovery. So consider these ten tips for tackling financial emergencies your very own emergency-response plan that will lessen the impact on your wallet and your credit.

Planning Ahead to Make a Difference

Companies develop disaster plans to help prepare for situations such as fire, theft, or customer injury onsite. As an individual or family, you also benefit from a plan for unexpected financial emergencies. You have homeowner's insurance to protect you if your home has a fire; you have car insurance in place to cover damage to your vehicle. But your preparations must extend beyond these measures for full protection from financial emergencies.

Why is planning ahead so important? Because if you're in the middle of a life emergency — say you just got laid off — you'll want to concentrate on the job crisis at hand, updating your résumé and setting up job interviews, for example, rather than worrying about paying the rent. Or if you're seriously injured, you want to focus on recovery instead of losing sleep and adding to unhealthy stress over mounting medical bills.

Your emergency plan starts with setting some goals: building a savings cushion of six months of living expenses in case of a job loss, for example, or making sure you have adequate insurance — health, medical, homeowner's, disability — to cover most emergencies. The key element to focus on is the plan. The results will follow.

Expecting the Unexpected

Save some room in your monthly spending plan for the unexpected. Many people have the tendency to spend what they have. Whether they make $30,000 or $250,000 a year, they spend it if it's there. That leaves them with no financial cushion in case of an unexpected cash crisis — from car trouble to medical emergency to job loss.

Most financial professionals recommend that you stash away between three and six months of expenses for unforeseen events. If this number seems impossible, let me assure you it is not. With time and commitment, you'll establish a habit of savings and then your emergency fund will take on a life of its own.

The key is to work the *unexpected* into your plan. For example, put away a set amount each paycheck into an emergency fund. Nothing left over? Trust me: The pizza you order each Thursday evening will not help much when your car needs repair, but the $20 put aside each week will add up quickly and help cover that $400 repair bill. Cut or trim back your weekly spending and you'll hardly notice the change. But the money set aside will make a huge difference when the unexpected occurs.

Paying Yourself First

The first rule of saving is to pay yourself first. Don't wait until the end of the month to put aside savings — you may not have any money left. Instead, put the money away as soon as you get paid. I strongly recommend that you have it taken from your check and direct-deposited into your savings account before you ever see it, much less get a chance to spend it. In addition, try to save at least half of any pay raises, bonuses, or tax refunds that you receive and, again, have the money direct-deposited if you can.

Your goal? As I mentioned earlier, to build a stockpile of three to six months of living expenses in your emergency fund savings account. It will not happen overnight, but your regular efforts will add up.

Increasing Income to Cover Expenses

After you've done all you can to reduce or meet your expenses, the next step is to look for ways to increase your income. *Income* is defined as what is left out of your paycheck after deductions for taxes and insurance. There are two ways to increase your income: Reduce your deductions or make more money.

Scrutinize your deductions carefully. Are you over-withholding for income taxes? Many people look at the IRS as a sort of savings account — they may purposefully claim fewer deductions than necessary in order to get that big tax-return check each tax season. But if you're getting more than $600 a year back in refunds, you may squeeze this category a bit. You'll be better off having that money on a month-to-month basis, earning the interest yourself, rather than letting the IRS hold on to it (without paying you any interest).

Here are some ways you can earn more money to be able to put aside something to fund that emergency account:

- **Get a second job.** No, not another full-time job. But a job with enough hours to make a dent in those emergency expenses — or to start your emergency savings. If you do the planning that I recommend earlier in this chapter, you'll know how much extra cash you need to build your emergency fund — sometimes a few extra hours on a Saturday is all it takes.

- **Work overtime.** Overtime hours can be a great way to increase your immediate earnings. I don't recommend building a budget dependent on overtime, but extra hours can help cover emergency expenses or fund savings.

- **Ask for a raise.** If it's been a year or more since your last raise, or if your job has changed significantly but your income hasn't, it never hurts to ask. Some things that you can do to increase your worth to your employer include getting additional certifications or education.

Selling Off Some Assets

In the face of a financial emergency showing up on your doorstop, some of your possessions may not hold the same value for you that they once did. If you're struggling with a medical condition, you may not have time to enjoy your sailboat on the weekends. If you're out of a job, the extra monthly payment for your second SUV, the motorcycle, and the snowmobile become a burden.

Consider selling off big-ticket items such as boats or vehicles. This will free up some much-needed cash to go toward your emergency expenses — and if you're still carrying a loan on the item, you'll eliminate that monthly payment, as well. Plus, getting rid of cars, boats — even jewelry — can reduce your insurance premiums. Review your assets: vehicles, boats, motorcycles, musical instruments, jewelry, artwork, and "toys" such as snowmobiles, jet skis, and golf clubs. Whether you sell your grand piano on eBay or gather your clutter and hold a garage sale, you just may be able to offset some or all of your emergency costs by turning your possessions into ready cash.

Borrowing Against Your Home

If you're a homeowner, I don't have to tell you that one of the most popular ways to consolidate debt or remodel your home these days is with a home-equity loan or line of credit. But if you own a home, have built up equity, and can afford an additional monthly payment, a home-equity line of credit may be just the ticket to help get you through a financial emergency. With a home-equity line of credit, you have access to the money if and when you need it, but not before. So your interest payments are only incurred if you draw on the line of credit, and they may be tax deductible.

Be careful not to over-borrow against your home. Because home prices can go down as well as up, I recommend that you try to keep the total amount of your mortgage to around 75 percent of your home's value. Consider this an investment in yourself — not investing for a vacation, but to get you through a rough financial spot before you sail into calmer waters.

Some lenders will provide an equity loan of up to 125 percent of your home's value. But being *upside down* on a home loan — where you owe more than the house is worth — is not a place your want to be. You won't be able to sell the house to downsize or move to take advantage of a job opportunity. And don't forget that your home is securing the home-equity line of credit. If you fail to meet your obligation, you could lose your home.

Calling On Friends and Relatives

A friend or a relative who has been more fortunate than you may be just the help you need to get through hard times.

If you have a supportive clan who can *afford* to help you overcome a financial hardship, you're fortunate, indeed. But I don't have to tell you that if money issues can destroy a marriage, they can also ruin a friendship and create family feuds. So, by all means, turn to friends and relatives for help, but do so with a careful and considerate approach. Neither bended knee nor flattery is what's called for. Responsibility and commitment are.

Here are some tips for borrowing from friends or family:

- ✔ **Make sure you put the terms of the loan in writing.**

- ✔ **Pay interest just as you would with a traditional loan.** Paying interest can keep your friends or family from feeling as though they're being taken advantage of.

- ✔ **Treat the loan just as you would an agreement with any other lender.** Establish a regular payment schedule — monthly, weekly, semi-monthly, annually — with a due date for each payment.

- ✔ **If you can't make a scheduled payment, communicate with the person immediately.** Offer whatever contingency plan you can — for example, making a partial payment or rescheduling a revised payment date.

- ✔ **Know that your failure to pay back the loan may damage your relationship with the person loaning you the money.** Do everything you can to set realistic terms and live up to them.

Deferring Retirement Contributions

If you're regularly contributing to a retirement plan — a 401(k), 403(b), or IRA, for example — you may want to consider foregoing these contributions and funneling the money toward your emergency expenses.

I advise this only as a short-term strategy. After all, the money in your retirement plan is tax-deferred (except in the case of Roth IRAs) and it grows with compounded interest. Additionally, you may be receiving an employer match when you contribute. If you aren't making your regular contribution, you miss out on these benefits. You can, however, make a commitment to make up the contributions you missed at a later date — and I would encourage you to do so.

Deferring your retirement contributions is definitely a better strategy than borrowing from your retirement account. But borrowing from your retirement account is an option if your situation demands it. If you do take money out of your account, you'll incur penalties and taxes that could take away 50 percent of its value. Only do this in the most dire of situations.

Seeking Professional Help

If you're at the end of your rope and see no other way out of your financial crisis, it may be time to call in the professionals at a credit-counseling agency. Check out Chapter 3 for help on finding someone who can help you get back on track.

Declaring Bankruptcy

Filing for bankruptcy is a legitimate way to handle a financial emergency if nothing else succeeds. Half of the personal bankruptcies filed in the United States are due to medical expenses. But bankruptcy is definitely a last-resort tactic.

The good part about a bankruptcy is that it works. If you're able to qualify for a Chapter 7, your debts will be wiped out and you'll have the opportunity to begin over again. That said, because bankruptcy is such a serious course of action, I only recommend it if you have no other option. What does that mean? Well, if you can do else to work your way out of debt, try it first. If you have a reason to hope that things will get better soon, wait. In short if you're hopeless and helpless, bankruptcy is for you.

In the end, the decision to file bankruptcy is a very personal one, and in the end, you're the only one to whom you have to justify that decision (aside from the court).

Turn to Chapter 9 for more on the pros and cons of filing bankruptcy.

Appendix A

Glossary

account: A record of transactions between the creditor and the consumer. Account examples include a mortgage, car loan, or credit card.

account number: A number assigned to an account by the creditor to identify the particular account and the person who is financially responsible for the account.

account reviews: Consumer credit history inquiries made by creditors with whom the consumer has a current relationship. This type of inquiry is the equivalent of just peeking at your file to be sure everything is ship-shape. Because you don't initiate the inquiry, it is not included in credit reports or credit scoring.

adverse action: Any negative action — such as the denial of credit, insurance, or employment — taken by a creditor or other person or company. The reasons for an adverse action must be disclosed to the person who was affected, as required under the Fair Credit Reporting Act, and the person is entitled to a free credit report from the bureau to which the adverse action was reported.

adverse information: Any information included in your credit report that a creditor or other interested party would view as reason to consider denying a loan or rejecting an applicant, such as past-due accounts.

application scoring: A statistical model used to evaluate and score credit applications and credit-bureau data. The score is used by banks and businesses to determine whether to accept or decline a credit application.

bank card: A general purpose credit card issued through a local, regional, or national bank that is accepted by millions of merchants, unlike store or gasoline credit cards, which may be accepted only by a specific merchant or brand. Most common are Visa, MasterCard, and American Express.

bankruptcy: A civil court proceeding in a district bankruptcy court that allows consumers legal relief from all or part of their debts. Bankruptcies appear on an individual's credit report for up to ten years.

business-version credit report: The business version of a credit report is an abbreviated version of a consumer's credit report that creditors see. The business version does not contain account reviews or promotional inquiries.

CCCS: *See* Consumer Credit Counseling Service.

Chapter 7 bankruptcy: A form of bankruptcy that requires consumers to pass a means test and give up some assets in order to be relieved of qualified debt. Excluded from relief is child support, alimony, taxes, debt incurred to pay taxes, and student loans. Also known as *liquidation.*

Chapter 11 bankruptcy: A form of bankruptcy, often used by corporations, that allows those who qualify to keep creditors at bay until the company or individual is able to pay their debts. This is the most well-known of the corporate bankruptcy chapters.

Chapter 12 bankruptcy: A form of bankruptcy that allows farmers to reorganize their debt and keep their farms.

Chapter 13 bankruptcy: A form of bankruptcy that allows consumers to keep most of their assets based on a means test and repay debt they can afford based on IRS allowances over a three- or five-year period of time under court supervision and protection. Chapter 13 is generally reported for seven years but may be reported up to ten years at the discretion of the credit bureau. Often referred to as *wage-earner bankruptcy.*

charge card: A form of credit card that requires payment in full each month and does not charge interest. Examples include the traditional American Express card and Diner's Club card.

charge-off: The status of an account when it goes unpaid for, typically, more than 180 days, and the balance of the account is written off by the creditor as a bad debt (for tax purposes only). The debt is still valid and collectible along with fees and interest.

COA: *See* Council on Accreditation.

collection: A past-due account that is transferred to an inside or third-party collector in an attempt to recover the balance due. Only third-party collectors as opposed to collectors who are employees of the company you owe the debt to are governed by the Fair Debt Collections Practices Act.

Consumer Credit Counseling Service (CCCS): A network of nonprofit counseling agencies that offer advice, budgeting, debt-management plans, and housing counseling. Look for accreditation by the Council on Accreditation.

consumer-version credit report: Credit report containing a consumer's credit information. Information may include your name, address, Social Security number, credit history, inquiries, collection records, and public records such as bankruptcy filings and tax liens. Creditors do not see this version of your credit report.

cosigner: An individual who signs a loan agreement in commitment to being responsible for repaying a debt if the primary borrower defaults.

Council on Accreditation: The largest accreditor of nonprofit organizations, including credit-counseling agencies, in the United States.

credit: The ability to create a debt by having a loan granted to buy now and pay later under designated terms based on a consumer's promise, ability, and track record of repaying.

credit bureau: A company that accumulates credit data on individuals, provided by creditors, and compiles this data in the form of a credit report.

credit card: A form of credit that enables a consumer to purchase goods and services and pay for them with scheduled monthly payments, and charging interest on balances that are not paid in full at the end of the month. A form of revolving credit.

credit check: A request to view a consumer's credit report to ascertain whether to extend credit to the consumer.

credit clinic: *See* credit-repair company.

credit file: *See* credit report.

credit fraud: Unauthorized use of credit by someone using fictitious personal information.

credit history: A record of a consumer's credit behaviors over an extended period of time, including credit account and payment activity. Negative information is usually reported for seven years with the exception of bankruptcy, which may be reported for up to ten years. Positive information will stay on indefinitely, sometimes for 20 years or more.

credit limit: An amount set by a lender establishing the maximum level of credit that can be extended on a particular account.

credit obligation: A legal agreement between a creditor and an individual that requires the individual to repay a debt.

credit-repair company: A business that alleges to be able to "clean up" or "erase" bad credit for clients. The abuses of such companies prompted passage of the Credit Repair Organizations Act to regulate their behavior. Also known as a *credit-repair clinic.*

credit report: A consumer's credit history as compiled by a credit bureau, including both credit and personal information about the consumer. Also known as a *credit file.*

credit risk: A determination by a potential creditor of a consumer's likelihood of repaying a debt as agreed.

credit score: A mathematical model used to assess a consumer's credit likelihood of default. The risk level is expressed in a three-digit number. A creditor gets your information from a credit-reporting agency and may order a credit score or apply its own credit scoring model to calculate a proprietary credit score.

creditor: A business or person who extends credit or lends money to individuals or businesses.

creditworthiness: A term used to describe a person's credit behavior on which a potential creditor bases the decision to extend that person credit. Those determined to have low creditworthiness will likely not be extended credit.

date closed: Point in time when an account or credit obligation is terminated.

date opened: Point in time when an account or credit obligation is established.

debt-management plan (DMP): A plan for repaying your debts, accepted by creditors and administered by a credit-counseling agency.

default: The failure to make a debt payment on time as agreed in the original credit agreement.

delinquent: The failure of a consumer to pay a credit account on time as agreed. A credit report lists delinquencies as 30 days, 60 days, 90 days, and 120 days late.

dispute: The official act of an individual challenging an item listed on his credit report; a dispute must be investigated by the credit bureau listing the item within 30 days of notification.

DMP: *See* debt-management plan.

Equifax: One of the three major credit-reporting agencies.

Experian: One of the three major credit-reporting agencies, formerly known as TRW.

Fair Credit Reporting Act (FCRA): Federal legislation enacted in 1970, assuring the accuracy, confidentiality, and proper use of information in the consumer files of every credit bureau.

Fair Debt Collection Practices Act (FDCPA): A law that amends the Consumer Credit Protection Act to prohibit abusive practices by debt collectors.

FICO score: A three-digit number devised by Fair Isaac, Inc., to measure a consumer's level of credit risk and based on information in the consumer's credit report.

fraud alert: A warning placed on a credit report by a consumer who believes he may have been the victim of identity theft; a fraud alert requires creditors to exercise caution when taking any action. Such an alert will prevent new credit accounts from being opened without the customer's express permission.

fraud statement: A notation placed on a credit report by a consumer that lets potential creditors know that the consumer may be a victim of identity theft or other credit fraud.

garnishment: A legal process by which a creditor obtains a judgment from a court on an outstanding debt, which authorizes permission to seize a portion of a debtor's assets — usually wages — to pay that debt.

grace period: A period of time during which a payment is accepted as "on time," thereby avoiding any additional finance charges or penalties. Credit-card accounts carrying a balance from one month to the next and delinquent mortgages do not have a grace period.

home-equity line of credit: A line of credit using your house as collateral. The amount of money available in the line of credit varies depending on how much you want to have available just in case you need it. You have a set period of time (called a *draw period*) when you can access the line of credit and a set period before which you have to pay it back.

home-equity loan: A loan for a specified amount of money, using your house as collateral. In a home-equity loan, you have an installment payment due every month usually at a set interest rate for a set amount of time.

identity: The unique traits and personal information that identify a particular consumer, including Social Security number, date of birth, address, and employer.

identity theft: Unauthorized use of credit by someone using another person's personal information, such as Social Security number, date of birth, or other identifying information.

inquiry: A request from a potential creditor, employer, landlord, or insurer to view an individual's credit report. The inquiry is listed on the credit report. Only those inquiries resulting from an application for credit are considered in the calculation of a credit score.

installment loan: A credit account that is paid in equal, periodic installments, usually monthly, of a specified amount for a specified length of time. An example of an installment loan is a car loan.

insurance bureau score: An insurance rating based on data from the major credit bureaus that helps insurers evaluate new and renewal auto and home-owner's insurance policies.

judgment: An official decision by a court relating to an action or suit. Typically, it is a ruling that a debt is valid and orders payment. A judgment is a public record and is listed on your credit report as a negative item.

late payment: A payment delivered to a creditor after the due date or time.

lien: A legal claim against real or personal property for the purposes of satisfying a debt.

line of credit: A specific amount of credit established by a lender that can be accessed by a consumer in whole or in part.

liquidation: *See* Chapter 7 bankruptcy.

manner of payment (MOP): Codes used on some credit-bureau reports that establish the payment patterns of the consumer — for example, "paid as agreed," "30 days late," and so on.

mortgage: A loan document that is recorded in official records and places a lien on real property until the creditor is paid in full according to the schedule and terms of the loan.

open account: A credit account that is currently active, still in use, and/or being paid.

paid as agreed: A term used on credit reports indicating that the account in question is being paid according to the terms of the agreement.

permissible purpose: Circumstances under which the Fair Credit Reporting Act deems it appropriate for a consumer credit report to be viewed by a third party.

promotional inquiry: A request to view a consumer's credit report for the purposes of consideration for an unsolicited promotional credit offer. Promotional inquiries are recorded only on the consumer copy of the credit report and do not count in credit scoring.

public records: Information included on a credit report such as bankruptcy court records, court judgments, tax liens, and other information available to the general public.

retail card: A credit account that is issued by a retail company such as a department store or electronics store.

revolving-credit account: A type of credit account that makes available a pre-determined amount of money that can be used at any time without additional approval.

scoring model: Formulas used to determine the likely future credit behavior of prospective borrowers and existing customers. A scoring model calculates credit scores based on data such as the information included in a consumer's credit report.

secured credit: A line of credit that is backed by real property such as a home, auto, boat, or securities.

trade line: A credit-industry term for an account listed on a credit report including bank loans, credit cards, mortgages, or any number of other credit accounts.

TransUnion: One of the three major credit-reporting bureaus.

TRW: *See* Experian.

universal default: A clause contained in many credit agreements allowing a current account that is paid as agreed to be converted to default status based on the default of another account or signs that the consumer is overextending and/or presenting a higher risk profile, as evidenced by information contained in the credit report.

unsecured credit: A loan or line of credit that is backed only by a promise to pay.

upside-down loan: A loan in which you owe more than the item securing the loan is worth — for example, you owe $10,000 on a car loan, but the car is only worth $7,000.

wage-earner bankruptcy: *See* Chapter 13 bankruptcy.

Appendix B

About the CD

System Requirements

Make sure that your computer meets the minimum system requirements shown in the following list. If your computer doesn't match up to most of these requirements, you may have problems using the software and files on the CD. For the latest and greatest information, please refer to the ReadMe file located at the root of the CD-ROM.

- ✔ A PC with a Pentium or faster processor; or a Mac OS computer with a 68040 or faster processor

- ✔ Microsoft Windows 98 or later; or Mac OS system software 7.6.1 or later

- ✔ At least 32MB of total RAM installed on your computer; for best performance, we recommend at least 64MB

- ✔ A CD-ROM drive

- ✔ A sound card for PCs; Mac OS computers have built-in sound support

- ✔ A monitor capable of displaying at least 256 colors or grayscale

- ✔ A modem with a speed of at least 14,400 bps

If you need more information on the basics, check out these books published by Wiley Publishing, Inc.: *PCs For Dummies,* by Dan Gookin; *Macs For Dummies,* by David Pogue; *iMacs For Dummies,* by David Pogue; *Windows 95 For Dummies, Windows 98 For Dummies, Windows 2000 Professional For Dummies, Microsoft Windows ME Millennium Edition For Dummies,* and *Windows XP For Dummies,* 2nd Edition, all by Andy Rathbone.

Using the CD

To install the items from the CD to your hard drive, follow these steps.

1. **Insert the CD into your computer's CD-ROM drive.**

   The license agreement appears.

   Note to Windows users: The interface won't launch if you have autorun disabled. In that case, choose Start íRun. In the dialog box that appears, type **D:\start.exe**. (Replace D with the proper letter if your CD-ROM drive uses a different letter. If you don't know the letter, see how your CD-ROM drive is listed under My Computer.) Click OK.

   Note to Mac Users: The CD icon will appear on your desktop, double-click the icon to open the CD and double-click the "Start" icon.

2. **Read through the license agreement, and then click the Accept button if you want to use the CD. After you click Accept, the License Agreement window won't appear again.**

   The CD interface appears. The interface allows you to install the programs and run the demos with just a click of a button (or two).

What You'll Find on the CD

The following sections are arranged by category and provide a summary of the software and other goodies you'll find on the CD. If you need help with installing the items provided on the CD, refer to the installation instructions in the preceding section.

Shareware programs are fully functional, free, trial versions of copyrighted programs. If you like particular programs, register with their authors for a nominal fee and receive licenses, enhanced versions, and technical support.

Freeware programs are free, copyrighted games, applications, and utilities. You can copy them to as many PCs as you like — for free — but they offer no technical support.

GNU software is governed by its own license, which is included inside the folder of the GNU software. There are no restrictions on distribution of GNU software. See the GNU license at the root of the CD for more details.

Trial, demo, or *evaluation* versions of software are usually limited either by time or functionality (such as not letting you save a project after you create it).

Software

The files on the CD are in Adobe PDF, Microsoft Word, and Microsoft Excel formats. In case you don't have Adobe Reader, Microsoft Word, or Microsoft Excel on your computer, I've included the following on the CD, so that you can read all the files I've included:

- ✔ **Adobe Reader:** Adobe Reader is a freeware application for viewing files in the Adobe Portable Document format.

- ✔ **OpenOffice.org:** OpenOffice.org is a free multi-platform office productivity suite. It is similar to Microsoft Office or Lotus SmartSuite, but OpenOffice.org is absolutely free. It includes word processing, spreadsheet, presentation, and drawing applications that enable you to create professional documents, newsletters, reports, and presentations. It supports most file formats of other office software. You should be able to edit and view any files created with other office solutions.

Acts

If you are, like me, a little strange, you may want to see the underlying legislation that spells out all the facts that apply to credit reports and debt collection. For all of you kindred spirits, I have included my favorite laws. If you're, like my wife — normal, or so she says — you'll go on to the next section.

- ✔ `Fair and Accurate Credit Transaction Act.pdf:` This is the famous FACT Act. It is an update to the Fair Credit Reporting Act (see the following bullet). It was designed to give you tools to help prevent identity theft, improve the credit-report dispute process, improve the accuracy of your credit data, and give you better access to your credit information as well as free credit reports annually.

- ✔ `Fair Credit Reporting Act.pdf:` This is the granddaddy of credit-reporting legislation. It deals with issues such as who can review your credit information and under what conditions, what information is kept in your report and for how long and what you rights are to access and dispute your data.

- ✔ `Fair Debt Collection Practices Act.pdf:` Here is the rulebook that collectors have to follow when contacting a person about a bill. What, when, and how they can do what they do is spelled out here. Your rights and what's fair and what's not are all included in this act.

- ✔ `Servicemembers Civil Relief Act.pdf:` This is an update of the Soldiers and Sailors Civil Relief Act. It covers the special rights that servicepersons have that allow them to concentrate on defending the United States — rather than defending *themselves* from creditors.

Bankruptcy

Understanding the means test that determines what chapter of personal bankruptcy you may qualify for can be very confusing. The handy `New Bankruptcy Code Filing Procedures Chart.pdf` is a graphic representation of the process used to determine which bankruptcy chapter an individual will qualify for under the Bankruptcy Abuse Prevention and Consumer Protection Act of 2005.

Credit-Report Letters

Here are samples of letters that get you started communicating effectively with your credit bureaus and creditors. *Remember:* Everyone makes mistakes, including the credit bureaus and creditors. You're just helping them to improve the quality of their records if you spot an error in your report.

- ✔ `Add 100-Word Statement to Report.doc:` This letter provides the format for adding a 100-word statement to your credit report explaining a negative item. This will not be picked up if your lender uses automated underwriting. The bureaus will assist you in writing a concise statement if you go over 100 words or (in the case of TransUnion only) if you ask them to.

- ✔ `Add Accounts to Report.doc:` If you have verifiable accounts that do not appear on your credit report, you can ask to have them added. There may be a fee and the bureau may refuse; however, often they'll add verifiable information to make your record more complete.

- ✔ `Annual Credit Report Request Form.pdf:` When requesting your free annual credit report, making your request on the official form is important. Use the `Request Credit File.doc` letter (see later in this list) as a cover letter.

- ✔ `Reinvestigation Request.doc:` This provides the basics you'll need to dispute an item in error or out of date on your credit report.

- ✔ `Request Credit File.doc:` This is a generic letter that you can use to request a free credit report for various reasons. If you're requesting a free annual credit report, attach the `Annual Credit Report Request Form.pdf` (earlier in this list).

- ✔ `Request for Creditor to Remove Error.doc:` This letter is helpful if your original request to a credit bureau did not remove a disputed item from your credit report. Asking the creditor directly may get you the attention you need.

Credit Reports and Credit Scores

If you've never ordered a copy of your credit report or credit score, this section shows you what to expect. A samples of the TransUnion credit report is included on the CD, as well as a sample credit score from Fair Isaac, to help demystify the process.

- ✔ `FICO Sample Score Report.pdf`: This PDF of a credit report order from the myFICO Web site shows you the reporting format used and what you should expect to see if you order a report from them with a credit score.

- ✔ `TransUnion Sample Credit Report.pdf`: This is a PDF of what you should expect to see if you order a credit report from TransUnion.

- ✔ `Understanding Your Credit Report.pdf`: This is a good credit report reference guide from the nonprofit agency Money Management International.

If you're interested in seeing sample reports from the other major credit-reporting bureaus (Equifax and Experian), as well as two of the major check-reporting bureaus (ChexSystems and SCAN), you can do so online:

- ✔ **ChexSystems:** Go to www.consumerdebit.com and, under "Consumer Assistance," click on "Sample Consumer Report." Then, next to "ChexSystems report," click "View Sample."

- ✔ **Equifax:** Go to www.equifax.com and, from the "Products" drop-down menu, click on "Equifax Credit Report"; then click on "See Equifax Credit Report sample."

- ✔ **Experian:** Go to www.experian.com/consumer_online_products/ credit_report.html and click on "View Sample Report."

- ✔ **SCAN:** Go to www.consumerdebit.com and, under "Consumer Assistance," click on "Sample Consumer Report." Then, next to "SCAN report," click "View Sample."

Creditor Letters

Communicating with your creditors can be a daunting task for many. This section has drafts of letters that will help you be precise, professional, and effective. In other words, get your way, with a minimum of fuss and worry.

Current Accounts

As a valued customer, your satisfaction is a primary concern of your creditors. These letters will help them be able to help you. Everyone will be happier with a few suggestions.

✔ **Billing Error.doc:** A short and professional letter aimed at getting billing discrepancies resolved quickly.

✔ **Change Due Date.doc:** Changing your due date with some creditors will allow you to spread your payments out to better match your pay-days. Here is letter to do just that.

✔ **Partial Payment Current.doc:** This letter shows you how to communicate with your creditor if you can't make a full payment due to circumstances beyond your control.

✔ **Request to Lower Interest.doc:** Service personnel on active duty can use the wording of this letter to reduce finance charges to the 6 percent legal limit allowed under the Servicemembers Civil Relief Act.

✔ **Unemployment Letter.doc:** When you can't make any payment to your creditors, it's better to tell them in advance than to let them guess why you didn't send in your payment. This letter will help set a professional and concerned tone for future communications with your creditors.

Delinquent Accounts

This list of letters contains suggested wordings that you should feel free to modify to fit your situation and tone. Using a professional tone is always best, regardless of your level of frustration or emotion. *Remember:* A letter will not resolve the situation, only a payment will — but documenting your efforts at trying to work out a solution is very important if matters should escalate to a court action. If you copy (cc:) a lawyer, be sure the collector knows about it. If you ask your lawyer to send a letter, expect the collector's attorney to respond to your lawyer. And always be sure to send correspondence certified mail with a return receipt requested to document your efforts.

✔ **Intend to File Bankruptcy.doc:** This is a short-and-sweet notice to your creditors that will stop any collection calls. It's usually easier and cleaner to send them a letter stating your intention rather than try to do this over the phone.

✔ **Offer to Return Secured Items.doc:** This letter puts you on record as trying to do the right thing in a difficult situation. Some items, like jewelry or hard goods, may be easier for the creditor to take back.

✔ **Partial Payment Delinquent.doc:** Contacting your creditors before you send in a short payment is a good idea. This letter asks that you be contacted in writing. They may call you at home if they have a current number, but you should not be called at work after they receive this letter.

✔ **Request a Settlement.doc:** Making an offer to settle an account for less than is owed is never the first choice of a creditor. Expect a push back from them unless you haven't made any payment in a long time. Also be prepared to answer the question about how you can come up with a lump-sum payment, but not an installment. (Perhaps a family member is willing to help out or you have a small windfall.)

✔ **Request No Future Contact.doc:** This letter will stop the phone calls but not the collection activity. Expect that the creditor will continue to want its money and will probably refer the matter to its lawyers.

✔ **Request to Stop Harassment.doc:** If you're being harassed, it is important to be on record with as much detail as possible. The Federal Trade Commission won't investigate, but your letter may help them identify a trend with some collection companies, which may move them to action. If you include your lawyer's name, be sure to run the letter by your lawyer first.

✔ **Request to Stop Work Calls.doc:** This letter will stop calls at work, but it's important to tell the creditor where and when they *can* contact you. They have the right to contact you, but only when it is convenient. If you don't let them know when it's convenient for them to contact *you,* they'll do it when it's convenient for *them*.

Forms and Worksheets

This section contains some handy tools to help you keep track of your communications with creditors and your money at home. You can use each of them individually or, if you want a soup to nuts approach, I suggest the Understanding Money and Credit.pdf, a comprehensive guide that will deliver much of what you get from visiting a financial professional (minus the personalized advice).

✔ **Communication Log.doc:** Being able to document all contacts with accuracy is essential to being credible and professional. This simple log will give you the essential categories to keep track of as you go through this process.

✔ **Cutting Expenses.doc:** Tracking your efforts is an important part of cutting back successfully. It's easy to think you aren't making progress unless you write it down. Having a goal on paper is much more powerful than having a goal in mind.

✔ **Future Plans and Goals.xls:** This worksheet gives you the elements you'll want to be sure to include as you set goals and track your progress. Expect this process to take more than one time to get right for you and your family. Be sure to go back and make changes as you go along to keep your goals realistic and achievable.

✔ **Money Gobblers.doc:** In the normal course of your day, you probably spend money almost as naturally as you breathe. Recognizing which of these money gobblers you really want to keep and which you don't need is an important part of getting back in control of your spending. The objective is to use this form to track where your cash goes so you can spend money on those things that you really want, not just on anything that comes along.

- ✔ **Monthly Expense Worksheet.doc:** The essential ingredient in controlling your expenses is to know where your money is going and decide if you want that to continue. This form can be customized to your needs but will give you a good starting point for identifying monthly expenses and beginning a livable budget.

- ✔ **Monthly Income Worksheet.doc:** The second essential ingredient in a good budget is knowing exactly how much you have to spend. Be sure to look at deductions from your paycheck to see if they can be reduced to increase your take-home pay. Reducing withholding for taxes if you always get a big refund is a good example.

- ✔ **Outstanding Debts.doc:** Fewer people than you would expect actually know how much they owe. This form will help you get a handle on the size of your debts and give you a reality check on which to base your solutions.

- ✔ **Understanding Money and Credit.pdf:** This is a great booklet that will help you assess where you are, set goals, prepare a budget and begin to save for the future. It has great worksheets and tips.

Identity Theft

Identity theft is on everybody's radar, newscast, and front page these days, and in this section you'll find tools to use if you think you've been a victim of identity theft, to keep the damage to a minimum:

- ✔ **Fraud Alert Letter to Credit-Reporting Agency.doc:** Quick and concise notification of possible identity theft is essential to limiting damage to your credit and those creditors who may be victimized as well. This letter has all the essential ingredients you need to stop identity theft from going any further and begin to recover from it.

- ✔ **Chart Your Course of Action.pdf:** This sample format will get you started on the path to organization, while tracking all your contacts with credit bureaus, creditors, and the law-enforcement agencies.

- ✔ **Identity Theft Letter to Institutions Directly Involved.doc:** Your identity has been stolen and so has their money, products, or services. Quickly letting creditors know about a theft not only helps your credit report but limits both your and the creditor's losses.

- ✔ **Identity Theft Letter to Institutions Not Directly Involved.doc:** Use this letter when you suspect your identity has been compromised but before you *know* someone is using it illegally. Placing passwords and safeguards on your account can help keep it and you credit safe from a thief who has your personal information.

Links

Following are some links to a few of the many sites out there in cyberspace that I think will be of interest and assistance to you. I hope you find one or more helpful. I don't endorse everything that these sites have to offer, but I do think they offer a good range of places to start looking at what type of information and help is out there.

- ✔ `www.bankrate.com/overkeyword/rate/calc_home.asp:` At Bankrate. com, you'll find many great calculators. The site became famous for its tracking of interest rates but has grown well beyond that into calculators, advice, and insightful articles. My mother thinks the "Debt Advisor" column is one of their best.

- ✔ `www.debtorsanonymous.org:` This site is an Internet treatment program for people who overspend because they can't help themselves. Similar to Alcoholics Anonymous, this site offers a structured program in well-defined steps. If you think your spending is out of control, if you've tried to stop spending but can't, this site may be of interest to you.

- ✔ `www.fool.com:` Similar to Bankrate.com, this site has calculators, advice, and investment information. I prefer Bankrate.com, but you may find this one fits your personal style better.

- ✔ `www.ftc.gov:` This site is the official Federal Trade Commission site that has a great deal of consumer-related information including credit- and identity-theft-related material.

- ✔ `www.guidestar.org:` GuideStar has detailed information on thousands of nonprofit organizations. They show detailed information you can use to decide if you want to use the services of or even give to a nonprofit organization.

- ✔ `www.lawdog.com:` Credit reporting, bankruptcy, and collection issues are covered by this legal site.

- ✔ `www.moneyadvice.com:` A financial planning site with good calculators and an interesting section on cash management.

- ✔ `www.moneymanagement.org/FinancialTools/:` Money Management International is the largest national credit-counseling agency accredited by the Council on Accreditation and the National Foundation for Credit Counseling. They have excellent tools and calculators to help you figure out purchasing options and get a handle on budgeting.

- ✔ `www.mymoney.gov:` This is the federal government's Web site covering topics like budgeting, saving, credit, and FACT Act legislation. In fact, the Fair and Accurate Credit Transaction Act (FACT Act) established the Financial Literacy and Education Commission and this is their site to coordinate many of the government's resources on personal financial matters.

- ✔ **www.naag.org:** This site gives you contact information for all states' attorneys general.

- ✔ **www.moneyclubs.com:** For the ladies, this is an inspirational financial site that has a club featuring a program to empower women to deal more effectively with money issues.

- ✔ **www.privacyrights.org:** This site offers fact sheets on a huge number of topics including identity theft and credit reporting, to name just two.

Troubleshooting

I tried my best to compile programs that work on most computers with the minimum system requirements. Alas, your computer may differ, and some programs may not work properly for some reason.

The two likeliest problems are that you don't have enough memory (RAM) for the programs you want to use, or you have other programs running that are affecting installation or running of a program. If you get an error message such as Not enough memory or Setup cannot continue, try one or more of the following suggestions and then try using the software again:

- ✔ **Turn off any antivirus software running on your computer.** Installation programs sometimes mimic virus activity and may make your computer incorrectly believe that it's being infected by a virus.

- ✔ **Close all running programs.** The more programs you have running, the less memory is available to other programs. Installation programs typically update files and programs; so if you keep other programs running, installation may not work properly.

- ✔ **Have your local computer store add more RAM to your computer.** This is, admittedly, a drastic and somewhat expensive step. However, adding more memory can really help the speed of your computer and allow more programs to run at the same time.

If you have trouble with the CD-ROM, please call the Wiley Product Technical Support phone number at 800-762-2974. Outside the United States, call 1-317-572-3994. You can also contact Wiley Product Technical Support at http://support.wiley.com. John Wiley & Sons will provide technical support only for installation and other general quality control items. For technical support on the applications themselves, consult the program's vendor or author.

To place additional orders or to request information about other Wiley products, please call 877-762-2974.

Index

• *F* •

• J •

• K •

• L •

• *P* •

Wiley Publishing, Inc.
End-User License Agreement

READ THIS. You should carefully read these terms and conditions before opening the software packet(s) included with this book "Book". This is a license agreement "Agreement" between you and Wiley Publishing, Inc. "WPI". By opening the accompanying software packet(s), you acknowledge that you have read and accept the following terms and conditions. If you do not agree and do not want to be bound by such terms and conditions, promptly return the Book and the unopened software packet(s) to the place you obtained them for a full refund.

1. **License Grant.** WPI grants to you (either an individual or entity) a nonexclusive license to use one copy of the enclosed software program(s) (collectively, the "Software") solely for your own personal or business purposes on a single computer (whether a standard computer or a workstation component of a multi-user network). The Software is in use on a computer when it is loaded into temporary memory (RAM) or installed into permanent memory (hard disk, CD-ROM, or other storage device). WPI reserves all rights not expressly granted herein.

2. **Ownership.** WPI is the owner of all right, title, and interest, including copyright, in and to the compilation of the Software recorded on the disk(s) or CD-ROM "Software Media". Copyright to the individual programs recorded on the Software Media is owned by the author or other authorized copyright owner of each program. Ownership of the Software and all proprietary rights relating thereto remain with WPI and its licensers.

3. **Restrictions on Use and Transfer.**

   (a) You may only (i) make one copy of the Software for backup or archival purposes, or (ii) transfer the Software to a single hard disk, provided that you keep the original for backup or archival purposes. You may not (i) rent or lease the Software, (ii) copy or reproduce the Software through a LAN or other network system or through any computer subscriber system or bulletin-board system, or (iii) modify, adapt, or create derivative works based on the Software.

   (b) You may not reverse engineer, decompile, or disassemble the Software. You may transfer the Software and user documentation on a permanent basis, provided that the transferee agrees to accept the terms and conditions of this Agreement and you retain no copies. If the Software is an update or has been updated, any transfer must include the most recent update and all prior versions.

4. **Restrictions on Use of Individual Programs.** You must follow the individual requirements and restrictions detailed for each individual program in the About the CD-ROM appendix of this Book. These limitations are also contained in the individual license agreements recorded on the Software Media. These limitations may include a requirement that after using the program for a specified period of time, the user must pay a registration fee or discontinue use. By opening the Software packet(s), you will be agreeing to abide by the licenses and restrictions for these individual programs that are detailed in the About the CD-ROM appendix and on the Software Media. None of the material on this Software Media or listed in this Book may ever be redistributed, in original or modified form, for commercial purposes.

BUSINESS, CAREERS & PERSONAL FINANCE

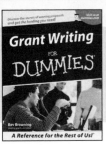

Grant Writing FOR DUMMIES

0-7645-5307-0

Home Buying FOR DUMMIES

0-7645-5331-3 *†

Also available:
- Accounting For Dummies †
  0-7645-5314-3
- Business Plans Kit For Dummies †
  0-7645-5365-8
- Cover Letters For Dummies
  0-7645-5224-4
- Frugal Living For Dummies
  0-7645-5403-4
- Leadership For Dummies
  0-7645-5176-0
- Managing For Dummies
  0-7645-1771-6

- Marketing For Dummies
  0-7645-5600-2
- Personal Finance For Dummies *
  0-7645-2590-5
- Project Management For Dummies
  0-7645-5283-X
- Resumes For Dummies †
  0-7645-5471-9
- Selling For Dummies
  0-7645-5363-1
- Small Business Kit For Dummies *†
  0-7645-5093-4

HOME & BUSINESS COMPUTER BASICS

Windows XP FOR DUMMIES

0-7645-4074-2

Excel 2003 FOR DUMMIES

0-7645-3758-X

Also available:
- ACT! 6 For Dummies
  0-7645-2645-6
- iLife '04 All-in-One Desk Reference
  For Dummies
  0-7645-7347-0
- iPAQ For Dummies
  0-7645-6769-1
- Mac OS X Panther Timesaving
  Techniques For Dummies
  0-7645-5812-9
- Macs For Dummies
  0-7645-5656-8

- Microsoft Money 2004 For Dummies
  0-7645-4195-1
- Office 2003 All-in-One Desk Reference
  For Dummies
  0-7645-3883-7
- Outlook 2003 For Dummies
  0-7645-3759-8
- PCs For Dummies
  0-7645-4074-2
- TiVo For Dummies
  0-7645-6923-6
- Upgrading and Fixing PCs For Dummies
  0-7645-1665-5
- Windows XP Timesaving Techniques
  For Dummies
  0-7645-3748-2

FOOD, HOME, GARDEN, HOBBIES, MUSIC & PETS

Feng Shui FOR DUMMIES

0-7645-5295-3

Poker FOR DUMMIES

0-7645-5232-5

Also available:
- Bass Guitar For Dummies
  0-7645-2487-9
- Diabetes Cookbook For Dummies
  0-7645-5230-9
- Gardening For Dummies *
  0-7645-5130-2
- Guitar For Dummies
  0-7645-5106-X
- Holiday Decorating For Dummies
  0-7645-2570-0
- Home Improvement All-in-One
  For Dummies
  0-7645-5680-0

- Knitting For Dummies
  0-7645-5395-X
- Piano For Dummies
  0-7645-5105-1
- Puppies For Dummies
  0-7645-5255-4
- Scrapbooking For Dummies
  0-7645-7208-3
- Senior Dogs For Dummies
  0-7645-5818-8
- Singing For Dummies
  0-7645-2475-5
- 30-Minute Meals For Dummies
  0-7645-2589-1

INTERNET & DIGITAL MEDIA

Digital Photography FOR DUMMIES

0-7645-1664-7

Starting an eBay Business FOR DUMMIES

0-7645-6924-4

Also available:
- 2005 Online Shopping Directory
  For Dummies
  0-7645-7495-7
- CD & DVD Recording For Dummies
  0-7645-5956-7
- eBay For Dummies
  0-7645-5654-1
- Fighting Spam For Dummies
  0-7645-5965-6
- Genealogy Online For Dummies
  0-7645-5964-8
- Google For Dummies
  0-7645-4420-9

- Home Recording For Musicians
  For Dummies
  0-7645-1634-5
- The Internet For Dummies
  0-7645-4173-0
- iPod & iTunes For Dummies
  0-7645-7772-7
- Preventing Identity Theft For Dummies
  0-7645-7336-5
- Pro Tools All-in-One Desk Reference
  For Dummies
  0-7645-5714-9
- Roxio Easy Media Creator For Dummies
  0-7645-7131-1

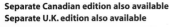

Separate Canadian edition also available
Separate U.K. edition also available

Available wherever books are sold. For more information or to order direct: U.S. customers visit www.dummies.com or call 1-877-762-2974.
U.K. customers visit www.wileyeurope.com or call 0800 243407. Canadian customers visit www.wiley.ca or call 1-800-567-4797.

SPORTS, FITNESS, PARENTING, RELIGION & SPIRITUALITY

 0-7645-5146-9

 0-7645-5418-2

Also available:
- Adoption For Dummies
  0-7645-5488-3
- Basketball For Dummies
  0-7645-5248-1
- The Bible For Dummies
  0-7645-5296-1
- Buddhism For Dummies
  0-7645-5359-3
- Catholicism For Dummies
  0-7645-5391-7
- Hockey For Dummies
  0-7645-5228-7

- Judaism For Dummies
  0-7645-5299-6
- Martial Arts For Dummies
  0-7645-5358-5
- Pilates For Dummies
  0-7645-5397-6
- Religion For Dummies
  0-7645-5264-3
- Teaching Kids to Read For Dummies
  0-7645-4043-2
- Weight Training For Dummies
  0-7645-5168-X
- Yoga For Dummies
  0-7645-5117-5

TRAVEL

 0-7645-5438-7

 0-7645-5453-0

Also available:
- Alaska For Dummies
  0-7645-1761-9
- Arizona For Dummies
  0-7645-6938-4
- Cancún and the Yucatán For Dummies
  0-7645-2437-2
- Cruise Vacations For Dummies
  0-7645-6941-4
- Europe For Dummies
  0-7645-5456-5
- Ireland For Dummies
  0-7645-5455-7

- Las Vegas For Dummies
  0-7645-5448-4
- London For Dummies
  0-7645-4277-X
- New York City For Dummies
  0-7645-6945-7
- Paris For Dummies
  0-7645-5494-8
- RV Vacations For Dummies
  0-7645-5443-3
- Walt Disney World & Orlando For Dummies
  0-7645-6943-0

GRAPHICS, DESIGN & WEB DEVELOPMENT

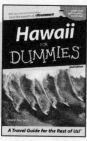 0-7645-4345-8

 0-7645-5589-8

Also available:
- Adobe Acrobat 6 PDF For Dummies
  0-7645-3760-1
- Building a Web Site For Dummies
  0-7645-7144-3
- Dreamweaver MX 2004 For Dummies
  0-7645-4342-3
- FrontPage 2003 For Dummies
  0-7645-3882-9
- HTML 4 For Dummies
  0-7645-1995-6
- Illustrator CS For Dummies
  0-7645-4084-X

- Macromedia Flash MX 2004 For Dummies
  0-7645-4358-X
- Photoshop 7 All-in-One Desk Reference For Dummies
  0-7645-1667-1
- Photoshop CS Timesaving Techniques For Dummies
  0-7645-6782-9
- PHP 5 For Dummies
  0-7645-4166-8
- PowerPoint 2003 For Dummies
  0-7645-3908-6
- QuarkXPress 6 For Dummies
  0-7645-2593-X

NETWORKING, SECURITY, PROGRAMMING & DATABASES

 0-7645-6852-3

 0-7645-5784-X

Also available:
- A+ Certification For Dummies
  0-7645-4187-0
- Access 2003 All-in-One Desk Reference For Dummies
  0-7645-3988-4
- Beginning Programming For Dummies
  0-7645-4997-9
- C For Dummies
  0-7645-7068-4
- Firewalls For Dummies
  0-7645-4048-3
- Home Networking For Dummies
  0-7645-42796

- Network Security For Dummies
  0-7645-1679-5
- Networking For Dummies
  0-7645-1677-9
- TCP/IP For Dummies
  0-7645-1760-0
- VBA For Dummies
  0-7645-3989-2
- Wireless All In-One Desk Reference For Dummies
  0-7645-7496-5
- Wireless Home Networking For Dummies
  0-7645-3910-8

ALTH & SELF-HELP

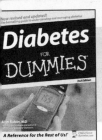

0-7645-6820-5 *†

0-7645-2566-2

Also available:

- Alzheimer's For Dummies
  0-7645-3899-3
- Asthma For Dummies
  0-7645-4233-8
- Controlling Cholesterol For Dummies
  0-7645-5440-9
- Depression For Dummies
  0-7645-3900-0
- Dieting For Dummies
  0-7645-4149-8
- Fertility For Dummies
  0-7645-2549-2

- Fibromyalgia For Dummies
  0-7645-5441-7
- Improving Your Memory For Dummies
  0-7645-5435-2
- Pregnancy For Dummies †
  0-7645-4483-7
- Quitting Smoking For Dummies
  0-7645-2629-4
- Relationships For Dummies
  0-7645-5384-4
- Thyroid For Dummies
  0-7645-5385-2

UCATION, HISTORY, REFERENCE & TEST PREPARATION

0-7645-5194-9

0-7645-4186-2

Also available:

- Algebra For Dummies
  0-7645-5325-9
- British History For Dummies
  0-7645-7021-8
- Calculus For Dummies
  0-7645-2498-4
- English Grammar For Dummies
  0-7645-5322-4
- Forensics For Dummies
  0-7645-5580-4
- The GMAT For Dummies
  0-7645-5251-1
- Inglés Para Dummies
  0-7645-5427-1

- Italian For Dummies
  0-7645-5196-5
- Latin For Dummies
  0-7645-5431-X
- Lewis & Clark For Dummies
  0-7645-2545-X
- Research Papers For Dummies
  0-7645-5426-3
- The SAT I For Dummies
  0-7645-7193-1
- Science Fair Projects For Dummies
  0-7645-5460-3
- U.S. History For Dummies
  0-7645-5249-X

Get smart @ dummies.com®

- **Find a full list of Dummies titles**
- **Look into loads of FREE on-site articles**
- **Sign up for FREE eTips e-mailed to you weekly**
- **See what other products carry the Dummies name**
- **Shop directly from the Dummies bookstore**
- **Enter to win new prizes every month!**

Separate Canadian edition also available
Separate U.K. edition also available

available wherever books are sold. For more information or to order direct: U.S. customers visit www.dummies.com or call 1-877-762-2974.
K. customers visit www.wileyeurope.com or call 0800 243407. Canadian customers visit www.wiley.ca or call 1-800-567-4797.